# Real Objects in Unreal Situations

# Real Objects in Unreal Situations
## Modern Art in Fiction Films

Susan Felleman

**intellect** Bristol, UK / Chicago, USA

First published in the UK in 2014 by
Intellect, The Mill, Parnall Road, Fishponds, Bristol, BS16 3JG, UK

First published in the USA in 2014 by
Intellect, The University of Chicago Press, 1427 E. 60th Street,
Chicago, IL 60637, USA

A catalogue record for this book is available from the
British Library.

Cover designer: Stephanie Sarlos
Cover image: Film still of Marlene Dietrich from *The Song of Songs* (1933)
Copy-editor: MPS Technologies
Production manager: Jelena Stanovnik and Claire Organ
Typesetting: Contentra Technologies

Print ISBN: 978-1-78320-250-8
ePDF ISBN: 978-1-78320-248-5
ePUB ISBN: 978-1-78320-249-2

Printed and bound by Hobbs, UK

To Hallie and Ben

# Contents

# Acknowledgements

This book has been a long time in the making and I have many debts to acknowledge and much gratitude to express, first to Intellect Press for taking it on, especially Jelena Stanovnik, Assistant Publisher for Film Studies, who acquired it, as well as Claire Organ, who oversaw the production, Stephanie Sarlos, designer, and Alice Gilliam in Marketing. It has been a pleasure. I also thank the two anonymous peer reviewers who will find their careful readings and thorough responses reflected herein.

I changed positions toward the end of my work on this book and I am unspeakably grateful for the year's research leave made possible by Mary Anne Fitzpatrick, Dean of the College of Arts and Sciences, here at the University of South Carolina. It was precisely what I needed to complete the project before undertaking a move and new teaching responsibilities, which I was then able to do with enthusiasm. The support of the Dean's office staff, as well as the Art Department's – especially Abby Callahan and Kim Gore – was invaluable. Thanks to Ashley Knox and Sara Chizari at University Libraries Special Collections, and to my colleagues Kathleen Robbins and Simon Tarr, for special help with photographic aspects of the book.

At Southern Illinois University, Carbondale, where I was on the faculty until 2012, I had the support of many university colleagues, including those in the Department of Cinema and Photography and the College of Mass Communication and Media Arts. I am particularly grateful for the consistent and capable assistance of Rhonda Rothrock and the department office staff and for the honor and funding of the William A. Minor Research Grant I was awarded for this project in 2010–2011.

Research for this book was conducted over considerable time and space and I am indebted to individuals and institutions of whose time, resources, and often hospitality I was the fortunate recipient: most especially the wonderfully generous Lola Scarpitta and her husband Jeff Knapple (Los Angeles); as well as Christoph Zuschlag and Andreas Hüneke (Berlin); Marshall Price and Rae Ferren (New York); and Evan and Joanna Jones (London).

I also wish to acknowledge the assistance, insight, expertise, and/or resources of: Alice L. Birney and the Library of Congress, Jeanpaul Goergen, Johannes von Moltke, Ed Meza, Deutsche Kinemathek, Berlin Filmarchiv-Bundesarchiv, Jenny Romero and the staff of The Margaret Herrick Library of the Academy of Motion Picture Arts and Sciences, James Saslow, Robert Pincus-Witten, Dallas Dunn, Bran Ferren, Chris Weedman, Johnny Davies and the BFI Library, Lin Jammet, Annette Ratuszniak, Jorge Luis Marzo, Genoveva Tusell García, Francesc Torres, Victoria Combalia, Gijs Van Hensbergen, and Juan Manuel Bonet (the last six of whom valiantly attempted to help me with the particularly thorny and, sadly, as yet unsolved mystery of the identity and 'reality' status of the artworks seen in *Muerte de un Ciclista*, which I added to Chapter 2 too late in the project to make a research trip to Spain).

I am also most thankful to Paul Mazursky, the late Ivan Karp, the late Paul Jenkins and his wife Suzanne Jenkins, Larry Cuba, Sydney Cooper, Susan Hambleton, Joseph Valle, Nick Jordan, Jacob Cartwright, Sean Doxey, Mark Rhodes, and the staff of Chatsworth House.

My thanks to Haelim Suh, Noah Springer, and Mark McCleerey, who all assisted me with research while I was on the faculty at SIU, and Nate Fortmeyer, who did so during my research leave. Liz Faber was at an early stage of this project my graduate research assistant and at later stages my writing partner, as she completed her brilliant doctoral dissertation and I this book, and then my editor, as I readied the manuscript for publication. There have been few relationships in my professional life as gratifying as this one with Liz, whose doctoral work I was privileged to supervise and who also for a time worked with me as a valued teaching assistant. For the intelligence, insight, skill, diligence, consistency, style, and grace she brought to the project and to our relationship, I am forever grateful, as well as for the time she took to help out, time I know she hardly had!

I would also like to acknowledge, with immense appreciation, colleagues who invited me to present and publish early versions of this material. The seeds of the project were to be found in two lectures I gave in late 2007: the first at the invitation of Steven Jacobs to the symposium, 'The Wrong Artist: Hitchcock and the Other Arts', at de Singel: International Kunstcampus Antwerp, in conjunction with the exhibition *Alfred Hitchcock & Pauhof: The Wrong House* and Cinema Zuid, Antwerp, and the second at the invitation of Dudley Andrew and Brigitte Peucker to 'The Human Figure: Painting, Film, Photograph' conference at the Whitney Humanities Center, Yale University.

An early version of Chapter 3 was presented as part of the session, 'Colour and Affect in Hitchcock,' to the conference, *Colour and the Moving Image: History, Theory, Aesthetics, Archive*, University of Bristol, in July, 2009; an early version of Chapter 6 to the session, 'The Place of the Museum in Film,' at the Society for Cinema and Media Studies, Annual Meeting, Los Angeles, 21 March, 2010; and a preliminary version of Chapter 4 to the session, 'Living Statues and Other Sculptural Subjects in Film,' at the Society for Cinema and Media Studies, Annual Meeting, Chicago, 9 March, 2013.

To those who were instrumental in affording me the opportunity to present my ideas and those interlocutors who helped me refine them at these conferences and symposia – including Paul Fry, and especially to my almost constant companions and collaborators on many of these occasions, Brigitte Peucker and Steven Jacobs – I am exceedingly grateful, as I am to the editors of *Jump Cut*, especially Chuck Kleinhans and Julia Lesage, who published a synoptic version of the material that constitutes the first half of the book as 'Decay of the Aura: Modern Art in Classical Cinema', in *Jump Cut* 53 (Summer 2011).

Finally, I must express my love, gratitude, and appreciation to friends and family, the relationships that have sustained me these many years. To the friends too numerous to name, to my father, my brothers, and my father- and brothers-in-law I am thankful. I owe particular thanks to my aunt Valerie Justin and to my niece Jessica Felleman, both of whom generously hosted and drove me to research appointments when I visited them in Sag Harbor and Los Angeles, respectively, although those mere facts do not convey the pleasure I had in their company. My good friends Carma Gorman and Harry Cooper are among the art historians to be thanked for help with identifications.

I cannot begin to put in words my love for, gratitude to, and appreciation of my husband Peter Chametzky. In addition to being an exceptionally supportive and tolerant spouse, he is a brilliant scholar, wonderful colleague, and true collaborator. His groundbreaking book *Objects as History in Twentieth-Century German Art: Beckmann to Beuys* (California, 2010) was underway as I was researching this. Together we uncovered and investigated the 'degenerate art' in the National Socialist film *Venus vor Gericht* (discussed in his Chapter 5 and my Chapter 2), and Peter's extensive knowledge of the German language, as well as German modern art and history, has been invaluable, along with his persuasive approach to the problem of the object (and its absence) in historical space and time. Finally, I am thankful for the patience, love, help and respect of my children, Ben and Hallie Chametzky. They truly inspire me. When I published my first book in 1997, Ben was 3 years old, Hallie was a baby, and I thanked them in my acknowledgments just for being and for doing very little to hinder my accomplishment. When I published my second book, in 2006, Ben was 11, Hallie was 8, and I promised in print that, were I to be fortunate enough to publish another, it would be dedicated to them. I have been fortunate! When this book is published they will be 20 and 17 and an award-winning scholar and author respectively. They lived a long time with and contributed much to this book, including, from Hallie, a wonderful word I had not known existed to replace one that I had invented. *Real Objects in Unreal Situations* is for Hallie and Ben, with my love, devotion, and admiration, and with thanks for all the great conversations, brilliant insights, and laughs.

Susan Felleman
Columbia, SC, February, 2014

# Introduction

The Work of Art in the Space of Its Material Dissolution

... we can readily grasp the social basis of the aura's present decay. It rests on two circumstances, both linked to the increasing emergence of the masses and the growing intensity of their movements. Namely: *the desire of the present-day masses to 'get closer' to things, and their equally passionate concern for overcoming each thing's uniqueness by assimilating it as a reproduction.* Every day the urge grows stronger to get hold of an object at close range in an image, or, better, in a facsimile, a reproduction. And the reproduction, as offered by illustrated magazines and newsreels, differs unmistakably from the image. Uniqueness and permanence are as closely entwined in the latter as are transitoriness and repeatability in the former.

Walter Benjamin
'The Work of Art in the Age of Its Technological Reproducibility' (2008: 23)

In *The Heiress,* William Wyler's 1949 film version of Ruth and Augustus Goetz's play based on Henry James's *Washington Square*, material things play an unusually important role. It is suggested that the charming Morris Townsend (Montgomery Clift) is a fortune hunter, even before Doctor Sloper (Ralph Richardson) proclaims it, by means of little bits of business involving the suitor's attention to things. To me, one of the most memorable moments has Morris, while waiting in the Sloper drawing room for Catherine (Olivia de Havilland), casually pick up a figurine from a table, turn it over in his hands, and glance at its bottom, presumably at its maker's mark. I find this memorable because it is a very realist action – the sort of small, mute, but meaningful, realist action one rarely sees in movies – but one more associated with shopping in an antique store than going visiting [Fig. 1]. *The Heiress* features one of the most carefully designed, dressed, and shot film sets of its era and is full of such details, which quietly convince us of the political economy of the relationships in the story, through the minute, fastidious staging and shooting of interactions between people and things. According to the production designer, Harry Horner, the Sloper house – a set to which most of the action of the film was restricted – was researched and designed to be a convincing representation of a wealthy, patrician New York household, ca. 1880, but also to frame and articulate the different experiences of the three principal characters: for Dr. Sloper, as a kind of personal museum and memorial to his dead wife; for his daughter Catherine, as a kind of prison (a gilded cage); and for her suitor Morris, almost as a shop window – a space full of attractive prospects, precious objects, and luxurious surfaces that he hopes to acquire (Gambill 1983: 227).

**Figure 1:** Montgomery Clift and Miriam Hopkins in *The Heiress* (Wyler, 1949).

One of the more costly problems was to find adequate furniture to match the description of exquisite taste and wealth, both of which were attributes of Dr. Sloper. Our expert on furniture, Emile Kurie [sic], went to New York and bought fine antique furniture, including the spinet, fine paintings, and ornaments, knowing that under the examining camera close-up the standard prop furniture would not convince anyone of the great wealth of the heiress.

(Horner 2002: 184)

One must count Horner and Kuri's efforts as successful. One is rarely, if at all, in the course of *The Heiress*, struck by historical anachronism (except, arguably, in the performances, which are strikingly but productively incompatible, deriving from three different schools[1]) or the impression of artifice or hollowness in its representation of the material world of Washington Square. Significantly, at the same time, despite the remarkably 'authentic' trappings with which the set is dressed, very few objects stand out. Really, it is just those to which the dialogue itself draws attention – Catherine's needlepoint, Morris's chamois gloves, the ruby buttons Catherine bought him in Paris – to which one attends. I have seen the film many times (albeit never in a true theatrical projection of a 35mm print), and I have taught it several times, too, but I cannot recall the figure whose underside Morris inspected. I did not see its mark – the 'mark of history' and index of authenticity.[2] As with the oil paintings, the spinet, the furniture, the ladies' jewels, I cannot attest to its quality or authenticity. This is the fate of the work of art in the age of its technological reproducibility, as we know from Walter Benjamin. What we remember is the action, not the object, even when the production designer and director have themselves scrupulously attended to aura.

Some time ago I learned, to my surprise, that one of the paintings on the wall of the Wendices' London flat in Alfred Hitchcock's *Dial M For Murder* (1954) is a landscape in oil by Rosa Bonheur (1822), a major nineteenth century French painter and the most famous woman artist of her time [Fig. 2]. According to a press release from the Warner Bros. Archives, 'because he is a man of taste and culture, Hitchcock hand-picked many of the props, including an original Rosa Bonheur oil painting, long hidden in Warner's property gallery, and a pair of valuable Wedgewood vases' (Jacobs 2007: 107). What of this? It is really not surprising that the vaults of Hollywood's major motion picture studios should contain some treasures, including 'original' art and 'valuable' antiquities. It would be surprising if they did not. As Horner's account indicates, their budgets sometimes permitted shopping trips to New York

**Figure 2:** Robert Cummings, Ray Milland, Grace Kelly, and a landscape painting by Rosa Bonheur in *Dial M for Murder* (Hitchcock, 1954).

galleries and auction houses. And, as with *The Heiress, Dial M for Murder* is a story almost entirely restricted to one domestic interior, the home of a couple to whose relationship (as with narrative) wealth is key. It is certainly not news that Hitchcock was a man of taste or that he exercised a great degree of control over particular elements of mise-en-scène. Many scholars – myself included – have explored the role of art in Hitchcock's oeuvre.[3] If there's any revelation associated with this 'discovery', it is that films do not and filmmakers, film audiences, and scholars (of film studies or art history) cannot – without the help of archives, press releases, and other documentary accounts, like Harry Horner's – really distinguish a fine oil painting by a major painter from a reproduction, an imitation, or from significantly lesser works seen on the screen. In the fine arts – the collectible ones – the connoisseur's work depends on the material presence of the object, and in movies the object is, like the actors, always absent. Moreover, does it really matter to us? What difference does it make whether a painting in a movie is 'real': an authentic object with provenance, as opposed to a photomechanical reproduction, an imitation, or an anonymous daub? Film itself is photomechanical; fiction is imitation; anonymity is the proper condition of the mutely indexical excess that constitutes the impression of reality on screen. And as Benjamin noted, the value of that unique, original object – the object that through its physical duration in space and time 'bears the mark of history' (21) and partakes of cultural tradition – has been liquidated in the age of technological reproduction. Mass media – film especially – has shattered tradition and 'substitutes a mass existence for a unique existence' (22).

Paradoxically, we are more likely to note the status of the art object in film when it is incommensurate to its task: when mere props or poor imitations must perform as masterpieces of art in scenarios about art and artists, as with two examples I have noted in previous work – Dolya Goutman's Gauguinesque pastiches in Albert Lewin's 1942 adaptation, *The Moon and Sixpence* (1997: 34–36) and Joseph Nicolosi's plaster 'Anatolian Venus' sculpture of Ava Gardner in William Seiter's 1948 film version of the Broadway show, *One Touch of Venus* (2006: 59–62) – or the ersatz Picasso paintings that James Cameron sunk with his 1997 *Titanic*, which included a diminutive *Demoiselles d'Avignon* (1907), a canvas that is not known to have sunk in the Atlantic and is in fact monumental. Even in such cases, though, authenticity is less pertinent than quality. High quality, scale reproductions, or excellent imitations and pastiches – the action paintings that are made in *Pollock* (Harris, 2000), for instance, or the bust of Darcy in *Pride & Prejudice* (Wright, 2005) that Nick Dutton made, mixing marble dust with resin, to stand among authentic marbles in the sculpture gallery at Chatsworth – can, arguably, perform their parts as well as museum pieces, perhaps sometimes better (if designed and crafted for maximum photogeneity). Indeed, after the production of *Pride & Prejudice*, the bust of Matthew Macfadyen as Darcy was put on view in Chatsworth's famous hall of marbles – itself made more famous by its appearance in the film – alongside all the 'real' sculptures, remaining there for some years in acknowledgment of the added value of fiction. Later, the bust was relocated to the gift shop, where its role in bolstering Chatsworth's commerce – trade in heritage tourism and Anglophilic romance – was tacitly acknowledged [Fig. 3].

**Figure 3:** The bust of Darcy/Matthew Macfadyen, made for *Pride & Prejudice* (Wright, 2005), on view in the Chatsworth House gift shop, November 2010 (photo: Susan Felleman).

It is fascinating to consider here, then, along Benjaminian lines, the vicissitudes of the aura's decay; perhaps it might be more apt to speak of its recycling, peregrinations, or dispersal. Wright's movie adapts the most cherished production of Jane Austen, an author who has one of the most fervent cult followings in modern literature. Of course, such a 'cult' is a function of technological reproduction – the rise of the novel follows from late-eighteenth-century innovations in printing – and is very different than the 'cult' value that, according to Benjamin, attends to works of art in their rarefied positions in sacred space and time. But 'Janeites,' as avid Austen fans are known, reinscribe aura by an almost fetishistic interest in the material world of Austen – in addition to 'getting closer' by means of collecting and reenacting – making 'pilgrimages' to places associated with and represented by her, including to Chatsworth, which Austen herself is said to have visited and which was known, even before the movie, to be a possible prototype for Pemberley (Greene 1988).[4] The devotions of 'Janeites' can sometimes extend to filmed versions of the novels, and those films, in turn, intensify the paraliterary phenomenon. Austen's Mr. Darcy, along with a few other temperamental dreamboats of nineteenth-century literature (including the Brontës' Rochester and Heathcliff), has had a remarkable hold on the private and collective imaginations of a largely female readership and the potency of this effect rubs off on many of the actors cast to play him (notably Laurence Olivier and Colin Firth). In them, the cult of the movie star, which Benjamin characterizes as a kind of reinscribed aura – associated albeit with a kind of 'putrid magic [...] of its own commodity character' – becomes conflated with the paradoxical aura produced by the immaterial or fantasy objects that are the literary characters. When – as with the bust of Macfadyen as Darcy – a portrait then reifies the actor, in character, the result is a confounding return of the work of art by way of its own decay. In theory reproducible – though it pretends to be marble, it is a resin cast – the bust comes to mingle among the unique marbles that exude the already somewhat withered, commodified – yet still rarefied – value associated with neoclassical statuary collected by the Duke of Devonshire (as opposed to the ritual value associated with their Classical and Hellenistic prototypes). The bust plays a part in the afterlife of Jane Austen and the moribund British aristocracy, in the nostalgia of 'heritage' consumers, as well as in the movie.

And what of that part? In what way does an object of art emerge from the background of a picture to perform as an actor? Benjamin made a point of distinguishing the photographic reproduction of a work of art from the work of cinema. In a film studio, he claimed, 'what is reproduced is not an art work, and the act of reproducing it is no more such a work than in the first case' (29). It is montage, he argued, that is the cinematic art, and he proceeded to identify the peculiar nature of a film actor's performance as the unique pro-filmic process. As the cinema, however, *does* sometimes reproduce works of art, even sometimes gives them starring roles, can Benjamin's observations about the fate of such objects in the age of their reproducibility be integrated with those that pertain to the nature of the processes peculiar to other film actors?

These are some of the many questions that arise around the question of the work of art as it appears in film, specifically the fiction film: questions I will address in the course of this study. They are questions that have not received adequate attention. Film studies tend to regard the art object as a symbolic or functional presence in film, of textual rather than material significance, so when the art object *mise en abyme* has been considered, its status as a material entity independent of the film – as a thing that might bear the unique 'mark of history' – has generally been neglected. This is in part a function of what the one medium does in representing the other – or misrepresenting, as is inevitable – but it also reflects a blind spot, one created by the withering of aura, the transformation of objects into images. Film cannot preserve the mark of history and, as Benjamin notes, it would not if it could. Films, as is especially evident in historical epics, shatter and disorient traditional culture and 'liquidate' its values. One such value that goes hand-in-hand with authenticity is authorship. The painters and sculptors of works featured in films – even those of some prominence – often receive no screen credit and are difficult to identify. This oversight was especially common during the classic period of cinema but is not unheard of today.[5]

There are obvious exceptions to this rule, in film and in film studies. Hitchcock's engagement with Salvador Dalí on *Spellbound* (1945) was highly publicized and has been thoroughly examined. My own work on the films of Albert Lewin attempted to illuminate the complexities of a rather unusual career; Lewin, one of Hollywood's notable art collectors, credited major artist collaborators and foregrounded artworks in his films, including Ivan Albright's titular portrait in *The Picture of Dorian Gray* (1945) and Max Ernst's *The Temptation of Saint Anthony* in *The Private Affairs of Bel Ami* (1947), for which producer-writer-director Lewin arranged a rather high-profile modern art competition (Felleman 1997). More recently, Olivier Assayas's *Summer Hours* (2008) was conceived as a collaboration with the Musée d'Orsay (on the occasion of its twentieth anniversary), by which objects from the museum's collection would be 'returned' via fiction to the kind of domestic life they might have known before becoming property of the French State, and the film is exquisitely sensitive to issues of art and objecthood, cultural patrimony, taste, and the lives that art surrounds and inhabits. Ironically, even a film such as *Summer Hours*, conceived around particular real objects of art – museum pieces – can reveal the extent of the 'decay of the aura'; several of the works selected from the Musée d'Orsay to be narrativized in Assayas's film – including paintings by Jean-Baptiste-Camille Corot and Odilon Redon – were deemed too fragile or valuable to be relocated to the house in which the film was shot, so were represented by copies (albeit high-quality painted copies, not mere photomechanical reproductions).[6]

Each of these exceptions, however, is doubly exceptional. Of them, only in *Summer Hours* does art play a realist role. Lewin, strikingly, used contemporary painting anachronistically and inserted Technicolor shots of it in his black-and-white movies, clearly with every intention of creating a vivid fissure in the narrative. Hitchcock credited artists for their contributions to dream sequences (also vivid fissures) – in *Spellbound* (1945 – Dalí) and in *Vertigo* (1958 – John Ferren) – but did not credit Ferren for the many paintings that performed the more realist role of Sam Marlow's work in *The Trouble with Harry* (1955). Assayas's film is exceptional in its foregrounded collaboration with French state museum and incorporation of the museum into the narrative and mise-en-scène. In general, to the contrary, movies tend to subsume and diminish art (and other media), even often when they celebrate it. The reasons for this tendency are complex and overdetermined (see Young and Elsaesser, among others). For this reason, along with snobbery, or doubts about the mass appeal and popular aspect of the medium, anxiety about how it will be received, or reluctance to give up control of the work, many artists have either passed up the opportunity to show their work in movies or have foregone the credit, an ambivalent acclaim. But such choices are fraught with economic implications. As a rule, the prominent acknowledgment of contemporary art in a movie has been a boon to the artist's career. This was certainly the case with S.C. Scarpitta, Elisabeth Frink, and Paul Jenkins, among the artists discussed in this study. But the anonymity of the many sculptors other than Scarpitta who lent work to *The Song of Songs* (Mamoulian, 1933), or of Ferren, as the hand behind Marlow's in *The Trouble with Harry*, left their reputations and their 'markets' more or less unaffected and their works more or less unnoticed. Publicity for and reviews of *The Song of Songs* make much, naturally, of Scarpitta's titular nude sculpture of Marlene Dietrich but do not mention the dozens of other works seen in the film (although censors noticed their nudity). Most accounts of *The Trouble with Harry* mention that Sam Marlow is a painter but say little about his paintings. Those that do mention them, generally treat the paintings as negligible, as jokes, or daubs. And, as I discuss in Chapter 3, the paintings do indeed seem oddly inconsequential; they lack aura, of course. They are diminished by cinema.

Understanding this diminishment – or decay – is one of the tasks of this study, in which I identify and examine a range of modern art objects (primarily, but not exclusively, paintings, drawings, and sculptures) as they enter, appear, and sometimes disappear in fiction films, from objects that appear to be playing 'themselves' (e.g. numerous examples of 'Degenerate Art' in *Venus vor Gericht*, 1941, a National Socialist romantic-comedy and polemic set in 1930; the content of SoHo's OK Harris gallery in *An Unmarried Woman*, 1978; the neoclassical marbles in *Pride & Prejudice*, 2005) to objects playing parts (e.g. figurative works by at least seven different contemporary sculptors as the work of fictional sculptor Richard Waldow in *The Song of Songs*; the paintings and drawings by John Ferren as the work of fictional painter Sam Marlow in *The Trouble with Harry*; sculptures by Elisabeth Frink as those of fictional sculptor Freya Neilson in *The Damned*, 1961; Paul Jenkins' paintings playing Saul Kaplan's in *An Unmarried Woman*, 1978, and Sydney Cooper's work as June Gudmundsdottir's in *The Player*, 1992). Some of the objects were made for and to some extent on film (the title sculpture in *The Song of Songs*, one or more of the Jenkins paintings in *An Unmarried Woman*, Sydney Cooper's works in *The Player*). These works are, in a sense, even closer to performances, and are perhaps liminally 'real,' in terms of the midway position they occupy between works that pre-existed their roles and props. In every case, this study is interested not only in the part played by the art, but also how it came to play that part, too: the social, economic, and material details of how the art came to be in the film and its recognition or reception thereby, along with the larger context of film's institutional and aesthetic engagement with art and artists.

This study, then, constitutes a new branch of the expanding intermedial field of and literature about film, material culture, and the other visual arts: one that attends to material, historical, personal, economic, and political realities around the artworks in films – including, where possible, the interactions between movie directors, producers, designers, and the artists engaged to work for movies – as well as to description and interpretation of their outcomes. I begin with a series of loosely connected case studies related to modern art in fiction films of the classic period (1930s–1950s), focusing on two Hollywood films – *The Song of Songs* (Mamoulian, 1933) and *The Trouble with Harry* (Hitchcock, 1955) – and two European films – *Venus vor Gericht/Venus on Trial* (Zerlett, 1941) and *Muerte de un ciclista/Death of a Cyclist* (Bardem, 1955). *The Song of Songs* and *Venus vor Gericht* feature sculptor–protagonists, and *The Trouble with Harry*, a painter. In *Muerte de un ciclista*, art plays a more supporting role. There are no artist-protagonists but there is a significant scene set in a gallery exhibition of modern art – as there is in *Venus vor Gericht* – and a significant antagonist is an art critic.

Politics play a vivid role, on screen and off, implicitly and explicitly, in these films, particularly in the European films, both made under dictatorships, in Germany and Spain. But while the earlier, *Venus*, is a work of propaganda made under the auspices of a Nazi-controlled film industry, the later, *Muerte*, is a somewhat more independently produced art film – made at a critical moment in postwar Spanish history – that couches a political critique within a meaningful aesthetic dialectic (switching between neo-realist and noirish styles) and a seemingly conventional – and scrupulously censored – melodrama. Both Hitchcock's *The Trouble with Harry* and Bardem's *Muerte* were released in 1955, when art and culture were becoming increasingly high profile and often controversial elements of Cold War political discourses and international policy. Modernism, abstract painting particularly, became emblematic of values such as freedom and democracy – in contradistinction to Socialist Realism – and, for some, the increasing dominance of US military and economic power. This was still the case when Joseph Losey engaged modern sculpture in his cautionary and dystopian *The Damned*, a genre hybrid made for Hammer in 1961 (although not released for two years in the United Kingdom and four in the United States[7]) that serves as something of a hinge between the classic films of the first half of this book and the later films that bring up the rear.

The sculptor and painter protagonists of the films considered in the first part – Richard Waldow (Brian Aherne) in *The Song of Songs*, Peter Brake (Hannes Stelzer) in *Venus vor Gericht*, and Sam Marlow (John Forsythe) in *The Trouble with Harry* – are, predictably, all men, as were the artists of the real objects that play their work, with one minor exception (one work by a woman sculptor among the pieces in Waldow's atelier). The sculptor character in *The Damned*, however, is a woman, as is the actual sculptor whose work plays hers. Freya Neilson (Viveca Lindfors) is not a protagonist but hers is a significant supporting role and her studio a major location; Freya's sculptures – made by Elisabeth Frink, with Barbara Hepworth one of the only women among the major British sculptors of the period – are prominent elements of the mise-en-scène, even the action. Views of them frame the film. *The Damned* was adapted from a 1961 novel, H.L. Lawrence's *The Children of Light*, that featured no sculptor or sculpture at all. The character of Freya was one of the many changes that Losey and screenwriter Evan Jones made to the story, according to the latter, expressly because Losey wished to feature Frink's work, which stands – at the same time its scarred, expressive figures embody an existential angst – for subtly gendered qualities of candor, compassion, and culture in the film, as does Freya's character herself, as opposed to more implicitly masculine characteristics of others in this dystopia: cold, secretive, technocratic empiricism and brutal, criminal aggression.

This view of culture is part of the film's political landscape; its considered alignment of art, science, and violence along gender lines is a novel element of *The Damned*. Although women artists had appeared very occasionally as characters in films of the classic period, they had rarely been represented seriously. If not a student, or the occasional society amateur, a woman artist in a Hollywood picture was likely to be represented as a working girl and commercial artist like Midge Wood (Barbara Bel Geddes) in Hitchcock's *Vertigo* (1958), or as silly and eccentric, like Louise Patterson, the batty lady artist Elsa Lanchester plays in *The Big Clock* (Farrow, 1948) or the Greenwich Village sculptress who is one of Jeff's neighbors in another of Hitchcock's films, *Rear Window* (1954). More typically, a woman played the role of model, muse, sympathetic or unsupportive wife or parent to the male artist, roles she still plays predominantly. Certainly women artists rarely, if ever before, occupied the moral high ground, as Freya and Frink's work do in *The Damned*. And certainly, too, an artist touted as a great talent or genius, be it in a major or minor part, was inevitably male. This bias, which follows from the reality of art historical reputation and regard, began to shift slightly as second wave feminism brought women artists – historical and contemporary – to light. The character of Freya Neilson, and the work made for her by Frink, who was given a prominent credit in the opening titles of *The Damned*, however, was most unusual in 1961.

After the late 1960s, women artists begin to appear across more serious and diverse characterizations but even then – as I have discussed in *Art in the Cinematic Imagination* (2006) – most are generally bound by myth. Historical women artists are more common and more significant characters than fictional ones but are always selected for and drawn along the lines of notoriety, sensationalism, and/or pathography, as for instance in *Artemesia* (Merlet, 1997), *Camille Claudel* (Nuytten, 1988), *Carrington* (Hampton, 1995), *Frida* (Taymor, 2002), and *Fur: An Imaginary Portrait of Diane Arbus* (Shainberg, 2006). In the modern period, the myth of the artist often fills in for the decayed aura around the art object. As Boris Tomasevskij sees it, the biographical legend is, in fact, part of the artist's oeuvre (1971). The astronomical prices paid at auction for paintings by Vincent Van Gogh and Frida Kahlo – artists whose work commanded little to nothing in their lifetimes – reflect this. The value that is sought is a kind of second-hand aura conferred by the sensational, abject, fascinating life that is also the stuff of movies. Robert Altman expressed this ironic exchange of one kind of cult value for another perfectly by inserting at the beginning of *Vincent and Theo* (1990) documentary footage from the 1987 Christie's London auction at which Van Gogh's *Still Life: Vase with Fifteen Sunflowers* fetched $39.9 million. But these films about artists are really almost the opposite of those considered in this book. *Vincent and Theo*, like several other filmed Van Gogh stories and most of the women artist biopics referenced above, as well as Julian Schnabel's *Basquiat* (1996), Merchant-Ivory's *Surviving Picasso* (1996), John Maybury's *Love is the Devil: Study for a Portrait* (1998, about Francis Bacon), Ed Harris's *Pollock* (2000), and Mick Davis's *Modigliani* (2004), were legally or financially prohibited from filming authentic works and were forced to use pastiches, copies, or, in the case of Maybury's film, completely absent art objects. That is, they feature *unreal objects in real(er) situations*. A biopic is, of course, very far from reality, indeed, at least as far as the works seen in those films are from their prototypes.

As is evidenced, perhaps, by that spate of artist biopics, the geopolitical and ideological discourses around modern art that informed many films of the atomic age (1941–1961) tend to give way after the mid-1960s to those that relate art to sexual and identity politics. The personal is, of course, political. Art is deployed in the films discussed in the second half of this book more sensually; its impact is less rhetorical, more psychological and sensory. In

Paul Mazursky's *An Unmarried Woman* (1978) and Joe Wright's *Pride & Prejudice* (2005), the female protagonist's engagement with art objects expresses a subjective experience of sensual awakening and pleasure, in the first case a liberatory, and in the latter, a revelatory experience. In Robert Altman's *The Player* (1992), a major character is both a woman artist and an obscure object of desire. The paintings of Sydney Cooper – pale, translucent, cryptic, and cool – crystalize the mysterious and phantasmal aspect of June Gudmundsdottir (Greta Scacchi), whose praxis is presented as opposite to that of Hollywood studio executive, Griffin Mill (Tim Robbins): non-narrative, anti-social, and not-for-sale. June's filmy paintings are very like her, and at the same time – in a formal sense – evocative of cinema itself; in them, fragmented photographic images and words are seen as if through glass, or a screen. The character of June, who always wears white, knows no one, and exudes a rather innocent sensuality, recalls spectral and dreamlike objects of desire from previous films about the movies and the men who make them, including Fellini's *8 ½* (1963), Fosse's homage to it, *All That Jazz* (1979), and Kazan's *The Last Tycoon* (1976). Indeed, Altman has said of June that she does not exist. Cooper's diaphanous pictures play the product, then, of a nonexistent artist; they instantiate the theme of this book. The recursive levels of real and fictional in *The Player* express, along with the juxtaposition of movies and painting, a complex and entertaining phenomenology of the arts. While a painting is made of stuff – its medium is oil or acrylic paint on a support of canvas or board – on film it is immaterial and absent, as is the actor. Altman points to this paradoxical aspect of the movies by making June 'unreal,' urging us to ask in what way she is less real to us than Griffin, or even, in a sense, than the many famous actors playing themselves.

A somewhat more realist and collective context – cultural and familial patrimony – is given to the experience of art in *Summer Hours* (Assayas, 2008). Yet, from very different directions, *The Player* and *Summer Hours* each engage with and narrativize the central problems of this study. The product of the highly publicized collaboration between the filmmakers, the Musée d'Orsay, and several private collectors, Assayas's film tells a story of people and things, the things being material works of art and the story about the fate of these things when their owners die. Theorists from Benjamin to Bazin to Barthes (1981) have contemplated the way that photography preserves the images of people at the same time as it testifies to their absence, their mortality. Film images, too, are of absent things and mortal flesh – and in them time annihilates matter – so a film about the question of preservation of art is inherently paradoxical. And *Summer Hours* presents other paradoxes. It features a few pastiches as the works of a fictional modern artist (a few sketches and supposed reproductions in an exhibition catalogue), whose own art collection is the patrimony around which the story is conceived. Prominent among this collection are a few works that are, in fact, in the collection of the Musée d'Orsay, where the fiction leaves them at the end. The film incorporated real objects from public and private collections (including furniture by Louis Majorelle and Josef Hoffmann), high-quality copies (two Corots in the Louvre and a fragile Redon painting that the Museé d'Orsay would not permit to go on location to the country estate where much of the film was shot), and pastiches into a fictional world that centered on richly sensory, aesthetic, and material pleasures and the problems of patrimony.

Assayas exits his story with a supremely cinematic scene, of youth in motion in the French landscape, a scene richly sensory, aesthetic, and consciously engaged with French culture's art historical and cinematic patrimony. Having emptied the real house in which the film was shot of the real objects around which its fictional life had been staged, and restored them to the mortified and mortifying space of muséal exhibition, where their withered aura will be preserved, he delivers the viewer over to pleasures that cannot be preserved: transitory pleasures of movement and color, the passing pleasures of a season, of youthful beauty. It is as though Assayas has told us a story about what Benjamin called the 'shattering of tradition,' and has sliced like a surgeon into the body of the world, excising that 'strange tissue of space and time.'

If, to continue with Benjamin's analogy, the painter is a magician and the cameraman a surgeon, the work of this book is something like that of a biopsy, a concentrated look at what remains of that excised tissue of space and time, the decay of its aura. Interestingly, though, Benjamin's analogy sets up a binary. If the painter is a magician and the cameraman a surgeon, what then is a sculptor? Benjamin overlooks practices like printmaking and sculptural casting that in history and praxis constitute a kind of link between the manual practice of fine artists and the mass media. Works that can exist in multiples stand somewhere in-between the magical, auratic, unique object of art and the accessible, mass-produced reproduction. The status of such equivocal objects – not unique, yet original – muddles Benjamin's argument somewhat and also reminds us of all the manual art and craft behind the immaterial reproduction that is a movie. I begin with a movie in which sculpture – some necessarily of the reproducible kind, in the case of *The Song of Songs* – stars.

## Notes

1   Ralph Richardson was a giant of the British stage, a veteran of many Shakespeare productions, as well as movies; Olivia de Havilland, although she did have a bit of experience on American stages as an ingénue, had been raised in the Hollywood studio system (beginning at Warner Bros.); and Montgomery Clift had trained as a method actor.

2   Of course, such marks can be and are often faked.

3   Notably, in addition to Steven Jacobs: Brigitte Peucker, Michael Walker, and Tom Gunning.

4   That Chatsworth was the model for Pemberley has been recently disputed by Janine Barchas (2013).

5   The reasons for this common oversight are multiple and difficult to discern archivally. One, however, must have to do with the fact that motion picture sets and productions, in Hollywood, at least, have been unionized since the 1930s. By the time Hitchcock used John Ferren's paintings in *The Trouble with Harry* in 1954, for instance, he may have been

trampling (or skirting) the contractual rights of studio employees represented by a newly independent (1949) local of Scenic and Title Artists.

6    See Ng (2009), Kahn (2009), and documentary film, *Inventory* (by Olivier Goinard), which is a special feature on the Criterion Collection DVD edition of *Summer Hours*.

7    When released in Britain in 1963, Hammer had cut Losey's film from 96 to 87 minutes; further cuts left it at 77 minutes when it was released as *These Are the Damned* in the United States in 1965 (Hearn 2010).

# Chapter 1

Doubly Immortal: *The Song of Songs* (1933)

A direct product of male desire and fetishistic transferral, art in this film simultaneously intensifies and displaces life; it causes both ecstasy and trauma. Though Mamoulian's camera frequently lingers on Dietrich's face itself in order to open intimate windows on her ever shifting appearances, it spends almost equal time to offer us images of her statue in scenarios of what Gaylyn Studlar would call 'iconic textuality', that is, highly choreographed scenarios emphasizing the sign as a creation independent of its referent.[1]

(Koepnick 2007: 47–48)

In 2011, the Deutsche Kinemathek received a gift for its Marlene Dietrich Collection: a sculpture – a life-sized bronze nude – *The Song of Songs*, a replica of the figure by Salvatore Scarpitta that had played a starring role, as Lutz Koepnick notes, in the 1933 Paramount film of the same title. Announcing the gift in its newsletter, the Kinemathek explained the origins of this bronze cast, made, 'as a replica of the original', in the 1990s (2011). But the term 'original' is something of a misnomer, or mystery here. As the short article about Stella Cartaino's (the artist's granddaughter) gift also notes, at least three identical sculptures were made for the film. The sculptures were all cast in plaster from the same mold, so there really was no original. But certainly the two surviving plasters (one was destroyed on film) are more original than the more durable bronze that was donated to the museum.

That object – the bronze figure of Marlene Dietrich, which came into being around the time of her death, more than 40 years after Scarpitta's, and some 60 years after he had modeled the sculpture; and which went on exhibit in the Kinemathek's ground floor showroom in 2011 – is a paradoxical artifact. Scarpitta generally destroyed his molds, so his son, Salvatore Jr. (also an artist), would have made the mold for the bronze cast from the plaster that his father had retained, which itself would have been cast in a mold, made from the impermanent clay original Scarpitta created 'of' Dietrich. The bronze is thus four processes removed from the hand of the artist and, you might say, five generations removed from the movie goddess whom it portrays. It is a reproduction of a sculpture made for the movies – one conceived as a movie star. The statue, director Rouben Mamoulian wrote when trying to cast the role, 'should be a masterpiece because it is not merely a prop in the picture but a central point around which the whole story revolves [...] it will have as many closeups as any star'.[2] Note here the double meaning of the word 'cast'. The Kinemathek's bronze is not exactly a work of art and not quite a prop. If it has an aura at all, it is a reconditioned aura; it is, in a sense, a reification of ephemera: the residue of the very particular type of aura that attaches to legendary stars such as Marlene Dietrich.

**Figure 4:** Poster for *The Song of Songs* (Mamoulian, 1933).

*The Song of Songs* was Paramount Pictures' 1933 adaptation of Prussian writer Hermann Sudermann's 1908 novel *Das hohe Lied*, a story that had seen two previous Hollywood adaptations: *The Song of Songs*, 1918, directed by Joseph Kaufman and starring Elsie Ferguson; and *Lily of the Dust*, 1924, directed by Dimitri Buchowetzki and starring Pola Negri, both for Famous Players–Lasky. The 1933 Paramount version was produced and directed by Rouben Mamoulian, who was a co-author with Leo Birinsky (as Leo Birinski) and Samuel Hoffenstein of the screen adaptation of Sudermann's novel and the American playwright Edward Sheldon's play based upon it. The film, then, not unlike the bronze sculpture that descended from it – and like all film adaptations, really – is generations removed from an original source (the Sudermann novel): a remake of a film adaptation of a play based on the novel. The question of authenticity or originality is moot; the aura is already withered.

In *The Song of Songs*, which is set early in the last century, Marlene Dietrich plays Lily Czepanek, an innocent but sensual, orphaned country girl who moves to Berlin. Working in the bookstore owned by her Aunt Rasmussen (Alison Skipworth), she meets Richard Waldow (Brian Aherne), a handsome young sculptor who lives and works across the street. She succumbs to his entreaties to pose for him and becomes the inspiration and model for his life-size nude, 'The Song of Songs,' and then his lover, marking the beginning of a precipitous fall from innocence. Taken with her, Richard's wealthy, decadent client, a retired Colonel, the Baron von Merzbach (Lionel Atwill), persuades the ambivalent and weak-willed artist to abandon Lily to him and purchases the cooperation of her aunt. Bereft, she is compelled into a loveless marriage to the Baron and turned into a beautiful but unhappy sophisticate (taken home to a neo-medieval, almost expressionist castle and instructed in piano, song, dance, French, and – it is implied – depraved sexual acts). A recriminatory act of infidelity (or the appearance of one, meant to hurt a visiting Waldow more than her husband) leads to her banishment and downfall, a (rather glamorous) downfall from which her reunion with Waldow at the end of the film redeems her. The loss of innocence theme was preserved from Sudermann's novel in Sheldon's play and both previous adaptations. The correspondence between art and sensual passion that comes to exemplify Lily's spirit and self-image also derives from Sudermann. Much of the narrative, however, was changed substantially in the Paramount adaptation and the sculptor character and modeling theme were wholly an invention of Mamoulian's film.[3] Sculpture, it can be inferred, was imported into the story to play a particular role (or roles).

Hermann Sudermann (1857–1928), the 'Balzac of the East,' although little remembered now, was a towering figure in drama and literature in the late nineteenth and early twentieth centuries. An editor of the radical newspaper Deutsches Reichsblatt from 1881 to 1889, and already the author of collected stories and a novel, *Frau Sorge* (1887), Sudermann gained enormous acclaim with his first play, *Die Ehre* (1889), which purportedly stirred Berlin youth to riot or protest over three days. Eleanora Duse, Sarah Bernhardt, and Helena Modjeska starred in famed productions of Sudermann's *Heimat* (*Magda* in English).[4] Sudermann's plays were performed in the premier theaters of Berlin, Vienna, Paris, Rome, New York, and as far as Japan.

Sudermann reached such heights of theatrical recognition that […] men all across Europe wanted their barbers to give them a 'Sudermann trim'. His visage was on postage stamps, tram tickets, ration cards, railway postcards and souvenir medals, and his whereabouts were a weekly feature in many Berlin newspapers. His literary reputation was such that major writers of that time, such as Bernard Shaw, Emile Zola and Henrick Ibsen, all attended productions of Sudermann's plays.

(Friesen 2011)

Among the forty-plus other filmed adaptations of Sudermann's works are F.W. Murnau's *Sunrise: A Song of Two Humans* (1927), based on Sudermann's short story 'Die Reise nach Tilsit'/'Trip to Tilset', and *Flesh and the Devil* (Brown, 1927), with Greta Garbo, based on his play *The Undying Past*.

Marlene Dietrich starred in *The Song of Songs*, her first Hollywood film *not* – for personal and contractual reasons – directed by Josef von Sternberg. She was not pleased about this; it evidently took a suit to bring her to work but, according to several sources, finally the production offered her a critical opportunity to wrest some control over her own image and craft (Anon 1933: 18).[5] There is a fascinating metacinematic paradox here, then. Dietrich – famously a creation of von Sternberg's ('Like an artist working in clay, von Sternberg has molded and modeled her to his own design, and Marlene, plastic and willing to be material in the director's hands, has responded to his creative moods' [Tolischus 1931: 28–29; 129]) – took on a role in the film in which she was literally modeled in clay by a sculptor, and in which the Pygmalion theme was telescoped ('you modeled her in marble but I modeled her in the flesh, so to speak; I'm a bit of an artist myself …,' says Merzbach, *Song's* ersatz Svengali), yet in undertaking the part without her Pygmalion (Svengali?), learned to master modeling herself in light.[6] Given that the sculpture theme had entered the *Song of Songs* script – after several revisions – sometime after Dietrich's services were secured, it is entirely possible that she inspired it. Although her prior film, von Sternberg's *Blonde Venus* (1932), had little to do with high art, posters and other elements of the advertising campaign featured variations on a sketch of Dietrich as the Venus de Milo, with the sculpted goddess's naked torso approximated by a skimpy, transparent, close-fitting bodice and her broken arms suggested by long black gloves [Fig. 5].

The motif effectively invokes art, beauty, eroticism, and Dietrich's status as a movie goddess, in one figure: one – as Mary Beth Haralovich points out – that is iconographically unrelated to the character, Helen Faraday, that Dietrich played in *Blonde Venus*. Perhaps this overdetermined image showed Mamoulian how he might give visual form to some of Sudermann's more problematic themes. It is perhaps no coincidence that in an epistle prepared in defense of the nudity of the statuary in *The Song of Songs*, Mamoulian asserted that the 'first synonym for beauty that comes to anybody's mind is always Venus de Milo' (Mamoulian 1933).[7] But contradictions around the significance and signification of nudity resound in *The Song of Songs*, as is vividly captured by discrepancies between the language of the letter contracting the titular sculpture and subsequent accounts.

**Figure 5:** Poster for *Blonde Venus* (Von Sternberg, 1932).

Dear Mr. Scarpitta:

You are hereby engaged to prepare and sculpture a life-size statue for use in our production entitled THE SONG OF SONGS. The head of such statue shall be a reproduction of Miss Marlene Dietrich who is the star in the said production, and the figure thereon shall be an ideal figure of your own composition. It is agreed that Miss Dietrich shall not be required to pose for you in any manner other than for the purpose of enabling you to reproduce her head.[8]

Marlene Dietrich, who wears trousers, and Sally Rand, who wears nothing, continue to oppose each other in loop theaters this week. However, it must be said of Marlene that in her picture, 'Song of Songs,' at the Oriental, she has several scenes wherein her statue is costumed as scantily as Sally herself at the Chicago.

In fact, it is Marlene's undraped counterpart sculped in marble by the inspired hands of Brian Aherne that causes as many gasps of amazement and approval from Oriental audiences as does Sally's fan-tasy at the stage showhouse [...]. That Miss Dietrich had no compunction about posing in the nude is ample tribute to the loveliness of the finished masterpiece. S. Cartaino Scarpitta [...] is the genius who molded Marlene's charms. Never before has a studio engaged an artist or sculptor of international repute for picture purposes.[9]

The contradictions revealed in two documents – a letter contracting sculptor Salvatore Cartaino Scarpitta (1887–1948) to create the titular sculpture for Paramount's film and a notice in a Chicago paper noting the proximate and competing attractions of Dietrich and Sally Rand in local theaters – are only some of those which attend the complex roles that real works of art play in this fiction film and others. The 'masterpiece in marble' that the newspaper item in nearly the same breath reveals to be an end run around the censors was indeed the work of an accomplished artist of some repute, but it is not made of marble. Indeed, *The Song of Songs* illustrates the process and the progress of the sculpture from its inception in a sketch, then a small maquette, to a full-scale armature upon which plaster is built up and then clay modeled. Numerous scenes show the sculptor working the pliable clay – in fact, much of the subtext depends upon such images. Generally, such an *additive* sculptural process results in a form from which a mold is made, in turn from which a sculpture is cast, typically either in bronze or plaster. Marble, on the other hand, must be carved; it is worked *subtractively*.

The anonymous Chicago reviewer was understandably confused about the medium, however. The movie itself wants to have its marble and mold it, too; it bares some of the devices of sculpture but not those of the movies: featuring a veritably documentary scene about process yet seeming to count on its audience's ignorance of or indifference to sculptural materials and techniques. Not only does publicity for the film tout the 'poem in marble conceived by the noted Italian sculptor S.C. Scarpitta,'[10] but the very script insists, too, upon the statue's marmoreal standing. 'Next the clay,' says Waldow, the fictional sculptor, as he completes his sketch, continuing – as if one could cast in stone – 'then the marble: *The Song of Songs* in marble!' Later, the libertine Baron von Merzbach echoes this material claim, saying to Richard of Lily, the model and inspiration for the figure, 'you modeled her in marble; I modeled her in the flesh.' Marble takes on metaphoric meaning again and again. Of course, a sculptor *might* make a clay study for a marble work, or two versions of one theme – one in each medium – but in this case, Scarpitta did not, Richard is *not* shown doing so, and when Lily, at the film's climax, attacks the work with a handy sledgehammer, it breaks apart readily, as plaster – revealing itself to be hollow and

**Figure 6:** Salvatore Cartaino Scarpitta with his maquette of the title sculpture for *The Song of Songs* (photo courtesy of Lola Scarpitta).

rather brittle, not solid and hard as marble – a material prized for, among other traits, its resistance to shattering. But what is in fact a significant semantic and artistic difference means little in the unfolding of the motion picture, becoming a minor detail, the kind of quibble destined for, at best, an IMDb entry under 'goofs.'[11] For, along with the aura of the work of art, what decays in the process of mechanical reproduction is its material facticity. In a museum the medium matters; in a film, the medium *is* film; the sculptural material is, ultimately, immaterial.

The incompatibility of what is shown and what is said about sculptural medium in *The Song of Songs* parallels the comparably equivocal treatment of sculptural signification, as suggested by the short Chicago item: the way that the prestige of fine art is used to throw an albeit thin veil over the more prurient purposes of the female nude sculpture. As Thomas Doherty notes, 'finding innovative ways to reveal women in states of undress and dishevelment was a creative challenge pre-Code Hollywood met unblushingly,' and this is without doubt one function of sculpture generally and the title work particularly in Mamoulian's film (1999: 118–119). Not only does the nude statue readily suggest and stand in for the star who could not be shown undressed, but it is often handled and beheld with open sensuality, as well as motivating suggestive scenes of undressing.[12] This equivocation between art and exploitation is certainly not new with the movies but takes on added urgency in a commercial medium in which profits are perceived to obtain more from the latter, while particular artists (writers, directors, production artists, actors) and critics value the former, and censorship bears down on all. These internal tensions are captured well by Dave Kehr's characterization of *The Song of Songs* upon its DVD release in 2011:

'The Song of Songs' proudly shows off its cultural credentials: a prestigious source novel (by Hermann Sudermann, whose short story 'The Trip to Tilsit' was the basis for Murnau's 'Sunrise'); a British supporting cast (Brian Aherne as the Berlin sculptor inspired by Dietrich's naïve peasant girl; Lionel Atwill as the decadent aristocrat who steals her away); a nonstop score composed of snippets from Chopin, Schubert and Strauss; and at its center a monumental nude sculpture of Dietrich, executed by Salvatore Cartaino Scarpitta (whose allegorical bas reliefs for the newly opened Los Angeles Stock Exchange were the sensation of the hour).

The sculpture, which might have been designed for the prow of an Art Deco ocean liner, depicts Dietrich as the embodiment of the eternal feminine, rising up on point with her arms open at her side – a pose that suggests great spiritual yearning but also exaggerates the lift of a pair of perky breasts.

Essentially the film is little more than an elaborate ruse to film Dietrich undressing (as the peasant girl – shyly at first, then with defiant pride – disrobes for the sculptor) and display the results in an aestheticized form that would not disturb the local censor boards.

(Kehr 2011)

There is something confounding, though, about Kehr's finally reductive assessment (film as elaborate ruse), which assumes that the film could not undertake a narrative having to do with sex and sexuality, test the limits of the Production Code, *and* have artistic intentions, integrity, or complexity. I believe it meant to be and do all that and that Mamoulian used the 'spiritual yearning' and 'perky breasts' of the sculpture to give visual form to – literally to embody – the foundational proposition of Sudermann's really quite radical narrative: that of a naïve, innocent, and beautiful young woman's idealistic attitude toward love, an attitude that is, over the course of the (very long) novel, gradually and inexorably exploited, degraded, and destroyed by men's lust and power and society's hypocrisy and corruption. As Adrian Danks notes, a 'focus on sexuality and class is a key, often troubling and unresolved theme of many of Mamoulian's films' (2007). We can understand the function of sculpture in the film, then, to be the opposite of a ruse. Rather, it gives form to an ideal – the innocent, even spiritual, sense of sexual love with which Lily enters the story – that is later contrasted to the actions of the players around it: the Baron's salacious gestures and Lily's own jaded sophistication at the end of the film. In fact, Mamoulian committed very much this view to paper, in a three-page memorandum, dated 5 June, 1933, to Paramount producer, A.M. Botsford, in anticipation of Hays Office challenges to his latest cut of the film:

> The key to the character of the girl is found in the beautiful lines of Solomon: 'Put me as a seal upon thine heart, as a seal upon thine arm, for love is strong as death.' This really is the thesis of the whole story. The Song of Songs of a human heart is symbolized on the screen orally through beautiful poetry and through the musical theme taken out of the Sixth Symphony by the great Tchaikovsky, and visually through the statue of a young girl listening in inspired awe to the distant melodies of a heavenly Song of Songs […]. The main statue, the SONG OF SONGS, as you probably know from newspapers, is on its way to the Chicago World's Fair, to be exhibited to millions of visitors who will be there from all parts of the world. I have tried not to be either obvious or unduly suggestive in any sense in the picture dealing with the love in its different phases between the sculptor and the girl, and I think that in every shot that includes statues, it is not 'nudity' that stands out, but beauty symbolized through the human form. It is not for nothing that through the many centuries of development, the human race, in its search for beauty and its desire to express it in a concrete visual form, has always chosen for its medium, the form of a human body. In this again art meets religion, for that which was created 'in His own image' is found by the artist in all the periods of history, pagan and Christian alike, to be the most sensitive medium of expressing beauty approaching divinity. The first synonym for beauty that comes to anybody's mind is always Venus de Milo, and whether it be under the sky of pagan Rome or in the sacred walls of the Chappela Sistina, beauty finds its expression through human form.[13]

Thus, the nude figure of the *Song of Songs* stands in on film for the biblical verse as it functions in Sudermann's novel as a leitmotif and touchstone for Lily; in the film the sculptural pose

**Figure 7:** Marlene Dietrich, as Lily Czepanek, with the title sculpture in *The Song of Songs*.

is represented as an expression of Lily's pure spirit. When she first visits his studio, Waldow shows her a sketch he has done after their first encounter in the bookstore:

RICHARD:        I've been making a sketch of you. Want to see yourself?

LILY:        Oh, yes! (looks) Oh, I haven't any clothes on!

RICHARD:        Clothes? Do you think I model people with their clothes on?

LILY:        How did you know I was like that?

RICHARD:        And just what does that mean?

LILY:        I mean, it is me and it isn't me.

RICHARD:        Go on, this starts to sound like criticism of the highest order.

LILY:        Oh, it's wonderful! I mean, it's the way I want to be. It's me as I dream of me. It's the girl in 'The Song of Songs.'

RICHARD:        Oh?

LILY:        The girl in 'The Song of Songs.' She's in the Bible.

RICHARD:        The Bible?

LILY:        She's the girl who feels in her heart that somewhere the perfect love is waiting for her. She says, 'I sleep but my heart waketh. It is the voice of my beloved saying, "open to me, my love, my own desire."' Oh, I know what she means; I know it, because I feel it inside; that's what I mean (rising on her toes, tilting her head toward heaven, arms by her side with palms opened as if to give or receive).

RICHARD:        Hold that pose! Now, don't move! Yes, yes, that's wonderful! Yes, there's my statue and we'll call it 'The Song of Songs.'

The dialogue here progresses from the very reflexive sort of prudishness embodied by the Hays Code ('Oh, I haven't any clothes on!') to an articulation of the paradox of mimesis ('it is me and it isn't me') – one that is important to the film as pertains to the censors (i.e. the sculpture is Marlene Dietrich and it is not Marlene Dietrich) – to art's capacity to inspire and move its audience and to give form to ideas ('It's me as I dream of me'), finally positing the expression of sexual love and desire as sacred. *The Song of Songs*, then – sculpture and film – walk a tightrope between exploitation and serious flouting of convention by means of art.

This act of funambulism – underscored by Romantic composers – falls for the most part to statuary, most notably Salvatore Scarpitta's titular figure. Although the contract with the sculptor (quoted above) expressly stated that Dietrich was to 'not be required to pose for you in any manner other than for the purpose of enabling you to reproduce her head' – she did probably, as did her character, disrobe for the sculptor.[14] And Paramount, regardless of its contractual caution, exploited the nude statue's embodiment (or signification) of Dietrich's sex appeal vigorously. A considerable portion of the publicity and exploitation campaigns for the film featured the sculpture, variously emphasizing its ennobling and titillating qualities. 'Marble Statue, Film Creation Motivates Plot,' the headline of one item prepared by the Paramount publicity department, repeats the misnomer about medium, while also indicating that despite his contractual deadline, the sculptor may have been permitted more time than the nine days given.

> Probably the most important inanimate actor ever cast for a motion picture is the life-size nude statue of Marlene Dietrich, which plays fully as important a role in the German star's newest Paramount picture, 'The Song of Songs,' as though it were one of the principal actors of the cast [...]. Rouben Mamoulian, director, commissioned S. Cartaino Scarpitta, one of America's best known sculptors, to design the statue [...]. Miss Dietrich paid numerous visits to Scarpitta's studio in advance of the picture so that he could outline the classic Dietrich figure. The task occupied over five weeks of his time. Never before, it is said, has a studio engaged a truly noted artist to create such a statue or painting for film purposes.
>
> (Paramount collection, Margaret Herrick Library)

Another short item entered the press kit after the Long Beach earthquake of 10 March, 1933, which occurred when the film was in production. 'Statue in Danger/Aherne Saves it,' the headline reads; the story relates that the 6.4 magnitude 'quake caused the statue, inspired by certain incidents in the story, to totter precariously, but Aherne clutched it in his arms and prevented it from falling and being smashed.' Even more imaginative and dependent upon the statue were some of the suggestions for theatrical exploitation devised by studio publicists.[15] Theaters were offered a 'Moving Still Display' for the lobby, 'an easily constructed, comp-board display using a cut-out from the three-sheet poster [an approximately life-size photographic image of the statue with Dietrich in costume at its base], slotted [right next to the statue's breasts] to show a moving display of stills. Stills move on a band, operated by a motor, as in the sketch illustrated.' Additionally, Paramount suggested that newspapers launch a contest in connection with the film's release. 'Famous Art Statues/Name Them! Prizes!' screams an exploitation headline of a full-page spread about a proposed contest in which Scarpitta's *Song of Songs* is pictured in inset next to four renowned sculptural masterpieces (the *Venus de Milo*, the *Discus Thrower*, Michelangelo's *Moses*, and Rodin's *Thinker*) that readers are encouraged to identify on sequential days, for prizes. More striking yet was a proposed theatrical exploitation. 'Sculptor Works in Lobby!' it was suggested to exhibitors; 'Artist Re-models Statue of Picture for Front-gazers.' 'A curious public will stand for hours gazing avidly at the prosaic performances of window-washers, street laborers, sign-painters, etc.,' the article begins. 'Imagine that public's reaction when they are afforded the opportunity of watching a sculptor at work in your lobby – creating in clay the nude image of a beautiful woman! This is not a lobby stunt. *It's a lobby spectacle!* A spectacle that will create more excitement and draw more crowds than a city hall fire!' The piece goes on to suggest procedures by which a hired sculptor might reproduce Scarpitta's Dietrich figure and gives specifications (the dimensions of the full-scale sculpture), adding that 'the services of a capable sculptor may be obtained by inquiring at a local art institute, or a commercial art service or your own poster artists can assist you in getting one. Perhaps a display ad in local classified columns would bring you a capable man and stir up some additional interest in the film.' It is not known how many exhibitors attempted or achieved this spectacular promotion.

Perhaps the oddest use of the image of Scarpitta's sculpture was in a merchandise promotion to exhibitors, a tie-in in the form of a tire cover, picturing the nude. 'Tell the town about Dietrich with Tire Covers…they cover the town! Every car carrying a Dietrich Tire Cover is a show salesman, busy 24 hours a day. After you plant the first few, your theatre will be besieged by car-owners *asking* for Tire Covers.' At 65 cents each, the colored spare tire covers of weatherproofed fabric were touted as 'beautiful! And practical, too!' From the rather ridiculous to the supposed sublime, a souvenir program cover features the most prevalent image used to promote the film, the photograph of Dietrich, clothed in her peasant garb, on her knees, embracing the base of sculpture (the same image used on the moving still display for lobbies). On the program, the image is accompanied by the poetic text:

'*Thou Art Beautiful*
*O My Love*'
    – The Song of Solomon, Ch. 6, IV
Poem in marble conceived by
the noted Italian sculptor S.C.
Scarpitta. Inspired by the beautiful –
Marlene Dietrich in 'The Song of Songs'[16]

'Poem in polished plaster,' despite its pleasant alliteration, does not quite work as well. But marble would not only have been a prohibitively expensive material for a film prop, it would also have been overly time-intensive and would not have worked with the narrative, which for shooting purposes required at least two identical figures, so an easily reproduced form. The contract he signed on 12 January permitted Scarpitta only nine days to produce both the preliminary maquette for approval and the final figure for casting, although evidence suggests he was finally given longer, and a whole paragraph of the contract was about the expenses, responsibility for, and final disposition of any casts.

Interestingly, the montage sequence in *The Song of Songs* documents some of Scarpitta's actual work on the sculpture; almost certainly his hands are those seen at work on Richard's initial sketch of Lily's pose and then the subsequent stages of work: a small, sculptural maquette, a full-scale armature, upon which first plaster, then clay is built up, then modeled. At least two – and probably three – plaster casts (later polished) were made from the clay figure, as one had to be smashed to pieces by its model [Fig. 8a–f].

Scarpitta, an academically trained sculptor, may have been unable to produce a 'masterpiece in marble' under the schedule and budget restraints imposed by the studio but he did, in fact, work often in stone, as with his many architectural commissions, portraits, and one of the most impressive among the dozen or more other sculptures seen in the Waldow atelier in *The Song of Songs: Transition* [Figs. 12–13], a massive, somewhat Rodinesque *non finito*,

**Figures 8 (a), (b), (c), (d), (e) and (f):** A montage sequence from *The Song of Songs*, showing the progress of the title sculpture.

a languorous nude in limestone.[17] Scarpitta was born in Palermo, Sicily, and trained at the Accademia di Belle Arti, Palermo. In 1910, he married and moved with his new wife to New York, where he became a member of the National Sculpture Society and commenced an active American career as a sculptor of, among other commissions, portraits, executing a bust of J.P. Morgan that very year. Some years later, his first marriage ended when he met and became involved with vaudeville acrobat, dancer, and actress Nadia Jarocki. By 1923, Scarpitta's second family had moved to Los Angeles, where Nadia appeared in occasional motion pictures (until, according to familial accounts, stopped by her husband's old-school jealousy), and Scarpitta received numerous public and private commissions, including most notably the decorative work for St. John's Episcopal Cathedral (1925) and for the main entrances of the Los Angeles County General Hospital (1934) and Los Angeles Stock Exchange (1929), the latter of which was awarded a prize by the American Institute of Architects[18] [Fig. 9]. By the time of his work on Mamoulian's film, Scarpitta was well known for statuary and portraits – including some among the movie colony – and had received a commission for a Mussolini portrait, which he completed that spring.[19] As with most of the other sculptors whose works were disposed around the set in the Waldow studio scenes, Scarpitta's academic training made him well suited to producing work believable as that of a turn-of-the-century sculptor.

Scarpitta was evidently not the first sculptor approached about the commission, however. Among the director's papers are copies of telegraphic correspondence between Mamoulian in Hollywood and Boris Lovet-Lorski, a prominent, somewhat more modernist sculptor of the day, in Paris. Lovet-Lorski was born in Lithuania in 1894 and trained at the Royal Academy in Petrograd. A naturalized US citizen by 1925, he was well known by 1933 for a series of 'bronze female figures with impossibly narrow, boyish hips, and bodies broadening as they rise to the shoulders and wide-spread arms held behind their heads like flowers on a stem' (Macklowe Gallery 2013).

It was almost certainly one such bronze, the celebrated *Venus*, 1925 (in the collection of the de Young Fine Art Museum of San Francisco), about which Mamoulian wrote to his friend on 5 January, 1933, by Western Union:

MY DEAR BORIS
HAVE AN INTERESTING IDEA WHICH YOU WILL LIKE STOP FOR MY NEXT FILM SONG OF SONGS WITH MARLENE DIETRICH I NEED A BEAUTIFUL STATUE OF YOUNG WOMAN STATUE SHOULD BE A MASTERPIECE BECAUSE IT IS NOT MERELY A PROP IN THE PICTURE BUT A CENTRAL POINT AROUND WHICH WHOLE STORY REVOLVES STOP IT WILL HAVE AS MANY CLOSEUPS AS ANY STAR STOP THERE ARE MANY STATUES AROUND HERE BUT I DON'T LIKE THEM I WOULD LOVE TO USE YOUR STATUE WHICH I SAW IN YOUR PARIS STUDIO AND THUS PRESENT IT TO THE ENTIRE WORLD AND MAKE IT DOUBLY IMMORTAL STOP UNDERSTAND BRONZE IS IN SAN FRANCISCO CANNOT USE BRONZE BECAUSE STATUE MUST BE BROKEN AS CLIMAX IN

**Figure 9:** An entrance to the Los Angeles Stock Exchange (1929), with sculptural program by S.C. Scarpitta.

THE STORY STOP WOULD LIKE TO MAKE PLASTER CAST OF SAN FRANCISCO BRONZE AND USE THAT IN DIFFERENT STAGES OF COMPLETION ON THE SCREEN STOP WILL NOT CONSIDER USING IT WITHOUT DUE FINANCIAL REMUNERATION TO YOU STOP PITY YOU ARE NOT HERE PLEASE CABLE COLLECT IMMEDIATELY GREETINGS AND LOVE ROUBEN

Lovet-Lorski replied with alacrity, the next day:

DEAR ROUBEN AM VERY ENTHUSIASTIC OVER YOUR SPLENDID IDEA WISH I WAS THERE TO SEE YOU AT WORK STOP I CAN BORROW THE BRONZE FROM THE MUSEUM STOP A PIECEMOULD COULD BE MADE OF HER FIRST COVERING HER SURFACE WITH TRANSPARANT VARNISH TO PRESERVE HER PATINE STOP I THINK FIVE THOUSAND DOLLARS WOULD BE REASONABLE FOR THE RIGHTS OF USING HER PLASTER COPY TO BE BROKEN STOP MOULD TO BE DESTROYED STOP THE LATER [sic] IS VERY IMPORTANT AS

THE BRONZE FIGURE OCCUPIES THE PLACE OF HONOR IN THE MUSEUM AND IS SCHEDULED TO BE THE CENTER PIECE AT THE CHICAGOS WORLDS FAIR STOP IF TERMS AGREEABLE TO YOU PLEASE WIRE I WILL CABLE THE DIRECTORS OF THE MUSEUM STOP A PARAMOUNT TRUCK COULD CALL FOR IT STOP THOUSAND WISHES AND BEST LOVE = BORIS

A week passed before Mamoulian's reply was sent, 13 January:

VERY SORRY ITS TOO LATE NOW YOUR PRICE WAS SO MUCH IN EXCESS OF WHAT STUDIO WAS PREPARED TO PAY THAT I DID NOT EVEN ATTEMPT MAKING A COUNTER OFFER AND AS MATTER WAS MOST URGENT MADE DIFFERENT ARRANGEMENT WITH A SCULPTOR IN HOLLYWOOD REGRETS AND LOVE

Evidently, Lovet-Lorski's price was indeed too high. Scarpitta's contract, dated 12 January, 1933 (one week after Mamoulian's initial cable to Lovet-Lorski), engaged him to prepare a preliminary maquette for approval and then the full-scale statue by 21 January (so, in nine days) for full compensation of $1,000, one-fifth of what Mamoulian's friend wanted to permit casting of an already finished work. But Scarpitta was not only the more cost-effective option. The film would have been a very different one had the job gone to Lovet-Lorski and a starring role to his Deco figure. This more stylized and abstract piece would have been a rather daring and anachronistic choice for a story set in the very first years of the twentieth century. The figure would also have had a much more abstract relationship to the image of Marlene Dietrich, neither whose face nor figure could be invoked (or exploited) by it, for either purposes of narrative or publicity.[20]

The figural sculpture's erotic impact depends very much on its verisimilitude but so does its function in the narrative as an image that preserves and embodies Lily's youthful innocence and idealism. Mamoulian uses it as an objective correlative against which Dietrich can perform the vicissitudes of her character's sexual awakening, initiation, disenchantment, and cynicism. This is, as Adrian Danks articulates it, following Spergel, consistent with Mamoulian's wont to explore the 'bifurcated identities' of his characters, most obviously in the case of *Dr. Jekyll and Mr. Hyde* (1932) – made the year before *The Song of Songs* – but also in relation to the metacinematic phenomenon of stardom and celebrity and its division between the public and private self, key subtexts of Mamoulian's films with both Dietrich and Garbo (whom he directed the same year in *Queen Christina*, for MGM): 'this theme plays along the fault lines of the divisions between actor, character, the public and the private self [...] many of his films feature characters who are either not quite what they seem or who are required to take on contrastive identities,' concluding with an observation that could not be more appropriate to *The Song of Songs* ('it is me and it isn't me'), which itself concludes with the destruction of the sculpture, 'the obliteration of one of these selves, or the closer alignment of the two, is often the key drama of the narrative' (2007).

If the titular, commissioned sculpture is, in a sense, the very star of *The Song of Songs* – 'not merely a prop in the picture but a central point around which [the] whole story revolves,' to quote Mamoulian – the dozen or more other sculptures seen in Waldow's atelier are more or less significant supporting players. Probably a couple of these other sculptures – two placed on either side of the door through which Lily enters the scene, which appear to be neoclassical bronzes of male nudes [Fig. 11] – came from the Paramount property department, but a number are works by contemporary Los Angeles area sculptors. There is little evidence of exactly how they came to be loaned to the production; however, a memorandum prepared by Mamoulian's office at the behest of Paramount production executive A.M. Botsford in May of 1933 – used to defend the film against censors' objections – identified (by artist, title, estimated value, and provenance/exhibition history) ten of these works seen in *The Song of Songs*.

In addition to Scarpitta's *Transition* and another rather celebrated contemporary nude, *Kneeling Aphrodite* [Fig. 10], by Montengro-born Vuch Vuckinich (also known under Vuk Vuchinich and variant spellings, 1901–1974), these included three works – *Captive* [Figs. 19–20], *Innocence*, and *Peasant Dancer* [Fig. 10] – by Bulgarian-born and trained Atanas Katchamakoff (1898–1988), who emigrated to the United States in 1924 and

**Figure 10:** *The Song of Songs*: Dietrich, Brian Aherne as the sculptor Richard Waldow, and Lionel Atwill as the Baron von Merzbach, in Waldow's atelier, featuring works by Harold Swartz (*Torso*), Vuch Vuckinich (*Kneeling Aphrodite*), and Atanas Katchamakoff (*Peasant Dancer*).

settled in the Los Angeles area a few years later, perhaps working for a time in production design.[21] Also included were two minor works – *Head of a Young Girl* and *Rhumba*, not publicly shown previously – by a 'young Los Angeles sculptor,' David Williams. Another of the sculptures, *Torso* [Fig. 10], was listed as by Harold Schwartz – certainly Harold Swartz (1887–1948), a New Mexico-born and European-trained modern sculptor, instructor at the Otis Art Institute, as well as briefly, in 1929, Commissioner of the Board of the Los Angeles Municipal Arts Commission. *The Bather* [Fig. 11] was by George Stanley (1903–1973), a student of Swartz, also later an Otis instructor, and designer of the 'Oscar' statuette, sculptor of the Isaac Newton statue at Griffith Observatory, and the Muse of Music, Dance, Drama sculptural fountain at the Hollywood Bowl; and there was a *Standing Nude* by Ella Buchanan (1869–1951), a Canadian-born teacher and librarian-turned-sculptor who both trained and taught at the Art Institute of Chicago, earned some renown with her allegorical *The Suffragist Trying to Arouse Her Sisters* (1911), and moved to California in 1915.[22]

The works by these legitimate, albeit in some cases little known, academically trained sculptors lend some credibility and artistic ambience to the lengthy scenes set in Waldow's studio, although the presence of several seemingly completed, fairly monumental, and

**Figure 11:** *The Song of Songs*: Lily enters the atelier, flanked by neoclassical bronzes, George Stanley's *Bather*, in rear.

presumably unsold works in stone and bronze seems perhaps somewhat unlikely in a period during which such ambitious and traditional works might result from commissions. Realistically, however, a few of the works are presented as in progress (clay, presumably, covered by cloths). Beyond their function as realist décor for an artist's atelier, many of the figures are vividly engaged by the narration. In fact, shots set in the studio are carefully composed around these sculptures; they fill what would normally be negative space with positively urgent sensual atmosphere, subtext, and innuendo.

From the moment Lily first enters the studio, figures point to and constrain her and all the action is staged to keep statues, particularly nudes, much in the frame [Fig. 11]. 'You mustn't think of me as a man,' Waldow assures the cringing Lily, 'a model means no more to me than a tree,' after she balks at undressing, but the staging has the two just in front of, and framing, Scarpitta's *Transition*, the most sensual nude in the space, belying such dispassionate attitudes. Lily looks quite small and helpless against the piece's monumental, languid eroticism as she attempts to rescind her agreement to model. She runs to the figure as if to hide behind it but ends up cornered next to it. Dietrich has several lines while she alone is up against the sculpture and then pointed dialogue between artist and model takes place with the players framing it on either side, the three heads – two of flesh and one of stone – forming a triangle [Fig. 12].

**Figure 12:** *The Song of Songs*: Waldow and Lily with S.C. Scarpitta's sculpture, *Transition*.

The work was the second version of this theme Scarpitta had executed. The first, referred to as *Nadia's Dream*, was a modeled piece, also life-sized or slightly larger, also showing a sleeping female figure – like Michelangelo's *Dying Slave* (1513–1516), rotated to the vertical axis.[23] The version seen in the film, one that may have been incomplete at the time of filming, echoes the basic pose of the earlier figure (Scarpitta's wife was the model for both) but like Michelangelo's other unfinished *Captives* (ca. 1525–1530), gives the impression of a figure half emerging from stone, as from sleep or unto death, the smooth skin of the sleeper offering a sensual contrast to the rough-hewn stone surrounding it [Fig. 13]. Like her male ancestor, the *Dying Slave* [Fig. 14] – probably the work's most salient intertext – Scarpitta's sleeping figure invokes an iconographic strain in the history of sculpture that began in antiquity – in the Hellenistic period – the most noteworthy antique example being the famous *Barberini Faun* (*Sleeping Satyr*, Munich Glyptothek), which shares with Michelangelo's and Scarpitta's figures the postural element of the bent, raised arm behind the sleeper's head and a potent sense of vulnerable eroticism [Fig. 15]. This Hellenistic trend of isolated figures, removed from narrative context and asleep or otherwise affectively closed off from the beholder, has been theorized as one that brings viewers into a kind of interactive circuit, in which the sculpture demands of its viewer an act of imagination – of fantasy – and is only completed by the act of beholding, with the mental construction of the setting and scenario to which the figure belongs.[24]

The viewer of *The Song of Songs*, however, is not alone in space and time with Scarpitta's sculpture, as an ancient viewer of the *Sleeping Satyr* would have been. Instead, spatio-temporal apprehension is taken over and constrained by the cinematic apparatus and the narrative context is reasserted by the placement of the work within the space and flow of the movie narration, as well as within the context of the other works in the space. The act of imagination or fantasy that such a provocative work induces, then, belongs in large part to the scenario: to fiction – and by implication as much to the beholder *within* the frame, to the fictional characters – as to us, the viewers. And rather than leaving *Transition* and the other sculptural works in the background, as realist trappings of the artist's studio, Mamoulian engages them in the action, giving them supporting roles in a scenario in which art, sensuality, and seduction are elided and sculpture performs a kind of sexual surrogacy.

With some seriousness, as well as more than a few knowing winks, *The Song of Songs* uses the artworks to express sexual passion, seduction, and thrall, to crystallize a certain image of Lily and to play hide-and-seek with the Hays Office. Conspicuous camera movements veer away at the last possible moment as Lily undresses for her first modeling session, to settle on the corresponding body parts of nude or partially nude statues, 'so we will know just what private part she is baring at the cutaway moment,' as Steven Bach puts it (2011: 167). Lily steps into a curtained changing area and sits down, pulls up her skirts, crosses her legs and begins to remove her stockings. A camera movement or special effect (it appears to be a swish-pan) whips from a close-up of her legs to a matching shot of the naked legs of a sculpted seated female nude, one that is not seen in any other shots of the studio [Figs. 16–17]. Back on Lily, still disrobing, the camera cuts to a long shot of Richard

**Figure 13:** S.C. Scarpitta. *Transition* (also known as *Nadia's Dream*), 1930s. The limestone sculpture as displayed in the artist's studio in 2009 (photo: Susan Felleman).

**Figure 14:** Michelangelo. *The Dying Slave*, 1513–1516. Marble. Louvre.

**Figure 15:** *Sleeping Satyr (Barberini Faun).* Hellenistic copy of bronze original, ca. 220 BC. Marble. Staatliche Antiken-sammlungen und Glyptothek München.

preparing the studio for the modeling session, then back to Lily, now framed in medium close-up, beginning to unbutton her bodice. The unbuttoning descends and the camera sweeps away in the nick of time, with another dramatic whip, to Richard ripping the drop cloth off the clay figure of a nude torso in progress. As with the swish to the sculptural legs that are not 'situated' anywhere in the narrative, this seems a rather gratuitous movement, as Richard is presumably preparing to draw Lily, not to work on this nude; there is no reason for this work to be exposed … no reason, that is, other than to suggest as explicitly as possible the anatomy that is nearby being revealed. It should be noted, though, that it is exactly at such moments in *The Song of Songs* – moments that focus on artworks – that the cinematic apparatus itself is most evident (here, in the prominent swish-pans; later, for example, in a highly reflexive use of voiceover in a scene in which Richard is alone with his statue). The

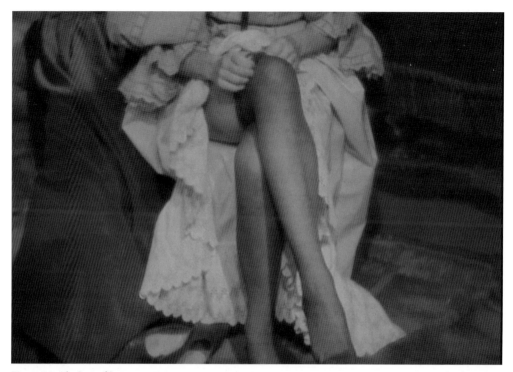

**Figure 16:** *The Song of Songs.*

sculptures are sexual surrogates, then; they expose what the movies cannot. But at the same time, cinematic artifice is exposed; movies are revealed to be art.

A year later, when the Hays Office had begun, under the authority of Joseph Breen and the Production Code Administration, to enforce the Code more strictly, this film could not have been released, and it was not without difficulties that it was, even in this last pre-Breen year of the Production Code. In fact, scenes featuring the sculpture were the ones that most concerned James Wingate, chair of the Studio Relations Committee of the MPPDA in his many communications with his staff and with Paramount about the film and also caught the attention of many of the local and international censor boards.[25] The film not only emphasizes the nudity of the statuary – particularly of the title work, as well as its likeness to Dietrich – it is quite explicit about the erotic equation of sculpture and model. In a second modeling scene, Lily has clearly grown comfortable with the regime. She arrives with a bouquet of flowers and teases Richard, who ends up chasing her about the studio [Fig. 18]. Lily pauses to employ sculptures in her game of catch-me-if-you-can, most notably two works by Atanas Katchamakoff that together express both the childlike silliness and incipient seriousness of the situation: *Innocence* (1930), a small marble sculpture of a pubescent nude with a dog, and *The Captive* (1931), a large, expressive plaster of a semi-naked female figure, bound and abject. At one point in the chase, Lily dangles her bouquet in front of the pubic area of *The*

**Figure 17:** *The Song of Songs.*

*Captive* [Fig. 19]; then, its solemn bowed head and bare breast soon frame her face [Fig. 20]. The chase ends with artist and model in an unanticipated clinch. Moments later, the film suggests Richard's certain sexual attraction to – indeed arousal by – Lily, as he stands kneading the statue's chest and shoulders, his fingers mere inches away from the figure's prominent, erect nipples, while watching the projected shadow of his model undressing [Figs. 21–23]. Mamoulian employs the artworks to evade the censors, certainly (although the censors were not inattentive to these striking scenes) and to evoke, extend, and enhance the viewer's visual and tactile engagement with the figure of Marlene Dietrich, keeping the sex goddess in view by proxy. But the equivalence that has a winking aura of fun in the modeling sessions takes on some gravity later in the narrative when Richard is seen ruefully alone with the statue after his abandonment of Lily. Here, as Lutz Koepnick puts it,

> [I]n what is the film's perhaps most uncanny and excessive sequence, we see Waldow despairing in his studio over his aborted affair with Lily while the camera captures a number of quasi-photographic shots of the statue's face [...]. Close-ups of Waldow's own

43

**Figure 18:** *The Song of Songs.*

face alternate with close-ups of the sculpture as seen from a variety of ideal viewing angles [Figs. 24–27]. Meanwhile the soundtrack carries us back to […] the time of the sculpture's making. Waldow's statue thus seems to gain a fantasmatic life of its own […] seems to hold the absent referent in what Studlar calls an 'I know-but-nevertheless' suspension […]. Mamoulian's camera engages our fantasy with a substitute of desire that sustains painful illusions of autonomy.

(2007: 48)[26]

Indeed, the presence of the statue seems not only to signal Richard's abject sense of Lily's absence but at the same time to remind us – by use of the disembodied voice from the past – of the spectral aspect of movies, the always already-absent status of the players. Even as it foregrounds sexuality in a story that centers on sexual desire and exploitation, then, the sculpture functions otherwise, too.

I have written elsewhere (2006) about sculptures of another 'sex goddess,' Ava Gardner, commissioned from academic sculptors for two of her films: Joseph Nicolosi's for *One Touch of Venus*, 1948 and Assen Peikov's for *The Barefoot Contessa*, 1954, which also perform

**Figures 19 and 20:** *The Song of Songs.*

**Figures 21, 22 and 23:** *The Song of Songs.*

multiple roles. Much of what I had to say about what was striking in relation to sculpture and Gardner pertains here, as well:

> [T]he way that the three-dimensional, spatial properties of sculpture mobilize the spatio-temporal properties of the cinema; the way that statues seem to emphasize the corporeal, even carnal problematics around cinematic bodies; the overdetermined valences of the statuary's signification, from fetish to cultural status symbol; and the relationship between classical statuary and a particular star of the classical Hollywood cinema [...]. The signification of the statue, for Hollywood, merges into the movies' perennial concern with class and status (etymologically and morphologically, statue and status are virtually the same word). As an undisputed emblem of Western culture, the (neo)classical statue signifies both Hollywood's claim to culture and, paradoxically, its association of classicism with suspect, effete qualities of the 'old world.' [...] the sterility, the decadence, and the obsolescence of European society.
>
> (58)

This last aspect is certainly also a factor in *The Song of Songs* and a possible subtextual rationale for the sculpture's ultimate destruction. The aristocratic Merzbach's decadence is vividly expressed in his rather prurient and rapacious admiration of art objects; in one scene, for instance, he leans in close to the sketch of the nude Lily, peering at it through a monocle, and blows smoke on it [Fig. 28]; a shot that was removed in the final cut of the film – one that had the censors up in arms – showed him touching a burning cigarette to the shoulder of the figure in the drawing on his and Lily's wedding night!

'And then,' I continued,
there is the common 'classicism' of such statues and of the Classical Hollywood films that they stand for and in: legible, legitimate, made with regular proportions and smooth, seamless contours, according to long-established canons. Overdetermined – magical idol, fetish object, memorial portrait, status symbol, bearer of cultural patrimony, classical canon – the statue somehow embodies many of the conflicts and contradictions effortfully suppressed by the classical Hollywood film. The unacceptable, repressed

**Figures 24, 25, 26 and 27:** *The Song of Songs.*

nakedness of the one statue (*One Touch of Venus*) returns metonymically in the focal bare feet of another (*The Barefoot Contessa*), as both condense, or displace the surplus of contradictory meaning around issues of gender, class, sexuality and desire in cinema and society.

(60–64)

The fetishistic emphasis on the naked feet of the Peikov statue of Maria d'Amata, the Countess Torlato-Favrini (Gardner) – which also express metonymically the earthbound, animal sexuality that is thematically central to *The Barefoot Contessa* but unable to be represented directly – seems to echo the focal bare feet of Lily Czepanek as shown in *The Song of Songs*, an idol of exalted female sexuality from 20 years earlier. These feet, upon which *The Song of Songs* rises up, were a feature of the Lovet-Lorski *Venus* that Mamoulian initially conceived as the film's central 'masterpiece' and it is more than likely that he urged this iconographic detail upon Scarpitta, especially given what Adrian Danks points out is an authorial 'focus on feet,' on Mamoulian's part, which 'appears numerous times in his work and the isolation

**Figure 28:** *The Song of Songs.*

of body parts and their relation to the objects around them also marks the most resonant scenes of many of his films …' (2007).

Somewhat later works for later films, the two sculptures of Ava Gardner were made by artists quite like those whose works are seen in Waldow's studio. Like Scarpitta, Nicolosi was an Italian-born and Academy-trained émigré and, like Katchamakoff, Peikov was Bulgarian-born and -educated, although he immigrated to Rome. Those two sculptural props meant to reify Gardner's erotic appeal, as Scarpitta's did Dietrich's, but a comparison to *The Song of Songs* points to the ways in which both Gardner figures fall short. Much of their inadequacy stems from greater censorship; very soon after Mamoulian's film, The Hays Office became more vigilant about enforcing the Code, and the human figure – now, whether as art or in the flesh – had to appear clothed. (Although, according to Gardner's autobiography, Nicolosi misunderstood this detail of his assignment, initially completing a nude version of her as a Hellenistic statue of Venus – which he assumed would be a nude and for which she happily consented to pose – much to the studio's displeasure; perhaps he remembered *The Song of Songs*!) Neither of the Gardner statues is so sensually 'handled' as Scarpitta's, either – in both senses of that term. But perhaps the most significant difference is the one most likely

**Figures 29 and 30:** *The Song of Songs.*

to be overlooked. In the absence of other 'real' works of art, such as those aesthetically and materially persuasive extras in the scenes set in Waldow's studio in Mamoulian's film, even sculptures made by 'legitimate' artists tend to become mere props.[27] The combination of the conditions around their creation – schedule and budget restraints, and the institution's probable conclusion that permanence of materials is irrelevant to the celluloid destiny of the work – censorship, and their origins on the page of a screenplay, rather than in the imagination and exertion of the sculptor, prevent them from acquiring the 'aura' – decayed though it may be – that surrounds the Dietrich nude as it comes into being in the context of art, both in the scenario and on the set of *Song of Songs*.

That aura is one of sensual force, if of withered facticity and salacious spectacle. Ironically, one way that artistic power is confirmed within the narrative is an action almost conventional in movies, although rare in life: the personal assault on and destruction of the object. At the climax of the film, encountering the sculpture – the image of her erstwhile pure and innocent sensuality – after many years of debauchery and degradation, Lily exclaims, 'I am dead! What right has she to live?!' and destroys *The Song of Songs* with several blows of a sledgehammer [Figs. 29–30]. Such assaults are near clichés of cinematic artist stories, especially assaults on portraits by their subjects and Oedipal assaults on parental portraits. As with many other art fictions, the destruction of the art object rectifies things. Here, it permits the restoration of Lily's relationship with Waldow. But the destruction of the art object like the object itself is always overdetermined in the movies.

Dramatically, the act allows Lily to lash out at Waldow and herself simultaneously. The entire narrative is, in a sense, contained and collapsed into the statue, which Mamoulian reinforces by incorporating the disembodied voiceover from the first scene set in the studio. So, the destruction of the art object signals the resolution and end of the story. It also expresses, however, an inevitable antagonism between the motion picture and 'fine' arts and allows the time-based action to triumph over the object (with its presumed aura); it fractures the static image, setting it into dynamic motion. Thus, the assault reifies what movies do to art in a phenomenological sense. The material object dissolves and is effaced by the inexorable, relentless replacement of one image by another.

## Notes

1   Koepnick is citing Studlar (1988).
2   Western Union Telegram, 5 January, 1933, from Mamoulian to Boris Lovet-Lorski, Rouben Mamoulian Papers, Library of Congress.
3   Of several outlines, scripts, and treatments by various writers retained from Paramount at the Margaret Herrick Library – including some connected to the earlier, silent production, *Lily of the Dust* – none introduces the Waldow character or the sculpture theme until a screenplay by Leo Birinski and Daniel Rubin, dated 12 July, 1932, about six months before production began on Mamoulian's film. Many accounts, ranging from scholarly works to IMDb, seem to assume that the basic stories of the novel, play, and three film versions are more or less the same, but they are not. In her account of censorship issues around *The Song of Songs*, Gaylyn Studlar (2007: 230) recounts how the story required considerable modification to conform to Hollywood and Code standards but mistakes elements of Mamoulian's story, with its artist and model theme, for the 'original' and mis-characterizes other aspects of the plot (mistakenly referring to the Prell character as a tutor, for instance). I have read Sudermann's epic work of Naturalism. In it, Lily – although she does find herself out in the world on her own – is not an orphan; her father walked out on the family and disappeared, then her mother went mad and was institutionalized. Preternaturally beautiful, idealistic, romantic, and suggestible, Sudermann's Lily is subject to a series of passionate crushes from a young age but remains virtuous until pressed into marriage by the libertine, Colonel von Merzbach. Her first act of infidelity – one that inevitably leads to divorce and disgrace – is with Walter von Prell, not an artist: rather a soldier-turned-farmer. Edward von Prell (Hardie Albright) – an underling of the Baron von Merzbach – is preserved as a secondary character in Mamoulian's film, becoming Lily's riding instructor and the instrument of an impulsive act of reprisal against both Merzbach and Waldow that is part of the narrative crisis that foretells the film's conclusion. In Sudermann's novel, Lily meets the man she believes to be her true love – Konrad Rennschmidt, a scholar, journalist, and art historian – too late, only after her divorce and several years of living among the demimonde, as the mistress of Richard Dehnicke, a friend of Prell's. In the movie, her first experience of love is her first experience of sex – the innocent but illicit affair with Waldow. Interestingly, although both stories appear to hurtle headlong toward tragedy, neither ends punitively for Lily. Sudermann brings her to the very brink of suicide upon her abandonment by Rennschmidt but then, surprisingly, after an ellipsis, adds a coda in which we learn she ended up married to Dehnicke. Mamoulian restores Waldow and Lily to one another. It is no doubt, at least in part, that Lily's transgressions went unpunished, that spelled censorial trouble for both novel and film. For compelling documentation of challenges to the British publication of the novel, see John Lane's publisher's introduction to the 1914 British edition of the novel.

4  In a previous publication (2011), I quoted Tino Balio, who indicated that *The Song of Songs* had already offered 'histrionic opportunities to Duse, Bernhardt, Modjeska, Pola Negri, and Elsie Ferguson' but Balio – perhaps misled by Paramount's souvenir program for the film, which features a photo spread, 'Famous Women Stars Portray Sudermann Roles,' with pictures of the five – seems to have confused or conflated two different Sudermann works; only Negri and Ferguson were in versions of *The Song of Songs*, both earlier film adaptations (Balio 1993: 244).

5  'LOS ANGELES, Cal., Jan. 2 – Paramount studios today sued in Federal court here Marlene Dietrich, the German film star, for damages of $182,850.06, said to have been spent in preparation for the filming of Hermann Sudermann's "Song of Songs" in which the actress is alleged to have refused to appear under a contract of $4,000 a week' (Anon 1933). There are various accounts of the exact circumstances surrounding this, but it is certain that Sternberg was on his way to Europe, his contract having expired, while Dietrich was still bound by hers. Mamoulian, initially reluctant to take on the project, had finally consented, partly at Sternberg's urging. But by all accounts, Dietrich was not pleased by the project or eager to work without Sternberg. Lutz Koepnick, engaging Maria Riva's and Helma Sanders-Brahms's accounts, considers *The Song of Songs* 'one of Dietrich's most important films' because 'it invites us to examine dominant narratives about the making of the Dietrich persona and its dependence on von Sternberg's authorship' (2007: 49).

6  See Riva 1993: 178–179. But as Lutz Koepnick notes, 'Dietrich at the time of the making of *Song of Songs* was far from ready to renounce the myth of von Sternberg's aesthetic genius and demiurgic power over her appearance […]. By severing her image from the ingenious talent of von Sternberg, *Song of Songs* in the eyes of Dietrich seemed to thwart her status as a singular artwork, an extraordinary creation, a fantasmatic masterpiece in which surface became essence and artifice the sign of overwhelming authenticity' (2007: 49).

7  Rouben Mamoulian to A.M. Botsford, 5 June, 1933. Motion Pictures Producers and Distributors of America (MPPDA) case file on 'Song of Songs,' Margaret Herrick Library of the Academy of Motion Picture Arts and Sciences (AMPAS). Hereafter referred to as 'Song of Songs,' MPPDA case file.

8  Contractual letter from Paramount Productions, Inc. to S.C. Scarpitta, dated 12 January, 1933, from Scarpitta family papers.

9  'Marlene Acted as Model for Statue.' Unidentified clipping, clearly from a Chicago area paper, likely from October 1933, from Scarpitta family papers. Sally Rand was a burlesque star famous for her 'fan dance.' As is noted in note 14, it is not certain whether Dietrich posed in the nude or not.

10  Paramount souvenir program for *The Song of Songs*, 1933. See: http://www.tcm.com/tcmdb/title/90852/The-Song-of-Songs/tcm-archives.html#tcmarcp-362850

11  But as of 2013, no such 'goof' is listed for *The Song of Songs* on its IMDb page.

12  Although *The Song of Songs* is a 'pre-Code' picture, it was not without censorship trials, including objections around the sculptural nude. For more on the censorship of nudity in American movies, and particularly nudity related to themes of artists and models in the silent period, see Chris (2012).

13  Rouben Mamoulian to A.M. Botsford, 5 June, 1933.

14  Dietrich's daughter, Maria Riva, contradicts this oft-reported claim: 'the Studio had come up with another demand. They announced that they expected her to pose for the nude statue that played an important part in *Song of Songs*. By now my mother concluded she had "prostituted" herself enough for this film […]. So she refused, informed the Studio they could use anybody's beautiful body, put Dietrich's head on it, release the news that Dietrich had posed nude for the statue in the film, and the tabloids would take it from there!' (1993: 169). The artist's granddaughter, Lola Scarpitta insists otherwise. Anecdotes associated with the episode are longstanding parts of family lore. It is fairly certain that Dietrich posed for the statue. Whether she posed entirely in the buff is harder to say and not particularly important.

15  'Exploitation' was an actual department of the major motion picture studio, 'charged with the responsibility of rendering aid to the exhibitor […] planning the ballyhoo campaign.' The director in charge of exploitation, according to Carl Laemmle, founder of Universal Pictures, 'must devise, create, and invent plans, schemes, or stunts which will link with the particular photoplay in question […]. This may be accomplished through the medium of newspapers, lobbies, theater fronts, window displays, printed matter, special showings, and the like.' Laemmle is amusingly specific about all aspects of making and selling movies in his article of 1927 (1976: 157–158).

16  Paramount souvenir program for *The Song of Songs*. The TCM DVD edition of *The Song of Songs*, released as part of a 'Pre-Code Double Feature,' also claims in a bonus article that Paramount distributed thousands of replicas of the statue (perhaps the smaller maquette?) to theaters with the film but I have not been able to confirm this. Were it true, there should be some in the movie memorabilia marketplace, but I've seen none.

17  As per Lola Scarpitta, the artist's granddaughter, who believes the sculpture was not completed until after the filming of *The Song of Songs*. In a previous account I mistakenly described this limestone piece as marble (2011).

18  Scarpitta was the father of two children (Maria and Guy) by his first marriage and three by his second, including noted postwar American sculptor, Salvatore Scarpitta (1919–2007) and actress Carmen Scarpitta (1933–2008).

19  According to Lola Scarpitta, whose father, Salvatore Jr., was living and studying in Italy from 1936, the senior Scarpitta was commissioned to create a second, monumental equestrian sculpture of Mussolini, which he and his son later connived to destroy after Italy declared war on the United States and both lost any illusions they had harbored about Il Duce. The family was trapped in Italy and both Salvatores joined the underground, Salvatore Jr. was involved with the so-called 'Monuments Men.' For more family lore, see Cummings (1975).

20  The Scarpitta statue does share one salient attribute with Lorski's *Venus* (1925): the figure stands on tiptoes. If Mamoulian was particularly impressed with his friend's work, he may have urged this iconography upon Scarpitta, when he undertook the commission.

21  A contemporary source (Anon 1931: 6) claims that he was designer for such moving picture epics as 'The King of Kings,' 'Helen of Troy,' and 'Noah's Ark,' but Katchamakoff's name appears on no movie credits in the 1920s, when these films were released, and I have encountered no other evidence he was employed in motion pictures. However, art production staff – other than the studio's department head – was rarely credited at that time.

22  A two-page document, found both in Mamoulian's papers at the Library of Congress and in the 'Song of Songs,' MPPDA case file, headed, 're: Statues Used in "Song of Songs,"' attached to a Paramount Productions, Inc. inter-office communication dated 26 May, 1933, from Rouben Mamoulian to A.M. Botsford reads, 'I am sending you herewith enclosed all the information concerning the statues used in SONG OF SONGS. I hope it will prove useful. I really feel that we have a very good cause to fight for and hope we have a good chance to succeed.' Mamoulian's concluding sentences suggest the information might have been employed in a dispute with the Hays Office.

23  Known to me only through the photograph from Lola, who also supplied the title, *Nadia's Dream* appears to be a painted plaster, probably no longer extant, although possibly cast and sold.

24  See Blanckenhagen (1975). In Chapter 6, in which I analyze other sculptural members of this iconographic family – several from the early nineteenth century at Chatsworth House – for their roles in *Pride & Prejudice* (2005), I return to Blanckenhagen's claims and relate them to Michael Fried's (1980).

25  Internal memo from J.B.M. Fisher to Wingate, dated 17 May, 1933; letters from Wingate to A.M. Botsford at Paramount, e.g. dated 18 May, 1933 and 21 June, 1933; and numerous reports of local, regional, and international censor board activity, 'Song of Songs' MPPDA case file, Margaret Herrick Library, AMPAS. For more on *The Song of Songs*' problems with the Hays Office, see Studlar (2007). For a fascinating study of censorship and nudity in artist and model movies of the silent period, see Cynthia Chris (2012). See also Lea Jacobs (1991).

26  Koepnick is citing Gaylyn Studlar (1988: 92).

27  Both *One Touch of Venus* and *The Barefoot Contessa* do include other artworks in their mise-en-scène. In the former, the supposed antiquity has been purchased for a department store art gallery that is furnished with an eclectic assortment of obvious reproductions. In the latter, a Renaissance period Italian palazzo is persuasively enough furnished. But in neither case do these furnishings create an entirely persuasive context for the central sculpture.

## Chapter 2

Suspect Modernism: *Venus vor Gericht* (1941) and *Muerte de un ciclista* (1955)

The art seen in *The Song of Songs* is indisputably modern. The sculptures that play the parts of Waldow's were made in the 1920s and 1930s by contemporary artists living in and around Los Angeles. Whether they are *modernist* is a trickier question but should probably be answered in the negative. By 1933, avant-garde movements and practices, from Expressionism, Cubism and Futurism to Dada and Surrealism, had left behind the kind of academic training and praxis that characterizes all the sculptors whose work is seen in the Waldow studio. Of course, the works of Scarpitta, Katchamakoff, Stanley, and the others play the oeuvre of a Berlin sculptor of the first decade of the twentieth century. In that context, verisimilitude is a given. And if one examines their larger oeuvres, several of these artists had assimilated a modern vernacular, one particularly associated with Art Deco, a decorative modernism evident across architecture, design, and the fine arts at this time. Katchamakoff and Stanley, particularly, displayed a rather Deco tendency toward geometric simplification and abstraction. This can be seen in the 'Oscar' statuette designed by Stanley – who was represented in the collection of the Museum of Modern Art – as well as his figures for the Hollywood Bowl fountain and in very abstract drawings and paintings and vaguely primitivist sculptural forms that Katchamakoff created in the 1920s and 1930s.

In the 1930s, Los Angeles was not yet the international metropolis it is today. It was relatively small, very remote, and only somewhat ironically referred to as a 'town.' That art directors made shopping trips to New York City galleries and auction houses, as recounted in Harry Horner's account of the production design for *The Heiress* (see Introduction), indicates that despite Hollywood's growing cultural capital, even in the 1940s, the center of American culture remained in New York. In international terms, probably even New York still claimed less cultural capital than London, Paris, or Berlin. Certainly the artists active in Los Angeles had less access to developments of the avant-garde. To those artists who had relocated to Los Angeles from points east, including Europe, Los Angeles's relative cultural infancy must have offered a sense of possibility and openness, compared to the more congested, competitive, established schools, studios, and galleries left behind, never mind more space and lower rents, as well as commissions from a new class of art patrons and sometimes from motion pictures. To be an artist in 1933 in Los Angeles was not at all the same as to be an artist in New York, Paris, or Berlin, although what it was would begin changing, dramatically, in the years to come. Indeed, 'scores of émigrés,' as Lawrence Weschler reminds us, 'fleeing the upsurge of European fascism, during the 1930s and the 1940s and tapering off into the 1950s, briefly transformed Los Angeles into one of the capitals of world culture' (1997: 341).

## Aestheticizing Politics

1933, the year that *The Song of Songs* was released, was, of course, not only the last year prior to the Hollywood Production Code Authority's crackdown on films with morally objectionable content; it was also the year Adolf Hitler and the National Socialists took power in Germany. Cultural actions were among the earliest and most decisive of the new government. Books were burned. Modern artists were dismissed from their teaching positions. Curators who had promoted modern art were fired and replaced with party members. By the end of the year, the *Reichskulturkammer* (Reich Culture Chamber) had been established, headed by Joseph Goebbels. Different divisions of the *Reichskulturkammer* were devoted to each of the arts. Censorship was a central function, along with propaganda, of the film division. *The Song of Songs* was submitted to Berlin censors at the beginning of 1934 and was not approved. Interestingly, this was not for exactly the reasons that had given it trouble with Joseph Breen and the Hays Office or those that had made it objectionable to some other national censors. Rather, *Ministerialrat* Dr. Ernst Seeger censored the film for political reasons, having to do with its representations of a decadent and corrupt bourgeoisie and nobility of pre-WWI Germany, although it was also noted that Marlene Dietrich was 'a German actress whose preference in America is to play the roles of whores' (quoted in Carter 2007: 196).[1]

It seems likely, however, that *The Song of Songs* was seen – perhaps in Vienna or Paris, where it did play in 1934 – by Hans Zerlett, the writer and director of a propagandistic German fiction film of 1941, *Venus vor Gericht/Venus on Trial*, that also told a tale set mostly in Berlin of a sculptor and his model. This otherwise minor film is distinguished by its dramatization of National Socialist art polemics and by its use of – as props – actual modernist works of 'Entartete Kunst' ('Degenerate Art'), which the narrative places into a dialectic with pseudo- and neoclassical sculpture, most prominently a nude rendering of the female lead.

*Venus vor Gericht* is set in 1930, that is, prior to the Third Reich, during the period of the Weimar Republic. Its protagonist is a sculptor, Peter Brake (Hannes Stelzer), obviously – from his name and his work – based on a sculptor favored by the National Socialists, Arno Breker. Breker (1900–1991) was German born and educated but had lived and worked in Paris from 1927 until the end of 1933 and was inspired there above all by the work of Auguste Rodin. At the time he returned to Nazi Germany he had been friendly with many modernist artists (Jews included) who would eventually be deemed degenerate, and he was not yet aesthetically or ideologically quite the paragon of a National Socialist artist that he would soon become. But between 1934 and 1936, Breker ingratiated himself with Hitler and leading NS authorities, gained major commissions and, ultimately, joined the Nazi party, in 1937. In 1936 Breker won the commission for two sculptures intended for the 1936 Olympic Games. It was at that time he ascended to the apex of National Socialist regard. 'Rather than accommodating his aesthetic to Nazi ideology, as some commentators contend,' argues Peter Chametzky, 'Breker in fact formulated a visual and material ideology of the object and of the body that informed Hitler at precisely the moment he intervened in Nazi artistic

**Figure 31:** Cover of *Illustrierter Film-Kurier (IFK)* film program for *Venus vor Gericht* (1941).

policy' (2010: 141). Breker, along with Leni Riefenstahl (especially in *Olympia*, her film of the 1936 Berlin Olympics), created and helped Hitler espouse an aesthetic that combined the classicism of antiquity with an aryanizing of the German population.

> The promotion of Breker's Germano-neo-Neo-Classical sculpture would help legitimate Hitler's imperial pretensions by virtue of its historical pedigree in the Greco-Roman empires, while his insistence that Breker worked from life could appeal to the contemporary populaces' narcissistic desire to imagine themselves literal embodiments of an age of renewal and progress.
>
> (Chametzky 2010: 45)

The fictional Peter Brake's sculptures echo Breker's, especially the muscular male figures, which embody an ideal of state-controlled militarism (the female figures are more reminiscent of those of another Nazi favorite, Fritz Klimsch) [Figs. 32–33]. But unlike Breker, who was *not* an early joiner, Brake is heroic in the terms of *Venus vor Gericht* because of his precocious fascism. In 1930 – when Arno Breker was in Paris, executing a sculpture of one of Germany's

**Figure 32:** A page from the *IFK* film program for *Venus vor Gericht* (1941), featuring a collage of scenes: Peter Brake's studio (top); the art dealer, Benjamin Hecht (center vignette); the excavation of the 'Venus of the Fields' (bottom).

**Figure 33:** View of Arno Breker's studio, during a visit by representatives of 18 nations, 8 November, 1942.

most significant poets, the Jewish-born Heinrich Heine – the fictional Brake is already an anti-Semite and quietly active in the Nazi party. He gets embroiled in a political, artistic, and journalistic brouhaha, and is taken to court for libel, after claiming authorship of the sculptural fragment excavated on a Bavarian farm in the film's first scene. The fragment, which becomes known as the *Venus vom Acker/Venus of the Fields*, is the head and torso of a female nude, missing most of both arms and legs. It is mistaken for an authentic antiquity by 'authorities' the film portrays as suspect (all coded as effete, Jewish, homosexual, etc.) [Fig. 34]. It causes a sensation in Berlin, where Venus frenzy takes over. Brake, it unfolds, had previously lived and worked in Bavaria and had buried the work not to commit art fraud, but to protect the identity of his model, Charlotte (Hansi Knoteck). Since then, he has moved to Berlin and Charlotte has become a respectable *Hausfrau*, married to a loutish small town *Bürgermeister*. Although the film portrays Brake's motivations as honorable and chivalrous (he is reluctant to call upon Charlotte's testimony to defend himself against libel, as it would besmirch her reputation), it also trades on the titillating equation of sculpture with model, as had *The Song of Songs*: before the court (*vor Gericht*), Charlotte, who finally comes forward on her own initiative – out of love and righteousness – as a witness for the defense, is briefly faced with the possibility of being asked to disrobe to prove that this Venus is no moldering antiquity.

Bildwerke heute noch beinah andächtig zu stimmen vermag. Hier erreicht der künstlerische Ausdruck einen Gipfelpunkt der Vollendung. — Immer haben die Künstler aus diesen Schöpfungen gelernt und Anregungen empfangen.

Und es erscheint uns heute nahezu unfaßbar, daß es überhaupt möglich war, daß gewisse Schichten einer Zeit den Sinn ihrer „Kunst" genau in das krasseste Gegenteil verbiegen und vergewaltigen konnten: sie zur Verkörperung des Abstoßend-Häßlichen, Grauenvollen zu machen.

Menschen mit grasgrünen Gesichtern, zinnoberroten Augenhöhlen, dunkelblauem Mund und violetten Haaren, zu entstellender Formlosigkeit verurteilt — Frauenfiguren aus unförmigen Klumpen gemacht, menschenunwürdig gedrungen oder statt der Verkürzung wie ein Totenskelett mager und überdehnt. Als Gegensatz zu Schönheit und Sinn eine ins Maßlose gesteigerte Häßlichkeit und eine an Ausgeburten des Wahnsinns grenzende Sinnlosigkeit.

Das heißt: auch in dieser scheinbaren Sinnlosigkeit der „entarteten Kunst" war messerscharf ein Sinn und ein Zweck eingefangen: die Aufgabe der Zersetzung, der Zerstörung jedes ethischen Willens, der Vernichtung. In dieser Auflösung suchte der jüdisch-liberalistische Zeitgeist seinen Vorteil und seine Stärkung, er benutzte sie als eine Waffe, und der Kampf gegen den Künstler eines gesunden und idealen Empfindens war zugleich ein politischer Kampf.

Der neue Hans H. Zerlett-Film der Bavaria zeigt das Ringen eines ehrlich und anständig gesinnten jungen Bildhauers gegen diesen „Zeitgeist", wie er sich in der Handlung des Buches am schärfsten in dem jüdischen Kunsthändler Benjamin Hecht (Siegfried Breuer) verkörpert und in dem Kreis der Personen, der sich um ihn gruppiert.

Benjamin Hecht unterhält eine „Permanente Ausstellung moderner Kunst", zeitgemäße Werke von Malerei und Plastik, wo man — wie der junge Bildhauer in spöttischer Erbitterung sagt — statt der Maler selbst nur ihre Bilder aufgehangen hat.

In diesem „Salon" spielt sich eine kleine, aber sehr bezeichnende Szene ab: zwei Besucher, ein Herr und eine Dame, sind dabei, eine Mappe mit großen Blättern zu betrachten, die Fräulein Rita, eine Person mit Monokel und Herrenschnitt, die einer dieser Zeichnungen entsprungen zu sein scheint, und die Sekretärin und Vertraute des Chefs ist (Eva Tinschmann), ihnen vorlegte.

„Er" hebt prüfend eines der Blätter hoch.

Fräulein Rita unterbricht: „Pardon, mein Herr, das Bild gehört s o herum . . ." (stellt es auf den Kopf).

Die Empfangsdame des Salons Benjamin Hecht führt im Film „Kunstwerke" vor, die wir heute als entartet ausgemerzt haben (Eva Tinschmann)

Der Herr Sachverständige (Hubert v. Meyerinck) äußert sich über die in einem Acker gefundene Venusstatue, um die ein großer Kunst-Skandal entbrannt ist (Vorn links Justus Paris,

„Sie" voller Ver- und Bewunderung: „Woher die das nur weiß?"

„Er", ein angekränkelter Kunstsnob: „Man muß wohl besonders geschulte Augen haben, um diese moderne Kunst zu verstehen . . ."

„Sie": „Ach, weißt du, verstehen wäre ja noch nicht so wichtig. Aber ich möchte doch wenigstens erkennen, was auf einem Bilde ist . . ."

Konnte, fragen wir uns heute voller Entsetzen, konnte sich ein Mensch — außerhalb der Irrenhäuser — überhaupt Mühe geben, diese Machwerke „verstehen" zu wollen? — Wir schütteln heute nur die Köpfe. Dieser spukhafte Irrsinn scheint uns nur in einem einzigen Punkt in etwa begreiflich: als notwendiges Symptom einer in allen ihren Grundfesten erschütterten Zeit.

So zeigt der Film den Weg auf, den wir einmal vor vielen Jahren gegangen sind.

Er tut es, um uns zugleich nochmals und in gegenständlicher Form die Gefahr vor Augen zu führen, der wir entronnen. Denn er war nur ein Mosaikstein aus einem wohldurchdachten Bau eines verheerenden Ganzen: der Jude Benjamin Hecht mit seiner „PermanentenAusstellung" zeit-

**Figure 34:** Metacinematic commentary on *Venus vor Gericht* in *Filmwelt* (1941), illustrating two suspect experts: Fräulein Rita (Eva Tinschmann), in Hecht's gallery, and Dr. Knarre (Hubert von Meyerinck), a scholarly witness, shown at trial with the sculpture and its model, Charlotte.

**Figure 35:** Marg Moll's bronze *Dancer* (ca. 1930), on display near a pastiche of a George Grosz painting, as seen in *Venus vor Gericht.*

More significant than the erotic and romantic fantasies around sculptor and model (who do end up romantically united), however, is the film's polemical representation of modern art and aesthetics. The story's main antagonist, a gallerist who deals in modern art but into whose hands the Venus falls, is called Benjamin Hecht. This is an overdetermined name: manifestly Semitic and also that of a well-known Hollywood writer, Zionist, and anti-Nazi activist, who was known in Berlin as well as Hollywood, having served there as correspondent for the Chicago Daily News from 1918 to 1919, in that capacity reporting on, among other matters, Berlin Dada activities, and associating with the avant-garde (Chametzky 2010: 45, 224, n. 25). In the movie, Brake is the mouthpiece for National Socialist (Nazi or NS) aesthetic values and Hecht at the receiving end of his invectives, both witty ('I haven't come here to look at your exhibit, in which you have unfortunately hung the pictures instead of the painters') – albeit unnervingly so, given the actual fates of some of the artists – and boorish ('we could give you such shit as you have displayed here in vast quantities if we had the effrontery. But we won't, because we don't cheat others, and because we believe that art is always still art!'). As Hans Schmid points out, *Venus vor Gericht,*

> tells a story set in 1930 that offers the audience of 1941, when it was released in German cinemas, a double satisfaction: it harkens back to the Weimar Republic, building anticipation for what will happen in 1933 and, at the same time, from 1941,

**Figure 36:** *Venus Vor Gericht*. In Hecht's gallery, two sculptures by Richard Haizmann, *Elephant* (left) and *Head* (right), and Wilhelm Morgner's painting of the *Deposition* (1912), on the far right, with other as yet unidentified 'Entartete Kunst'.

looks back with satisfaction upon the vanquished *Systemzeit* [an NS term for the Weimar period]. 'Democracy' is a dirty word in *Venus vor Gericht*. Zerlett peppered his 'comedy' with scenes, propagandistically arranged to demonstrate that everything would be much better if there were no free elections, no free press, no rule of law, and no Jews.

(Schmid 2011, my translation)

… And no modernist art, it should be added. Yet, the 1941 audience for *Venus vor Gericht* must have been thought to be well indoctrinated (or 'coordinated'[2]), for scenes that to a contemporary audience – indeed most any audience – might seem celebratory, introduce its 'damning' picture of the decadence of Weimar Berlin. These scenes, strikingly, seem rather like cinematic correlatives of the 'Entartete Kunst' employed in the film; they consist of footage obviously excerpted from period films shot in the city; most of it evidently documentary and much of that identifiably from Walter Ruttmann's 1927 *Berlin: Die Sinfonie der Großstadt/*

**Figure 37:** *Venus vor Gericht*. In Hecht's gallery, on the left, Wassily Kandinsky's *Two Kinds of Red* (1916), with Erich Heckel's *Grosse Stehende* (*Large Standing Woman*, 1912), and an unidentified painting.

*Berlin: Symphony of a Great City*. But such film work was not equally reviled, although some of the phenomena it captured may have been.

There are layers of irony here. Ruttmann's *Symphony* – conceived by Carl Mayer, who later distanced himself from its ultimately overly formalist, insufficiently critical 'surface approach,' shot by Karl Freund, and inspired by Dziga Vertov's radical and innovative Soviet films of the 1920s (Kino-Pravda, etc.) – is an undisputed masterpiece of Weimar cinema, and it, in turn, helped inspire a series of international 'city symphonies' on film at the end of the decade (see Kracauer 1947: 182–187). Ruttmann was additionally one of the earliest innovators of abstract film, having made numerous experimental shorts – animated abstractions to musical compositions – that would later, one would think, have been regarded as degenerate, as comparably abstract paintings were. Yet the NS politics of cinematic form and style were more complex than those of painting and sculpture; the latter were overdetermined by the Führer's personal sensibilities; and different Nazi authorities and policies were employed in different domains of culture. A Hollywoodish 'realism' dominated features such as *Venus vor Gericht*. And, 'to be sure,' as Barry Fulks has written,

> the formal devices and experimental techniques of the 1920s were not integral components of Nazi feature films. However, in other genres, such as the newsreel, the documentary, and the various permutations of the educational film (Kulturfilm), the cinematic innovations of the 1920s were continued, perfected, and infused with new ideological messages.
>
> (1984: 28)

What the Soviets had learned in their editing exercises at the Moscow Film School was a lesson not lost on the Nazis, as it turned out; meaning in cinema is readily constructed, deconstructed, and revised through editing and context.

Walter Ruttmann's career is instructive in terms of the politics of style. In the conclusion of his prescient essay, Walter Benjamin asserts that in granting expression to the masses without granting them rights, Fascism aestheticizes political life. '*All efforts to aestheticize politics culminate in one point. That one point is war.* War, and only war, makes it possible to set a goal for mass movements on the grandest scale while preserving traditional property relations' (Benjamin 2008: 41, emphasis in original). Ruttmann was very much a modernist in formal terms but *not* a member of the avant-garde in any larger political sense. Indeed, *Berlin Symphony* was greeted with praise and fairly harsh criticism, not only by one of its own initiators, Mayer, but also by progressive critics, including Siegfried Kracauer, who wrote in the Frankfurter Zeitung in 1928,

> Ruttmann, instead of penetrating his immense subject-matter with a true understanding of its social, economic and political structure [...], records thousands of details without connecting them, or at best connects them through fictitious transitions which are void of content. His film may be based upon the idea of Berlin as the city of tempo and work; but this is a formal idea which does not imply content either and perhaps for that very reason intoxicates the German petty bourgeoisie.
>
> (Kracauer 1947: 187)

Ruttmann's future course bears out both Benjamin's warning and Kracauer's critique. Although putatively apolitical, he returned to Germany from Italy in 1933, writing to his (leftist and Jewish) friend Hans Richter that he could not leave his Fatherland in such a time. He joined the Nazi party in 1934 and brought his sensibilities to bear on work done in the service of the Third Reich (Goergen 1989). Indeed, Ruttmann excerpted some of his own Berlin footage into *Blut und Boden/Blood and Soil* (1934), as Michael Cowan and Kai Sicks note, 'to oppose the unhealthy conditions of Weimar urban life to the beauty and strength of the blood-and-soil lifestyle propagated by Nazism' (258). Furthermore, Ruttmann, who was Leni Riefenstahl's assistant on *Triumph des Willens/Triumph of the Will* (1935), was originally assigned – according to Cowan and Sicks – to create a prologue for it about the decadence of

Weimar. It is entirely possible, given the consolidation of NS control over the entire German film industry, that some of the footage – excerpted from his own work and other Weimar documentaries and *Querschnitts* (cross-section) films – originally destined for Riefenstahl's *Triumph,* ended up later, long after the sequence had been eliminated, being used in *Venus vor Gericht.* Ruttmann himself died on 15 July, 1941 in Berlin from complications of surgery, less than six weeks after *Venus vor Gericht* was released.[3]

The Weimar sequence in *Venus vor Gericht* – really a very short city symphony, repurposed as propaganda – is supposed to set the stage for the action of Zerlett's story. It consists of about twenty shots, beginning with establishing shots of Berlin's Cathedral (Dom) and wide views of bustling city streets, and is a dynamic montage of pedestrians, including some orthodox Jews, cars, buses, and trains, a man hawking clothing, another stridently gesturing from a soapbox, policemen in a park, a caravan of vehicles with passengers waving flags, newspaper hawkers, sidewalk cafés, outdoor dance halls, night clubs, with dancers dancing the Charleston, jazz combos, chorus girls, a scantily clad dancer, and a black drummer, all accompanied by a lively jazz tune. It is a testament to the thoroughness of National Socialist *Gleichschaltig* ('coordination') – as well as paracinematic support in the form of press kits, movie programs, advertising, etc. – or to Zerlett's hubris, that German audiences by 1941 could be expected to properly understand as offensive, revolting, or decadent such scenes, or those showing Hecht's contemporary art trade (there is scant evidence, however, that they did, in fact). These scenes all flow together in a sequence that begins with the Weimar decadence shots, then by way of a montage of newspapers with bold headlines rolling off the press, transitions back to the film's action, introducing a muckraking newspaper reporter; then moves on to Hecht's gallery and then to Peter Brake and friends in his studio, where his monumental statuary is seen. The newspaper montage – employing a cinematic cliché that dates back to the silent period – is a critical buffer between the archival footage of Weimar Berlin and the contemporary fictional scenes, for it must be noted that due to the impression of age, bygoneness, and a residual iconicity that attends photographic and cinematic images of Berlin in the 1920s generally and Ruttmann's *Symphony* particularly, that footage retains a kind of aura that is lacking in *Venus vor Gericht*'s conventional fictional scenes, ironically even in those that contain significant, and now lost artworks of the period.

At first glance, Hecht's gallery of modern art looks quite plausible, civilized, and benign. It is introduced in a sequence in which some customers are shown strolling amidst the works, stopping to study them. And why should it not be plausible? The gallery is furnished with real modern works – of the Weimar period and earlier – most of which director Hans Zerlett managed to borrow from the government cache of so-called 'Entartete Kunst' ('Degenerate Art') through the authority of Nazi Cultural Commissioner Hans Hinkel. 'Entartete Kunst' had been confiscated from collections of NS victims and refugees and seized from public collections – programmatically in 1937; some 16,000 works were purged from German museums – some then exhibited in a series of now infamous exhibitions, beginning that same year.[4] Zerlett's letter to Hinkel, written in October 1940, to request access to 'degenerate' works, made the case for realism. 'It goes without saying that it would be desirable to show real originals in this art gallery, rather than obvious fabrications,' he wrote.[5] Pride of place in Hecht's exhibition of contemporary art is given to perhaps the most major work obtained by Zerlett, Ernst Ludwig Kirchner's wooden sculpture, *Das Paar (The Couple)*, which had been confiscated from the Museum für Kunst und Gewerbe in Hamburg. The forcefully 'primitive,' Expressionist sculpture of a male and female nude couple appears in the window of the gallery, with a sign – 'Benjamin Hecht/Permanente Austellung Moderner Kunst (Permanent Exhibition of Modern Art)' – at its feet. *Das Paar* also had appeared prominently in photographs of the 1937 Munich exhibition of 'Entartete Kunst' [Fig. 38].

Other known 'degenerate' works seen in the gallery include Paul Kleinschmidt's large, garish image of a pair of prostitutes, *Duet in the North Café*; Richard Haizmann's sleek, rather deco sculptures, *Elephant* and *Head*; an Expressionist *Deposition* by Wilhelm Morgner; a

**Figure 38:** *Entartete 'Kunst' Austellungs-führer (Degenerate 'Art' Exhibition Guide)*, published after the original exhibition in Munich, in 1937. Heckel's *Large Standing Woman* and Kirchner's *The Couple* were included with others on page 19, under the heading, 'No comment necessary!'.

67

cubist-expressionist hybrid, Arnold Topp's *Picture with Foal*; Erich Heckel's *Große Stehende*, a large primitivist carved-wood female figure; and at least two other works that had been in the 1937 'Degenerate Art' exhibition in Munich: Wassily Kandinsky's abstract painting, *Two Kinds of Red* (1916), seized from the National Gallery in Berlin and Marg Moll's somewhat cubist bronze *Female Figure* or *Dancer* (ca. 1930), from the Museum in Breslau.[6] A few works appear to be pastiches or copies. According to Andreas Hüneke, the two apparent George Grosz paintings are pastiches: 'apparently there weren't enough socially critical paintings among the available inventory, so two pages from the portfolio *Ecce Homo* by George Grosz were translated by a scene painter into large paintings' (2008: 43, my translation). Hüneke also identifies a couple of small, sleek sculptures of cats seen in Hecht's office as copies of works by Haizmann and Naum Slutzky. The works are modern – or, as the Nazis would have it, 'degenerate' – in a wide variety of styles. Only a few are entirely nonobjective – the Kandinskys and a Suprematist abstraction that resembles a *Proun* by El Lissitzky – while the others are figurative and characterized by abstraction associated with of a range of modernist practices and aesthetics: Expressionism, Cubism, Futurism, Primitivism, Neue Sachlichkeit, Dadaism, etc. This array of objects illustrates the diversity of modernist art practices to be found in German collections prior to the NS period and the wide swath of contemporary art purged. Combining numerous authentic works with a few pastiches in the context of an anodyne, albeit fiercely polemical movie, *Venus vor Gericht* also illustrates the profound 'decay of the aura' of the artworks. As I shall return to, they seem rather negligible, hardly more than objects of ridicule as incorporated into a flimsy narrative in which artistic merit is defined by antiquity and grandeur and is, above all, a rhetorical concept.

Almost all the 'degenerate' works seen in Hecht's gallery disappeared during the war; only one of those that could be identified was known to have survived, until recently. Then, in January of 2010, during excavations for a new subway station in Berlin, workers dug up a bronze head that turned out to be a lost modernist work by Edwin Scharff. In subsequent months, fifteen other sculptures were excavated nearby; all appear to have been among those withdrawn from public collections and deemed degenerate by NS authorities; two – works by Marg Moll and Otto Freundlich – were among the works seen in *Venus vor Gericht*. On the site where they were discovered in Berlin Mitte, an apartment building destroyed during allied bombing of Berlin once stood. Even more recently, since the excavation and the speculation about how the works came to be there, evidence has turned up in the form of an order from the Reichspropaganda Ministry that 'Entartete Kunst' exhibits be moved to a storage facility at that address (Wemhoff 2012: 22–23). It is almost certain then, that these sixteen damaged works are all that remain of the 200–300 (quite likely including most other borrowed items seen in *Venus vor Gericht*) that were stored together on Königstrasse.[7]

The unearthed works were cleaned and displayed in an exhibition that opened at Berlin's Neues Museum, not far from where they were found, and in 2012 traveled to two other locations in Germany: the Museum für Kunst und Gewerbe, Hamburg and the Neue Pinakothek, Munich (Stiftung Preussischer Kulturbesitz 2010)[8] [Fig. 39]. It is as difficult

**Figure 39:** Marg Moll's *Dancer* on view at Berlin's Neues Museum (2011) as part of the Skulpturenfund (photo: Susan Felleman).

to imagine from the roles in *Venus vor Gericht* of two of the surviving but badly damaged sculptures – Otto Freundlich's black-glazed terra cotta *Head* (1925) and Marg Moll's bronze *Dancer* (ca. 1930) – the catastrophic destinies of these modest modernist works and their makers as it is to comprehend the offense that they are supposed to have constituted when subjected to public ridicule by the NS propaganda machine. But as Michael Kimmelman reminds us, 'the Nazis seized the Freundlich from a museum in Hamburg in 1937, then six years later, in France, seized the artist and sent him to Majdanek, the concentration camp in Poland, where he was murdered on the day he arrived' (Kimmelman 2010). The sculpture's offense was its strong, minimal primitivism; the sculptor's his Jewish origins. As Sabine Schulze, director of Hamburg's Museum für Kunst und Gewerbe, says about the scarred and broken sculptures dug up in Berlin: 'These works suffered the same fate as many people did at that time. They were despised and destroyed. As artworks, they don't work any more; too much has happened to them. Their surfaces are destroyed [...]. These shells with their wounds – they show the horrors of that time' (My translation; Museum für Kunst und Gewerbe 2012).[9]

It is more than a little ironic then, that *Venus vor Gericht* begins with – and its plot set in motion by – the sensational excavation of a buried sculpture. Sigmund Freud often used archaeology as a metaphor for psychoanalysis; the return of the repressed visualized as artifacts returned from the oblivion of a long-buried site of human habitation. *Venus vor Gericht*'s fictional excavation of the fictional Brake's ersatz antiquity embodies the specious connection the Third Reich posited between classical antiquity and its cultural program, while the actual excavation of those surviving works of real modern art, despised and savaged by the real consequences of National Socialist policy, come to embody quite literally the return of the repressed. The actual sculptor of the unearthed Venus and the other ersatz works that appear as Brake's in *Venus vor Gericht* is uncredited and unknown. These works appear to be props (made of plaster for the film); they are similar to, but not clearly the works of, a number of prominent sculptors – in addition to Breker, Fritz Klimsch (1870–1960) and Josef Thorak (1889–1952) – who employed the basically reactionary, neoclassical, and often monumental style favored by Hitler and Goebbels. The *Venus vom Acker*, which is less monumental than the other Brake pieces, plays its part reasonably well; it looks like it could have been carved in stone and one can accept it as a contemporary academic nude that – dug out of the ground and fragmentary – just *might* be taken for an antiquity.

I must note a troubling paradox around the relationship of these sculptures to the sculptures used in *The Song of Songs*. Those seem more than modern enough in the turn-of-the-century setting in which they perform and downright daring, risqué – even avant-garde – in terms of the censorship conventions they flout in Mamoulian's film, but at the same time, most of them could be described stylistically as comparable to the 'Brake' Venus and other sculptures in *Venus vor Gericht*, which perform decidedly reactionary roles. This points to a number of interrelated problems, many situated around political and aesthetic discourses of classicism, some of which were discussed in Chapter 1. Salvatore Cartaino Scarpitta, after all, was sculpting for Mussolini at about the same time as for Mamoulian. Fascist aesthetics evolved out of and borrowed from well-established academic traditions that were not necessarily inherently reactionary but were often merely aesthetically conservative. If the conservative, the reactionary, and the totalitarian are on a political spectrum, there may not be a neatly parallel aesthetic one. Italian Fascist aesthetics embraced not only the classicism and monumentality favored by the Germans, but also incorporated modernist tendencies, including Futurism. To further complicate any facile alignment of art and politics, Scarpitta grew to revile Mussolini and engaged with the partisans, while Arno Breker had been associated professionally and stylistically with Parisian modernists and modernism only a few years before his reinvention as the heroic Nazi artist par excellence. And, as scholars including Patrice Petro and Sabine Hake have observed, popular cinema in the Third Reich 'was in fact sustained by well-established generic conventions, cultural traditions, aesthetic sensibilities, social practices, and a highly developed star system – not unlike its Hollywood counterpart' (Hake 2001: back cover). It was, that is, a 'classical' cinema, as well as a popular one.

*Venus vor Gericht* is positively rife with paradox. It stages a confrontation between modernism and anti-modernism in which the latter is obviously the victor – in the terms of the movie's unambiguous ideology – but at the same time underestimates and overestimates the former, as played by authentic examples of 'degenerate art.' Unlike the notoriously propagandistic displays of the Nazis' Entartete Kunst exhibitions, where works were displayed and framed polemically, to assert their inherent madness and degeneracy and where anti-modernist screeds – in bold gothic type – filled the space between and around them, Benjamin Hecht's display of contemporary art is plausible as a Berlin gallery exhibition of circa 1930: the paintings are hung from moldings at reasonable intervals on white walls; the sculptures stand on pedestals; works on paper are kept in portfolios; objects are identified with small labels. It is all rather civilized and somewhat tame. And although – as is often the case with prints, drawings, easel paintings, and small-scale sculptures seen in black-and-white film – one cannot experience the sensory power or immediacy of works we know might have had vivid modern 'aura' in the flesh, for the very same reason the film seems unable to persuade us to encounter these objects so reviled by the state with the perplexity or contempt that NS aesthetics demand. The decay of the aura cuts both ways. Additionally, since the modest, degenerate objects' adversaries are – despite their grand scale – mostly rather indifferent plaster pastiches of a type of statuary that at its best was heroic but bland and at its worst mere kitsch, modern art feels like something of a straw man, or even a Macguffin here, in this movie that, aside from its polemics, is a rather conventional and lightweight romance. As Peter Chametzky notes,

The film scholar Linda Schulte-Sasse has argued that the popular cinema of the Third Reich was structurally similar to earlier and later film. This holds true for *Venus vor Gericht*. The film employs familiar narrative and entertainment devices: boy meets girl, boy loses girl, boy gets girl back; the hero is wrongly accused; things look bad for him, as only he and the audience know he is telling the truth; final vindication and happy ending. Rather than Nazi propaganda with conventional entertainment inserted, it is essentially a conventional entertainment film that includes some not very compelling Nazi propaganda. Perhaps realizing the film's weakness as a potential propaganda vehicle (the scenes of decadent Berlin nightlife look much more entertaining than Brake and his friends' *gemütliche* gatherings, and Siegfried Breuer plays a Hecht who is a more interesting and certainly less annoying character than Hannes Stelzer's Brake is), an extremely polemical article appeared in the journal *Filmwelt* in April 1941, which clearly explicated the film's ideological lessons. The article concentrated almost exclusively on art, juxtaposing the Classical, beautiful work of Brake to the 'degenerate' work shown by the Jewish Hecht: 'Artworks characterize their times and their world views, their spiritual and moral stature [...]. [T]he apparent absurdity of "degenerate art" had a razor sharp purpose and meaning: The corruption of all ethical values [...] this spirit is embodied by the Jewish art dealer Benjamin Hecht (Siegfried Breuer) and the cabal surrounding him.'

(2010: 151)[10]

Yet, in the case of this silly, polemical film, the 'real' status of the art objects could hardly be more significant. The film not only embodies paradoxes and polemics associated with modern art in Nazi Germany, but is, in effect, lasting evidence of state crimes. It is also vindication of the prophetic insights of Walter Benjamin, who, writing from exile in Paris the year before the Nazis seized from real state collections most of the objects seen in *Venus's* fictional Berlin gallery – virtually all of which were liquidated in the bombing of Berlin – saw clearly how mass culture could and would be deployed to liquidate cultural heritage. He may have used the term figuratively – and he did not think this liquidation was unequivocally bad – but he was certain that war would be the outcome of NS culture. His death by suicide when facing deportation from the Catalan village to which he had escaped occupied France occurred just as *Venus Vor Gericht* was going into production.

In its denunciation of modernism in art, *Venus vor Gericht* ranges from vitriolic (Brake's rhetoric) to comical. One of its more clichéd little jabs is a familiar trope in the cinema and indeed, according to Bruce Barber, 'one of the most common popular critiques of modernist abstraction' (2009: 156): the disoriented, or 'upside-down' abstract picture. In Zerlett's film, the work is a print or drawing, probably by Kandinsky. A couple visiting Benjamin Hecht's gallery exhibit of contemporary art are looking at a piece from a portfolio of works on paper when Hecht's assistant, Fraülein Rita (Eva Tinschmann) – a stout, severe woman with a monocle and a necktie, plainly coded and despised as a lesbian – happens by and corrects them, rotating it to the 'proper' orientation (a rather clever way to impugn her 'inverted' sexual orientation, along with the artwork) [Fig. 40]. The implication of the scene is that the work and the 'refined' sensibility that purvey it are utter nonsense. This, of course, is a criticism of nonobjective art (art with no recognizable subject matter) that neither began nor ended with the anti-modernism of the Nazis. *That Uncertain Feeling* (Ernst Lubitsch, 1941), a wonderful Hollywood film of the same year, treats modern art with pretty much equivalent ridicule. Hollywood films certainly had fun with the upside-down picture trope prior to and after 1941 (including in Stanley Donen and Gene Kelly's *On the Town*, 1949, and Vincente Minnelli's *An American in Paris*, 1951) and it made a noteworthy appearance in *The Trouble with Harry*, Alfred Hitchcock's droll black comedy of 1955, the subject of my next chapter.

This antimodernist cliché seems to adapt readily to a range of ideological contexts. In addition to being the butt of jokes in the popular cinema of Nazi Germany and Hollywood, bewildering and disorienting modern art starred in Francoist Spain in 1949 in a No-Do (the colloquial name for the state-controlled series *Noticiarios y Documentales/News and Documentaries*) newsreel about the 2nd Salón de Octubre, held in Barcelona. In it, paintings spin (suspended by threads), rotate, and seem to disappear from their frames. In a recurring leitmotif, a quasi-cubist painting appears 'properly' oriented, but some of its spectators are sideways, seen walking past the picture at a 90-degree angle from the bottom of the screen to the top. A woman spectator interacts with a Calder-like mobile, an abstracted figure, suspended from above. In another series of shots, a man (the painter?) seems to reorient a sideways or upside-down abstraction, and the camera alternately views the scene from behind him and from 'behind' the painting, seen from this reverse angle as an empty frame

**Figure 40:** *Venus vor Gericht.* In Hecht's gallery, Fraülein Rita corrects the orientation of an abstract drawing.

through and around which one views the man turning the edges [Figs. 41ab]. Another conceit has a painting suddenly disappear from its frame, followed – in turn – by the frame (like the emperor's clothes) as two men discuss it, the artist gesticulating emphatically in explanation. A young Antoni Tàpies – the year after he cofounded *Dau al Set* and exhibited in his first group exhibition – is also shown explaining one of his surrealist canvases to another man, who perceives it to flash brilliantly, like a flicker film.[11] The newsreel is fascinating for the playful admixture of ridicule of and pleasure in abstraction it seems to display.

This more equivocal and lighter form of ridicule reflects not only a less comprehensive and ideologically centralized approach to modern art and culture by Franco's regime – despite its authoritarian grip on politics, speech, and religion – but also a historical moment at which Spain was on the verge of economic and cultural 'normalization'. As Genoveva Tusell García notes in her discussion of Spanish abstraction in the 1950s:

[L]ate 1930s modernism associated with the Republic had been erased from the map. Many of its protagonists had died in the war, others were exiled, and only a few remained in what was to be called 'interior exile'. In this latter group, young artists were looking

**Figures 41ab:** A 1949 'No-Do' newsreel about the 2nd Salón de Octubre, Barcelona.

for their historical link with the avant-garde movements prior to 1936, a connection that they would make through Surrealism, following the example of Joan Miró. In the 1940s, a period of profound international isolation, opposition to what was considered the establishment in the art world had clear connotations of political rebellion. As Franco's regime had not been able to define a true Fascist art, academicism ended up assuming that official role. Consequently, all that was opposed to academicism was seen as insubordination – artistic, social and political.

(2006: 241)

Despite intensive government censorship, inner exile seems to have been a somewhat less stifling destiny for modern artists active in post-war Spain than it had been in Nazi Germany, as aesthetic practices were of less interest than morals and political activities to the regime.

If official Francoist propaganda did not know exactly what to do with modernist art in 1949, by 1951 there was a distinct thaw in its approach to cultural products that did not directly challenge Franco or any core state values (Nationalism, Catholicism, etc.), with the appointment of Joaquín Ruiz-Giménez as Minister of Education. By this period, US leadership had determined that Francoist Spain was preferable to a Communist one, and had embarked upon a policy of détente. This rehabilitation culminated in the Pact of Madrid, signed in 1953. Alliance with the United States and Western Europe in the Cold War had enormous impact on Spanish culture. As Tusell García continues,

[T]he political scene of the 1950s can be seen as transitional, moving toward a different international status. Diplomatic relations with the United States resumed and in the artistic sphere this decade broke once and for all the postwar isolationist cycle by initiating something new. Although the general situation within the regime changed little, it was now an unexpected advocate of modern art. Coinciding with the onset of international political détente, interest in promoting an image of cultural normality took hold.

(2006: 241)

This image of cultural normality was paradoxical, however. The regime retained its iron grip and exercised strong control over political discourse and public life. Suddenly, after years of being regarded as subversive, modern art was mainstream. Indeed, as Jorge Luis Marzo points out, because of its incorporation into official state policy, what had been vanguard was now, ironically, conservative (2006).

## Politicizing Art

Such is the aestheticizing of politics, as practiced by fascism. Communism replies by politicizing art.

(Benjamin 2008: 42)

This irony – by which art that was vanguard and disapproved became, almost overnight, official and conservative – is perhaps nowhere more evident than in one of the foremost artistic accomplishments of the Spanish cinema of the 1950s, Juan Antonio Bardem's 1955 *Muerte de un ciclista/Death of a Cyclist*. 'A communist, Bardem stayed, struggled, and was jailed more than once; he was in prison when he won an award at Cannes for this creepy, claustrophobic 1955 melodrama,' Jonathan Rosenbaum notes (2007). In *Muerte de un ciclista*, an adulterous upper-class couple (Lucia Bosé and Alberto Closas) returning from a tryst by car, accidentally run down a cyclist. María José persuades Juan that they must leave the gravely injured cyclist, out of fear that their relationship will be revealed if they help him. They later learn from the newspaper that he died. The rest of the film deals with the moral fallout from and psychic toll of this act on the two individuals and their relationship. María José, who provides the beauty and status in a marriage to which her husband brings the money (and lots of it), will not jeopardize that marriage, and a selfish fear of discovery is her primary response. Juan, on the other hand, suffers from a progressively corrosive guilt and sense of responsibility.

*Muerte de un ciclista* combines influences from Hollywood (Film Noir, Hitchcock, and Welles) and Europe (especially Antonioni and Italian Neorealism) in a dialectic that couches a political parable in moral melodrama. The complex and intriguing relationships and shifts between different visual and narrative codes foreground style and signal the viewer to look for hidden meaning. 'In his juxtaposition of neo-realism with the mise-en-scène of melodrama, Bardem effects a grammar of film-making that maximizes and antagonizes the political implications of both' (Stone 2002: 48). Just as the Communist Party, of which Bardem was a doctrinaire member, survived in Francoist Spain by going underground, ideological critique and taboo themes survive in Bardem's film by going underground in plain sight. As Marsha Kinder notes, 'the film goes beyond Bazinian realism to create a reflexive structure in which the aesthetic discourses of Hollywood melodrama and neorealism can be ideologically repositioned' (1993: 74). The foregrounded style and ideological repositioning speak to political and social ideas that, due to stringent censorship, Bardem had to cloak. María José represents a self-interested, historically forgetful materialism with which the film implicates the expedient capitalism associated with new government policy and haute bourgeois sensibilities in the 1950s. She and her businessman husband, Miguel (Otello Toso) live in a home that displays conspicuously modernist art and design, and she wears modish – possibly couture – clothing. This is contrasted to the brooding, morally troubled war veteran, Juan, a university lecturer, to whom María José had been engaged before the war and who lives with his patrician mother in a dark, rather Victorian, traditional home (his father and brothers were Nationalist martyrs). As Kinder notes of a sequence that intercuts between the two lovers, each at home, 'the Manichaean contrast in lighting, décor, and tone helps to underline the moral difference in the way the two lovers cope with the manslaughter – to escape or to brood, the same respective reactions they had to their separation during the Civil War' (1993: 77–78).

An added irony of the editing is that Bardem cast very similar men in the parts of husband and lover. 'The husband, Miguel, and the lover, Juan, are astonishingly similar physically. Both have thick dark hair, thin moustaches, somewhat prominent and hooked noses, and slightly dimpled chins. For the first half of the film we never see them in the same frame together, and through montage we are actually encouraged to confuse them' (Martin-Márquez 1992: 513). Although interpreters have offered various explanations for this clearly intentional casting decision – more than one of which may be and probably is valid – it is certain that one effect is to induce a wary vigilance on the part of the viewer. Following the plot requires ascertaining with some certainty at every turn whether one is watching husband or lover. As Kinder and Martin-Márquez note, in the first half of the film the two men cause confusion by being separated in diegetic space but often elided through editing. In the second half, they are often in the same space, watching and being watched in an atmosphere that the editing renders paranoid. The watchfulness and vigilance required to keep them straight is implicitly paralleled to a watchfulness and vigilance that the protagonists display in their actions, not only because of their frequent conducting of taboo activities and suspicious conversations (adultery, blackmail, etc.) in public spaces, but also because those taboos are, in a very real sense, surrogates for political activities and speech that are disapproved and censored.

The characters are essentially self-censored. As a woman and visible exemplar of her class in a social order that imposes patriarchal, authoritarian, and conservative values, María José, as Martin-Márquez puts it, is inscribed 'within pre-established paradigms, since the bourgeois society which she inhabits is obsessed by form and structure' (1992: 512). Lucia Bosé plays her with a mask-like placidity of expression.[12] Her opposite and antagonist is the rather repugnant and grossly expressive Rafael ('Rafa') Sandoval (Carlos Casaravilla),

**Figure 42:** *Muerte de un ciclista* (1955). Left to right: Rafa (Casaravilla), the husband, Miguel (Toso), Maria José (Bosé), and lover, Juan (Closas).

'a kind of court jester in the form of art critic and snarky hanger-on [...] who views himself as outside enough to be able to tally up her [María José's] inner circle's quotidian corruption and crimes like a dark-eyed accountant with a permanent smile forming at the end of his lips, waiting for his day to exact blackmail' (Koehler 2009: 73). Rafa is flagrantly different than the other characters, with large, broad features and many of the same attributes and mannerisms that have been used to stereotype Jews and homosexuals in popular culture. Early in the film, as he plays piano at María José and Miguel's party, Rafa reveals – somewhat cryptically, while singing a song called 'Chantaje'/'Blackmail' – that he had seen Juan and María José together in the car. It remains unclear to the adulterous lovers, however, exactly where and when he saw them, and whether he knows anything of their terrible crime. This uncertainty torments María José. At a key scene set at a gallery exhibition of modern art, she and Rafa have a conversation that is equally cryptic, underscoring the risks attendant to speech and expression in Franco's Spain, and pointing to the way that the entire film is structured, reflexively, by codes – implicit and explicit. From discourse on modern art to a game of hot and cold, the dialogue in the scene accompanies the moving pair and the tracking camera, past and among a series of modernist canvases and sculptures, circling rather abstractly around the question of what Rafa knows and what he wants.

The gallery scene begins with the two standing before a painting reminiscent of some Joaquin Torres-García and Adolph Gottlieb pictographs of the 1930s and 1940s.[13] It is worth noting that this first artwork shown, and the only one to which the dialogue attends, in its use of pictographic forms, points to the semiotic potential of images. It is very much like a rebus, a similarity implied by Rafa's question for María José, after reading the accompanying text in a catalogue or brochure:

RAFA:                    Number 21 ... 'Summer.' Do you get it? It lacks clarity; has an insecure contour and color scheme. It's very ... very tentative [*vacilante*], don't you think? ...

Having moved screen right, Rafa pauses in front of the next painting, which is abstract with nested, shard-like geometric forms.

RAFA:                    Well, that's all. Now you tell me why.
MARÍA JOSÉ:              Why?
RAFA:                    Yes. Why we've come here today.

The two begin moving back toward screen left as they converse. They pass no. 21 (*Verano*), and pause in a space foregrounded by an abstracted seated figural sculpture, along the lines of Henry Moore or Isamu Noguchi, and with their backs to a bold, geometric abstract painting.

RAFA:                    Why this interest in a third-rate art show? Just what is it you want?
MARÍA JOSÉ:              To know.
RAFA:                    To know? Abstract art?
MARÍA JOSÉ:              Cold.

The next several lines of dialogue are exchanged as they continue walking through the space. They pass four more paintings – a couple reminiscent of William Baziotes's work of the early 1950s and other artists working in an abstract vernacular that hovers historically and aesthetically somewhere between the Surrealism of Miró and Abstract Expressionism – and an abstract, atomic age sculpture apparently made of bent wire.

RAFA:                    The influence of Paul Klee on contemporary art?
MARÍA JOSÉ:              Cold.
RAFA:                    How much I earn as an art critic?
MARÍA JOSÉ:              Freezing.
RAFA:                    How much I like you?
MARÍA JOSÉ:              Warmer.
RAFA:                    What suspicions?

**Figures 43–48:** *Muerte de un ciclista.*

| | |
|---|---|
| MARÍA JOSÉ: | Hot |
| RAFA: | What I want? |
| MARÍA JOSÉ: | Burning up. |

They pause, backs to an oblong grid of simple geometric, and presumably chromatic – forms, similar to paintings by Giorgio Cavallon, Bradley Walker Tomlin, and others inspired by the innovations of Paul Klee. In the foreground is a vaguely figural, attenuated, seemingly bronze sculpture, not unlike a work by David Hare. It is the first of three or four sculptures set prominently in the foreground, which María José glances at as she avoids eye contact with Rafa, who sneers at her as his tone becomes contemptuous.

| | |
|---|---|
| RAFA: | (laughs) You see, it's all simple, very simple. The hard part is finding out where to start. |

They move on, passing before several more paintings – one similar to Picasso's figural abstractions of acrobats and swimmers of the late 1920s and early 1930s – and behind a few abstract sculptures – including a white plaster Abstract Expressionist style piece, one with aggressive, flame- or talon-like forms, along the lines of a work by Theodore Roszak, Seymour Lipton, or Herbert Ferber – as Rafa pronounces.

| | |
|---|---|
| RAFA: | I am Rafael Sandoval, or Rafa. Good for nothing, but granted entrance to the most exclusive circles. At your charity balls, at parties for wealthy merchants and landowners, I, art critic, represent culture with a capital C. I eat your caviar, drink your whiskey, and smoke your cigarettes. In exchange – and I'm the loser in the bargain – I endure you all. |
| MARÍA JOSÉ: | And you're bored stiff. |
| RAFA: | No, I'm really not. It's fun observing you. I see your sins, classify them, file them away … and wait. |
| MARÍA JOSÉ: | For what? |
| RAFA: | The right opportunity. |

He pauses again in front of a painting vaguely reminiscent of some of Picasso's work of the 1930s. The two remain there, in a tight two shot in the shallow space before the canvas as he continues.

| | |
|---|---|
| RAFA: | All the ugly things you hide, I dig them up and lay them before you. It's a means of purification. |
| MARÍA JOSÉ: | Or blackmail. |
| RAFA: | (tsk-tsks and shakes his head) That's an ugly word, and not really even Castilian. |

Rafa's remark about the etymology of the word *chantaje* (blackmail) alludes to Francoist linguistic politics. Castilian Spanish was declared the official language; others, including

**Figures 49–54:** *Muerte de un ciclista.*

Catalan, Galician, and Basque, were suppressed, along with the separatist movements that advanced them. The public use of languages other than Castilian was forbidden, and films and mass media were censored for linguistic noncompliance, as well as political and religious.

| | |
|---|---|
| MARÍA JOSÉ: | But the meaning is clear. |
| RAFA: | If you say so. |
| MARÍA JOSÉ: | And what do you want? |

They have begun to move left again. His next line is uttered as they move behind and are framed on either side of a rather large white stone or plaster sculpture on a pedestal. The work is vaguely figural, with forms suggestive of a torso and buttocks, but is abstract and ambiguous.

| | |
|---|---|
| RAFA: | Not much. A., stop taking me for such a fool. |
| MARÍA JOSÉ: | Granted. |
| RAFA: | B., don't try to see my cards. If you want to see my hand, you'll have to pay. |

The scene's dialogue comes to an end as the two suddenly are in a larger and more public part of the space – what appears to be an entrance to the gallery. The wall, upon which hung the many paintings they have passed before, ends, and one can see deeper into the space behind them, where two other people are visible – a seated elderly woman and a younger man who appears to have just entered the gallery – as well as a large abstract painting and a couple of abstract sculptures, one very tall and tree-like.

| | |
|---|---|
| MARÍA JOSÉ: | I suppose there's no other way. Very well. Anything else? In fairy tales, the evil fairy always asks for three things. What's your third wish? |
| RAFA: | You. |
| MARÍA JOSÉ: | (back to him, smiles). I'll have to tell my husband. |
| RAFA: | Just what I intend to do. |

It is ironic that María José invokes the rule of three. This foreshadows, or corresponds to the tri-logical deaths of the film's narrative. For, when her troubled lover Juan resolves to come clean and report the death of the cyclist to the police, María José – who will not take responsibility for the accidental killing and plans instead to leave for abroad with her husband, Miguel – contrives to kill purposefully. She returns with him to the scene and runs Juan down in exactly the place where the bicyclist had died. It is a stark and illuminating scene. An ellipsis has brought them there from their tryst, presumably in the same remote getaway they had been to before the opening events of the film. We do not know why they have stopped; perhaps to confirm the cliché that a criminal always returns to the scene of the crime. Juan, newly liberated by his decision to take responsibility, stands in the barren landscape by the road and speaks of the past and the future with an almost rhapsodic sense of redemption, revealing significantly that that very stretch of landscape had been the site of a Civil War battle at which many died and where he had languished in the trenches, longing for María José. Thus, the film's final sequence provides the key to the allegorical level of the story. The death of the cyclist stands for the scores of others; as Jo Evans points out, it 'becomes symbolic of the unrecognized Republican victims of the Civil War, so that the couple's attempt to dissociate themselves from him becomes, in turn, a reflection of Nationalist disregard' (2007: 258).

María José embodies this disregard: the denial of responsibility, the selfish, amoral, hypocritical values of the elites under Franco. The film reinforces the multiple signification of the faceless victim by repeated images of anonymous bicyclists. In several overdetermined sequences, cyclists traverse the mise-en-scène, reminding us of the cyclist left behind on the road, at the same time intertextually invoking *Ladri di Biciclette/Bicycle Thieves* (Vittorio De Sica, 1948), an iconic source for identifying bicycles with the working masses. Finally, racing home in the rainy night after murdering Juan, so as to meet Miguel's deadline for departing for their evening flight, María José swerves to avoid another cyclist on a bridge, careens over the edge, crashes, and dies. According to Kinder, Bardem's scenario ended with Juan dead, just below the frame of the film, as had been the eponymous cyclist at the beginning. But the Spanish censors (not unlike their equivalents in Hollywood) insisted that María José – an adulteress and murderer – not go unpunished, so Bardem complied, adding a third fatal car crash, this one spectacular – the only one of the three in which the victim is seen, in lurid close-up, spotlighted by the flashlight of the cyclist she had swerved to avoid hitting (2008: 19).

The political connotations of *Muerte de un ciclista* emerge around the censorship by means of such gaps, analogies, and codes. One of its most pointed political critiques is of the hypocrisy and contradictions of 'normalization.' In a couple of contiguous scenes, all the principals (Juan, María, Miguel, and Rafa) are together at a party for and outing with some visiting American VIPs. Bardem sets the tense melodrama around the adulterous affair and Rafa's prospective blackmail amid action that points to *españolada* (the performance of 'Spanishness') as a charade. Rafa says as much, from the piano: 'this one's in honor of the USA ... Something 'typically Spanish' ... Olé, olé, toreador!' The most vivid sequence takes place at a tavern where gypsies perform flamenco and sing: the Andalusian cliché that – with bullfighting – was promoted by Franco (and avidly taken up by Hollywood, it should be added[14]), while most ethnic difference was suppressed.

The scene between Rafa and María José in the gallery exhibition of modern art points to another aspect of this charade: the pretense of cultural relaxation. The works in the exhibition might be 'real' or might be pastiches. Extensive research, including correspondence with authorities on Spanish modernism of the period, is inconclusive, with the visual evidence leaning slightly toward the conclusion that the works are authentic, although mostly lesser and derivative works, possibly on view in Galeria Buchholz (founded 1945) or Galeria Fernando Fe (founded 1954) – a couple of Madrid galleries that specialized in contemporary art and modernism at this time.[15] They resemble those of any number of artists of the period – European, American, and Spanish – mostly in a rather derivative way. But many of the artists whose works they resemble were themselves in the early 1950s derivative – at early and transitional stages of their careers. Rafa may be overstating it by calling them third-rate but certainly few are better than second-rate, if rating is necessary. By the late 1940s, when the No-Do newsreel had its fun with modern art, there was a burgeoning revival of modernism in Spain. Rafa mentions the influence of Paul Klee, and, in fact, there had been an 'Homage to Paul Klee' exhibition in Madrid in 1948. By the time Bardem shot *Muerte de un ciclista* in 1954, there were a few galleries dedicated to modernism, there had been some major international exhibitions, and modern art, architecture, and design were associated with international capital and the technocratic interests behind normalization. For a strident leftist like Bardem, that would have been enough to make modernism suspect.

In 1955, soon after *Muerte de un ciclista* won a prize at the Cannes Film Festival, Bardem participated in the celebrated Salamanca Congress, organized by critic and director Basilio Martín Patino to establish a dialogue between the more liberal representatives of the state cultural apparatus and the moderate leftists among cineastes. Bardem's contribution was the least moderate and would become the most renowned. In his 'Report on the Current State of Our Cinema,' he famously declared Spanish cinema 'politically ineffective, socially false, intellectually worthless, aesthetically nonexistent, and industrially crippled.' Proceeding to elaborate on these claims he excoriated Spanish films for their disingenuous patriotism, political cowardice, and general falsity; for turning their backs on reality, for their anti-intellectualism, and their vapidity. 'Our films lack form,' he insisted, 'because they lack content. Not even our style is any good. At best it is at times simply correct. On the other hand, I don't believe in style for its own sake. The lack of rigorous and true content produces an absurd aesthetic' (Bardem 2008: 22–23). This essentially Marxist critique is the same as was often leveled at the 'empty' formalism of abstract art and other modernist practices and is almost an elaboration on Rafa's aborted critique of the works in *Muerte de un ciclista*'s gallery scene. That abstract art performs two almost contradictory operations: it functions as objective correlative to the abstracted public language – the obscure and cryptic code – that his characters, like Spaniards generally under Franco, by necessity, speak; and it embodies the empty materialism and decadence of international capitalism.

Thus, the Marxist critique that Bardem implicitly levels at modernist art is not entirely different from that of the Nazis. But Marxism regards it less as degenerate and dangerous and more as hollow and elitist, as an alienating signifier and specious commodity. In this respect, Bardem's scene was bound to be more successful than the scenes set in Hecht's gallery in *Venus vor Gericht*. Where the latter fails to create an atmosphere of insanity or danger around the 'Entartete Kunst' on view, *Muerte de un ciclista* has little trouble making the art seem without content. Crowded into the scene, passed behind and in front of, barely paused over, shot in black-and-white – not only stripped of their color, their texture, their material facticity, their aura, but also rendered as background and scripted as 'third-rate' – the objects become ciphers, always already unreal.

## Notes

1   The censors' decision of 14 March, 1934 is available at http://www.deutsches-filminstitut. de/filme/f035202.htm (9 August, 2007); it is discussed in Anon (1980: 45). On Dietrich and Nazi Germany, see Carter (2007).

2   I am referring to 'coordination' as a translation of the term *Gleichschaltung*, used during the Third Reich for the process by which the NS regime successively and forcibly established a unified system of control and coordination over all aspects of society.

3   Widespread claims that Ruttmann died of wounds suffered on the Eastern Front while shooting an NS newsreel are untrue. Ruttmann was never at the front and made no such film. See Goergen (1989: 56, n. 55), where he traces the origins of the mistaken assertion to Lotte Eisner, who made it in the context of the Walter Ruttmann retrospective that was part of the 9th Westdeutschen Kurzfilmtage (West German Short Film Festival) in Oberhausen, 1963.

4   See Petropoulos (1996, 2002) and Kunsthistorisches Institut (2010), as well as Barron et al. (1991). The relationship between Zerlett and Hinkel, as well as – to my knowledge – the first scholarly indication that *Venus vor Gericht* featured actual seized works, is mentioned in Giesen (2003: 265).

5   My translation. 'Es liegt auf der Hand, dass es sehr wünschenswert wäre, in dieser Kunsthandlung wirklich derartige Originale, die sinnfällig als Machwerke wirken, zu zeigen' (Zerlett correspondence in the Deutsche Kinemathek, Schriftgutarchiv, as per Hüneke [2008: 42]).

6   Many of these identifications were made by Andreas Hüneke and Christoph Zuschlag, both at that time associated with the Forschungsstelle 'Entartete Kunst', of the Freie Universität Berlin, to whose attention the author and Peter Chametzky brought the movie in 2006. According to Chametzky:

> [T]he Kleinshmidt, *Duett im Nord-Café*, 1925, formerly Staatsgalerie Stuttgart, is visible in the 1937 Munich showing of 'Degenerate Art' in Stephanie Barron, *'Degenerate' Art: The Fate of the Avant-Garde in Nazi Germany*, 56, # 15988. It is also visible in a still, with the caption: 'The receptionist (*Empfangsdame*) in Benjamin Hecht's Salon presents "artworks" that these days we have eliminated as "degenerate". Ellie Tschauner, 'Benjamin Hecht macht in "Kunst"', *Filmwelt: Das Film- und Foto-Magazin* (Berlin) Nr. 16 (18 April, 1941): 410–411. The *Empfangsdame* wears a monocle and a necktie, identifying her as a Weimar period lesbian. The possible Grosz is also reproduced, captioned as 'Das Erlebnis' (it is captioned 'Die Begegnung' in the film itself), 'a concoction of Jewish corruption'. The Kirchner is *Das Paar*, 1923–1924, acquired 1930, Museum für Kunst und Gewerbe, Hamburg.
>
> (2010: 242–3, n. 8)

7  In my earlier account of this then-very-recent excavation (Felleman 2011), I quoted Kimmelman who reported official speculation about how the works came to be where they were unearthed, at 50 Königstrasse, across from City Hall.

> German investigators now believe, the likeliest candidate to have hidden the art was Erhard Oewerdieck, a tax lawyer and escrow agent. Oewerdieck is not widely known, but he is remembered at Yad Vashem, the Holocaust memorial in Israel. In 1939, he and his wife gave money to a Jewish family to escape to Shanghai. He also hid an employee, Martin Lange, in his apartment. In 1941 he helped the historian Eugen Täubler and his wife flee to America, preserving part of Täubler's library. And he stood by Wolfgang Abendroth too, a leftist and Nazi opponent, by writing him a job recommendation when that risked his own life. The current theory is that when fire from Allied air raids in 1944 consumed 50 Königstrasse, the contents of Oewerdieck's office fell through the floor, and then the building collapsed on top. Tests are being done on ash from the site for remains of incinerated paintings and wood sculptures. How the lost art came into Oewerdieck's possession in the first place still isn't clear.
>
> (Kimmelman 2010; Felleman 2011)

Compelling as these speculations were, the true explanation seems to have been much simpler, and less redemptive.

8  The works have since traveled to the Museum für Kunst und Gewerbe, Hamburg (9 August, 2012–27 September, 2012) as 'Verlorene Moderne: Der Berliner Skulpturenfund.'

9  As this volume goes to press, there is breaking news of the recent discovery of an enormous cache of art, some missing since the war, recovered in Munich from the son of Hildebrand Gurlitt, a dealer entrusted by NS authorities with selling 'Degenerate Art' and probably art from Jewish collections (Eddy et al. 2013).

10  Chametzky cites Schulte-Sasse (1996) as well as Tschauner (1941: 410–411). In an earlier publication (Felleman 2011), referring to an earlier manuscript version of Chametzky's book, I misquoted it.

11  I am indebted to Jorge Luis Marzo for information on this film and the identification of Tàpies. See Marzo (2006; 2009).

12  Lucia Bosé (born Lucia Borloni in Milan, 1931) was a former Miss Italy (1947), turned actress who had just previously appeared in Antonioni's *La signora senza camelie*, 1953.

13  My descriptions of the artworks in the scene depend on comparisons to well-known work of the period, one in which there was an evolving international style. Among the comparatives, American painters and sculptors are dominant, along with a few of the best-known Spanish artists of the prewar generation, mainly because of the limitations of my knowledge of and literature on their contemporaries in Spain. See note 15.

14  Flamenco performances figure in, among other Hollywood films with Spanish settings of the Franco years: *Pandora and the Flying Dutchman* (Albert Lewin, 1951), *The Barefoot Contessa* (Joseph L. Mankiewicz, 1954), *Around the World in Eighty Days* (Michael Anderson, 1956), *The Sun Also Rises* (Henry King, 1957), and *The Pleasure Seekers* (Jean Negulesco, 1964).

15 Juan Manuel Bonet and Genoveva Tusell García, leading experts on Spanish art of the period, do not recognize any individual works but both say the style of most of the work is consistent with work that would have been shown in Spain mid-century, including by painters such as Fermín Aguayo, Santiago Lagunas, Eloy Laguardia, Modesto Ciruelos, Mathias Goeritz, Manolo Millares, Planasdurá, Luis Feito, Pablo Palazuelo, and Will Faber; and sculptors such as Carlos Ferreira, Placido Fleitas, and José Planes.

## Chapter 3

The World Gone Wiggy: *The Trouble with Harry* (1955)

Modern art is related to the problem of the modern individual's freedom. For this reason the history of modern art tends at certain moments to become the history of modern freedom.

Robert Motherwell (quoted in Rose 1968: 130)

In the previous chapter, I could only begin to suggest the complexity of political discourse around abstract art in the postwar period, a problem that has been the subject of considerable controversy and scholarship. In Western Europe in the aftermath of the war, debates tended to polarize abstraction and realism polemically, dogmatic elements of the left favoring the latter, as I suggested in my reading of Bardem's film. A longstanding rhetoric of freedom associated with abstraction came in the course of the 1950s – according to one prominent strain of social art history – to cause the dominant abstract American art movement, Abstract Expressionism, to be regarded as an international ambassador of the dominant Western power – the United States – and its military-industrial form of democratic liberalism. Not only in New York, however, but throughout Western Europe, as Martina Tanga puts it, 'artists used the brushstroke and painterly gesture as a symbol on many fronts: victory over fascism and totalitarianism; over state and institutionalized artistic styles; as a rejection of societal constraints and even commodification' (n.d.: 1). Among the many ironies of this association is that from the 1930s into the 1950s, abstract art had been regarded by many in the United States, including in government agencies, as subversive and associated with Communism. Indeed, a number of New York School artists and their most forceful advocates (i.e. critics Clement Greenberg, Harold Rosenberg, and Meyer Schapiro) were known leftists. While arguments about the propagandistic role of Abstract Expressionism as an element of American triumphalism regard it as a 'weapon of the cold war' (Cockcroft 1985; Guilbaut 1983), it is also certainly the case that during the decade that followed the end of the Second World War, the artistic triumph suggested by this view was far from a given and the political role of style was highly contentious in the United States as well as in Europe.[1] 'Freedom,' associated with abstraction in a range of sometimes contradictory discourses, is a very broad concept that denotes personal, political, and philosophical values.

Moreover, Abstract Expressionism was only one arm of the avant-garde and only one of several abstract vernaculars of the period. While I was able to compare each artwork seen in *Muerte de un ciclista* to vanguard work by European and American artists, only a few of those artists were regarded as Abstract Expressionists, and the comparable work of even those was mostly of a transitional style. It should be noted that there is some irony that this controversy arises here in the context of a discussion about movies. Abstract art generally and Abstract Expressionism particularly – whatever their kinetic elements inspired by or borrowed from music, cinema, and other action-, process-, and time-based practices – were in a sense antithetical to popular film. The arguments made for realism and against abstraction in postwar art discourse included salient claims about the popular accessibility of the former and recondite and alienating properties of the latter. Almost all movies (and here I distinguish movies from 'films,' a broader designation that includes avant-garde and experimental films along with other less commercial short forms – documentaries, educational films, etc.), be those by Paramount Pictures or Juan Antonio Bardem, are for a 'popular' audience. The motion picture is a mass medium, and artists and intellectuals of the New York School regarded mass media skeptically. 'The Abstract Expressionists saw their own works as expressions of a marginalized and counter-cultural political ideology,' Claude Cernuschi notes in his substantive review of David Craven's *Abstract Expressionism as Cultural Critique: Dissent During the McCarthy Period*, a book that carefully reexamines the actual politics and political impact of the movement (Cernuschi 1999: 35). Cernuschi and Craven, following Meyer Schapiro – one of the major theorists of Abstract Expressionism – observe that the elements of haptic immediacy, craft, and individual gesture in an abstract painting were regarded as antithetical to the industrial, technological, and highly capitalized products of mass media. Hollywood, especially with its industrial mode of production, its commercial aesthetic, its self-censored moral and narrative orthodoxies, opposed all the values of the action painter, whose individual psyche and phylogenetic connection to nature and myth were expressed through an authentic and soul-searching engagement of technique and bodily process.

Popularity could be regarded as problematic too. As John Ferren (1905–1970), president in 1955 of the Club, the Greenwich Village hub of Abstract Expressionist debates and activities – founded in 1949 by, among others, Franz Kline, Willem de Kooning, and Ad Reinhardt – wrote in his 'Epitaph for the Avant-Garde':

> The avant-garde artist accepted his status as an outsider. He faced the consequences of this status, and then, curiously, derived some benefits from it. In the early days of the Club on Eighth Street, I remember often hearing the remark – I said it myself – 'Well, we don't sell anyway, so why not?' In short, by accepting our isolation we acquired its rewards. We were alone with ourselves; we painted by ourselves, and in some degree we became better acquainted with ourselves. Our complete divorce from the official art world, from magazines and the museums – in a word, our hopelessness – gave us the possibility of unknown gestures. The 'crazy,' the 'gone,' had no terror for us. We were in limbo. It was in this situation that Pollock kicked over his first can of paint.
>
> (1958: 26)

The past tense employed in Ferren's 'Epitaph' reflects the remarkable speed with which Abstract Expressionism had gone from being a loose association of 'hopeless,' uncommercial, outsider artists in 1949, the year the Club was founded, to the dominant and most canonical artistic phenomenon of the postwar period. Ferren's elegy could also have been for his own avant-garde status. In 1958, he had a prominent screen credit on a motion picture produced by Paramount Pictures, one of Hollywood's major studios. The movie was Alfred Hitchcock's *Vertigo*, and Ferren designed the special sequence that illustrates Scottie's nightmare [Color plate 1].

And *Vertigo* was Ferren's second contribution to a Hitchcock picture. The first had occurred three years earlier, in 1955, the same year Ferren acceded to presidency of that bastion of vanguard art, the Club. John Ferren was by then both a central and incongruous presence among the New York avant-garde. In the years that most of its members were young artists being educated in and then rebelling against the regionalism and realism that dominated art in the United States during the years of the Great Depression, Ferren had lived and worked in Europe and established a very European abstract vernacular. Although there was no one school of political thought among the artists in his New York circle, communism, socialism, and anarchism were favored. Ferren – more a philosopher than an ideologue – was less aligned and more politically aloof. Indeed, after his somewhat inadvertent return to the States in 1938, Ferren, having been turned down by both Army and Navy (as per his 1968 interview with Paul Cummings[2]), obtained a position with the Overseas Operations Branch of the Office of War Information (OWI), a civilian position with no rank associated. Ferren served in North Africa, then in Europe as chief of publications for the US Psychological Warfare Division.[3] This commitment and service suggest Ferren took a less countercultural position than most of his peers. Intellectually, politically, and sartorially, Ferren, although he was surrounded by them, was not one of the 'Irascibles.'[4]

> His fellow artists scorned conventional society and its stifling mores in the Eisenhower era and in this sense were rebels […]. John was a gadfly, quick to point out hypocrisies […] he twitted his colleagues on their boastful claims to being avant-garde, pointing out that abstract expressionism had become 'established' – and he was one of the first to recognize that it had. But he always had an even-tempered, soft-spoken manner. Indeed, he looked like anything but a maverick, more like a professor (and he was that as well as an artist) – jacket and tie, clean-shaven, with his mustache neatly trimmed.
>
> (Sandler 2003: 101)

Ferren, despite – or perhaps because of – his differences from the 'typical' New York School artist, made an ideal president for the Club due to his gentlemanly intellect, open-mindedness, and equanimity. He was involved in many public discussions of art and its contexts.

In 1952 alone, as Marshall Price points out, Ferren moderated 'Abstract Expressionism II' (the Club, January), participated in 'The Purist Idea' (the Club, March), and moderated the interdisciplinary discussion, 'The Problem of the Engaged Artist' (which included John Cage, dance critic Edwin Denby, and poet Emmanuel Navaretta; the Club, April), and the panel discussion by three distinguished critics, Robert Goldwater, James Fitzsimmons, and

James Thrall Soby, 'American Criticism of American Painting' (the Club, December). And Ferren gained considerable visibility in the coming months for activities beyond Eighth Street. In May of 1953, he was asked to speak about common approaches to art and industry at the annual meeting of the Industrial Research Institute. His remarks on 'The Problem of Creative Thinking in Painting' were subsequently published as 'Art and Creative Thinking' in the December 1952 issue of *Arts and Architecture* (Price 2011: 172–173). In July of 1952, Ferren had a solo exhibition at the Santa Barbara Museum of Art and early in 1953, another at Iolas Gallery, his first one-man exhibition in New York in four years. Ferren was the subject of a profile in *Art Digest* in March 1953; a feature article in *Art News* in February 1954; and was included in a photo feature, 'New Means for Moderns,' in *Life* in November [Color plate 7]. Additionally, he was thrice more published in 1953 and 1954, as a member of an *Art Digest* 'Symposium: The Human Figure' and with essays in two volumes edited by R.M. MacIver and issued in 1954 by The Institute for Religious and Social Studies: 'New Art and Old Morals – Another View' in *New Horizons in Creative Thinking* and 'An Artist Pursues the Reality Beneath the Appearance' in *The Hour of Insight: a Sequel to Moments of Personal Discovery*. However difficult had been his transition from Europe to the United States 15 years before, however hopeless and 'divorce[d] from the official art world, from magazines and the museums' he had been, by 1953 John Ferren was a well-established, visible, and well-connected working artist, teacher, and public intellectual.

How exactly John Ferren and Alfred Hitchcock became acquainted is not known. Ferren, who was raised in California and had family there, spent summers in Los Angeles regularly after 1949. The two could have met socially or at a gallery or museum event. As is well known, Alfred Hitchcock was an art lover and was wont to figure art in his films – including abstractions. In fact, a dialectic between mimetic and abstract artworks appears in subtle variations across a number of them. In *Suspicion* (1941), for instance, a visiting police detective, Sgt. Benson, is distracted by a small Picasso still life in the entrance hall,[5] while a portrait likeness of Lina's father, General MacLaidlaw (Sir Cedric Hardwicke), bears down Oedipally on the entire household. *Rear Window* (1954) features another modernist still life, a reproduction of Henri Matisse's *Still Life with Asphodels*, 1907, over the mantel in Jeff's apartment, and an abstract quasi-figurative sculpture – by one of Jeff's neighbors – in progress. Despite that one of its main protagonists, Sam Marlow (John Forsythe), is a modern artist, that a couple of rather lengthy scenes feature a dozen or more of his works, and that those works are by John Ferren, art as a theme in *The Trouble with Harry* has rarely been seriously treated by film studies (or art history).[6]

In his chapter on *The Trouble with Harry* in *Laughing Hysterically: American Screen Comedy of the 1950s*, Ed Sikov is one of the few scholars or critics to note how central Sam Marlow's paintings are to the film: 'Sam's art breaks *Harry* open into a yawning gulf, a disturbance of epic proportions out of which Harry's sexual symbols fly.' At the same time, Sikov fails to appreciate those paintings. 'Wiggy's store and outdoor market are both crammed with Sam's work,' Sikov notes, 'most of it fairly dreadful (though the script describes him as "an extremely talented painter") ...' (1994: 168). Of course, he is entitled to his opinion. But

**Figure 55:** Mrs. Wiggs (Mildred Dunnock), Sam Marlow (John Forsythe) and paintings by John Ferren in *The Trouble with Harry* (Hitchcock, 1955).

Sikov's dismissal seems uninformed and cavalier. And if the film regards Ferren's works equivocally, as is almost inevitable, even as it depends upon them in a number of ways, probably Hitchcock did not. It might seem like a joke to insert abstract art into the bucolic New England countryside of *The Trouble with Harry*, but color and abstraction function at two levels in this droll picture, operating within the setting and the narrative, as well as within the paintings seen *en abyme* as indices of psyche and freedom.

John Ferren, so well known in New York art circles in 1954 and so relatively forgotten now, may be best remembered for his other Hitchcock collaboration, *Vertigo*, on which he received a prominent credit for the dream sequence he designed and for which he is said also to have painted the Carlotta Valdez portrait.[7] Ferren, whose association with the New York School I have emphasized, was actually perhaps better known and is better characterized as a European artist, having lived in Europe from 1929 to 1938, mainly in Paris where he worked among and associated with major modernists: Jean Hélion of the Abstraction-Création group, Picasso, Miró, and others.

During Ferren's eight-year stay in Europe he consciously transformed himself into an essentially European personage. His marriage to Laure Ortiz de Zárate, his participation in exhibitions of European artists, his entrée into Parisian artistic circles all point to this transformation from a provincial representational artist in San Francisco with an earnest desire for, but little understanding of modern art, to one of great sophistication who helped codify the language of geometric abstraction in the 1930s, and through exhibitions in the U.S., helped transport it to America. He had consciously shed his American identity – the artist himself even indicated that he was not part of expatriate circles, but had become integrated into a group of European artists in Paris.

(Price 2011: 111–112)

Gertrude Stein confirmed Ferren's view of himself as more European than expat, when, in 1938, she referred to him as 'the only American painter foreign painters in Paris consider as a painter and whose painting interests them' (108). So assimilated to the European art scene was Ferren that he is one of very few Americans to be seen in the famous group portrait of 'Artists in Exile,' taken in 1942 at Peggy Guggenheim's New York City apartment. And he may have been the only American artist among those exhibited in the opening exhibition at Guggenheim's Art of this Century Gallery.[8]

Ferren's work, including much among the selection visible in *The Trouble with Harry* – drawings and paintings in styles typical of his work in different periods, from the mid-1930s to the film's present (1954–1955) – was deeply influenced by Wassily Kandinsky, by a range of other modernists, including Paul Klee, Joaquin Torres-García, Fernand Léger, Hélion, Miró, and by the ideas generated around William Stanley Hayter's Paris Atelier 17, the foremost modern printmaking studio (which Hayter relocated to New York, from 1940 to 1950). Tensions between figuration and abstraction, both within individual pictures and across his oeuvre, characterize Ferren's work. Although much of it is nonobjective, at a few key junctures in his career Ferren returned to figuration. Evidence of an oscillation between abstraction and figuration can be seen in *The Trouble with Harry* [Color plate 2]. There are several works seen that are clearly schematic views of human heads and figures, in different styles, including a couple of drawings that would seem to date from 1938 when, just before leaving Europe and as his first marriage was ending, Ferren executed a series of vividly distorted human heads, which resemble and anticipate formally, by 30 years, Francis Bacon's portraits of the late 1960s and 1970s.

Ferren was, above all – and more than most of his New York peers – a colorist. *New York Times* art critic Roberta Smith's pithy assessment of Ferren's work suggests its consonance with Hitchcock's Technicolor films: '[…] undiluted color and flashes of pictorial wit' (1993). And most of the Marlow paintings in *The Trouble with Harry* are characterized by intense and varied color. Ferren's widow, Rae Ferren, also an artist, recalls that the director was expressly interested in her husband's paintings for their vivid use of color, which Hitchcock connected to the colors of the autumnal New England landscape. The Ferrens spent a few days on location in Vermont, as John Forsythe had to be advised on technique for the scenes in which Marlow drew. Rae Ferren recalls, too, that her husband and Hitchcock got along famously and shared a predilection for French wine. She also revealed to me that it was she, at the time very recently an art student and one with a more representational disposition – not her husband, as generally assumed – who drew the sketch of the dead Harry Worp's head that figures prominently in the film[9] [Fig. 56].

Disorientation is a central trope in *The Trouble with Harry*, beginning with the titular corpse itself. Sikov points out that the stocking feet of the dead man are part of a somewhat

**Figure 56:** *The Trouble with Harry.* The portrait of the dead Harry Worp.

lewd joke, in terms of color and orientation. 'Hitchcock lends Harry's feet a whimsical touch by having him wear blue socks with bright red tips.' The feet [Color plate 3], Sikov says, are

> a key element in the pervasive displacement of sexual energy that underlies each of the central characters' progression through the film [...]. The joke stands on the fact that the dead human body is metonymically reduced to the feet: while the rest of Harry's corpse lies flat, his feet stick up in the air [...] standing at priapic attention.
>
> (1994: 160)

The question of orientation is addressed directly, in dialogue that often has a suggestive aura. Jennifer (Shirley MacLaine) says of Harry, 'he looked exactly the same when he was alive, only he was vertical.'

So, when Hitchcock engages the trope of the upside-down picture – that old chestnut we saw in *Venus vor Gericht* – it is a joke, but an overdetermined one, that alludes to the upside-down world and affect of the film. In the scene where the picture is inverted, Mrs. Wiggs (Mildred Dunnock), at whose country store and post office Marlow attempts to sell his work, is all admiration: 'Ah, Mr. Marlow; it's wonderful!' she exclaims, looking at Sam's new canvas, one that, coincidentally – or not, based on its style – was in fact then a very recent Ferren; he had begun creating just such busily and vividly chromatic, all-over impastos of fruit- and flower-like forms with ambiguous or absent figure-ground relations no earlier than about the time *The Trouble with Harry* was in production [Color plate 4]. Marlow inverts the picture she is admiring [Color plate 5]. 'I've been in a tortured mood lately,' he explains, quite casually, turning her error into something of a matter of interpretation, artistic and psychological. 'What is it?'

Mrs. Wiggs asks. 'Good ol' Wiggy: my sternest critic,' responds Marlow. But again, Hitchcock fails to drop it here at the point where one can laugh at the obscurity of abstract painting. 'I don't understand your work. I think it's beautiful,' says Wiggy almost rapturously, without taking her eyes off the picture, having the last word: implying that art appreciation is no mere matter of academic mastery. The film itself, like Mrs. Wiggs, spends considerable time looking at Ferren's luminous canvases. Wiggy and Miss Gravely (Mildred Natwick) both respond to the paintings with aesthetic appreciation that harbors a hint of eroticism. They function as surrogates for us, and perhaps for Hitchcock too – whose favorite painter, Paul Klee, like Ferren, made somewhat mysterious and vividly chromatic pictures that shift between and across abstraction and figuration. Several of the paintings feature biomorphic forms, which, although in no way descriptive, vaguely suggest sexuality, be that human, animal, or botanical. The bright colors dominant in several of the paintings are also evident in the autumnal landscape of New England: yellow, orange, red, blue, green. In fact, the painting with which Marlow makes his first appearance very clearly echoes colors and textures from the autumnal scene.

## A Natural Distance from Reality

> I'm not self-indulgent where content is concerned. I'm only self-indulgent about treatment. I'd compare myself to an abstract painter. My favourite painter is Klee.
>
> (Alfred Hitchcock, quoted in McGilligan 2003: 476)

Although the abstract aspect of Marlow's work has generally been regarded as a joke – how ridiculous that an abstract painter would work in *plein air* – this view is misguided. Abstract does not equal nonobjective. Several of the pictures used in the film have evident representational content and Ferren's work of the 1940s and 1950s in fact includes numerous abstract landscapes, works whose forms, colors, and textures are responses to the subjective, sensory experience of place, rather than mimetic representations of it [Color plate 6].

Moreover, as Bruce Barber points out, abstraction signals Hitchcock's attitude toward his subject matter, toward life and art. 'On one level this film is about the abstractions we live in daily life, time and space, the question of being ...' Continuing, Barber calls *The Trouble with Harry*

> an allegory about the value of art, life and death, or more specifically a dialogue between the art in death and the death in art [...]. Harry functions as a still life (*nature morte*), treated as an object for disinterested contemplation and Sam's abstract paintings take on a life through the association with the various characters' desires.
>
> (2009: 182)

Painting maintains, to quote Walter Benjamin, 'a natural distance from reality' and abstract painting, it would follow, a greater one; it is this distance that allows Hitchcock to employ the paintings as images of disorientation, play, sensuality, mystery, and freedom. The art in death and death in art to which Barber points, also correspond to those properties of media that preoccupied Walter Benjamin. The indexical quality of the film cuts (like a surgeon) to the very material quick of the world, while the magic of painting, through the laying on of hands, delivers us over to something else, something more unreal, chimerical, and disorienting (Benjamin 2008: 35).

But is it the painting or the viewer that is disoriented, one wonders? Does not Sam's nickname for Mrs. Wiggs – Wiggy – imply that there's something dizzy in this otherwise very down-to-earth viewer of his pictures? Earthiness and color are dialectically engaged in *The Trouble with Harry*. Richard Allen, in his analysis of Hitchcock's color designs, asserts – employing a metaphor that seems especially apt here – that Hitchcock approached the color film as a 'blank canvas in which every element of color placed in the frame is put there for a reason' (2006: 131). With few but significant exceptions – most obviously Harry's socks and Jennifer's garb (both combining blue and red) – sartorial color in *The Trouble with Harry* is generally neutral, dark, and/or earthy. The neutrality of their appearance underscores the characters' absurd nonchalance and the darkness and earthiness of the morbid and sexual humor that pervades the story (e.g. 'I'm grateful to you for burying my body.' 'Marriage is a comfortable way to spend the winter.'). Thus the brilliant colors of both landscape and art are very much in contrast to the behavior and appearance of the characters. The colors and forms of the paintings manifestly excite the two middle-aged women: Wiggs and Gravely, as well as – it seems – the elderly millionaire who stops to admire and later purchase them. This excitement is expressed in a sense by the inversion. These sensual, stimulating objects turn the world inside out, or upside down. As Sikov suggests, they represent unconscious, repressed currents (1994: 169). It is then utterly silly and yet at the same time quite serious when Marlow turns his painting right side up.

It ought to be noted that Ferren had some experience with his work's inversion and the incumbent ridicule. *The New Yorker* in its 'Talk of the Town,' 17 October, 1942, reported under the heading, 'Cliché':

> Our philosophy is that we must take things as they come, and it is with a high consciousness of duty that we report the hanging upside down of a painting by the Museum of Modern Art. The composition involved is an abstraction by John Ferren, and is upside down – or was last Friday – and no two ways about it, unless the artist had the irrational whim of signing it upside down in the upper left-hand corner. We have a feeling that Royal Cortissoz will simply accept this happening as confirmation of his worst suspicion about the way things are going.
>
> (14)[10]

On 7 November, 1942, 'The Talk of the Town' followed up on this amusing item, under the heading, 'Upside Down':

> A couple of weeks ago we reported in these columns that the Museum of Modern Art had apparently hung a picture, a modernistic composition by John Ferren, upside down.

We said the picture must be upside down unless the artist had had the irrational whim of signing his name upside down in the upper left-hand corner. Well, as you might guess, Mr. Ferren's whim is just that, and probably no odder than lots of other whims we've heard of. Accordingly, we eat our words about the Museum of Modern Art. We'd feel perfectly terrible if we weren't able to report, in the light of this information about Ferren's signature, that another of his compositions *is* hung upside down, in the new Art of This Century museum – that is, unless he has lately taken to signing his work right side up in the lower right-hand corner. If this is the case, just let the matter drop, please.[11]

These little items from one of America's foremost cultural forums are informative. They confirm that in 1942, the year after *Venus vor Gericht*, the upside-down abstraction could be regarded as a 'cliché', and that it was amusing to stage an imaginary face-off between the irrational whims of abstract artists and the worst suspicions of anti-modernist critics. By highlighting the fact that he had works exhibited simultaneously at the Museum of Modern Art and Art of This Century they also reveal that, even as Ferren was struggling to adapt to the New York art scene, he was receiving significant recognition.

Although it may seem like mere cliché and a throwaway laugh, there was a more serious side (so to speak) to the disoriented painting. Ferren himself would certainly have known that his artistic forebear, Wassily Kandinsky, famously claimed that his own move toward nonobjective imagery was inspired by an encounter with one of his own paintings in the dark, set upside down, which upon returning home one night he found unrecognizable but 'of extraordinary beauty, glowing with an inner radiance' (Hamilton 1993: 208). Ferren would have known, too, that the cryptic, colorful pictures of Hitchcock's favorite painter, Paul Klee, were profoundly influenced by the art of children and, especially, the insane, the latter through Hans Prinzhorn's influential publication of 1922, *Artistry of the Mentally Ill*. Perhaps, whether he was in on *The New Yorker*'s joke in 1942 or not, the painter was in on Hitchcock's in 1954.

Such jocular reorientation in a sense celebrates the 'craziness' of modernism and its freedom. As has been noted, by the late 1950s, discourses linked abstraction, particularly Abstract Expressionism, to freedom during the Cold War; the Museum of Modern Art, the United States Information Agency (USIA), and other agencies employed this rhetoric in their presentation of contemporary American art abroad, even as popular audiences in America remained skeptical. The equation of abstraction and freedom is echoed in *The Trouble with Harry* in a rather feminist exchange. Marlow says to Jennifer, 'if you marry me, you'd keep your freedom', to which she replies, 'you must be practically unique, then.' 'I respect freedom,' he confirms. 'More than that, I love freedom. We might be the only free married couple in the world.'

But the rotating canvas takes on other overtones when considered in cinematic terms. One element of the cliché of the disoriented painting may be the dynamic possibility afforded by its reorientation. Do the movies turn abstract pictures around because they can? A perennial problem in the representation of painting in film is its stasis, which can act upon the flow of cinema like a stop sign. The still picture, whose stillness does not bother us upon the gallery wall, looks dead in moving pictures ... like Harry. *The Trouble with Harry*, it could be argued, is just this: his inexorable horizontality and stasis. Sikov points out that Harry's reorientation is a sexual joke, his erect feet 'standing' for the organ he could not get up in life. But in moving pictures, even the dead must – and, as I have noted elsewhere, often do – move (the movies' ubiquitous zombies, for instance, and Hitchcock's own variously reanimated dead: Rebecca, General McLaidlaw, Madeleine Elster, Mrs. Bates [Felleman 2006: 14–24]). This mortified property of the still image is not only the source of the often morbid poignancy of the cinematic freeze frame (Truffaut's, for instance) but also gives rise to the much abused impulse in documentaries on art to zoom in on and pan across canvases, as with still photographs: the inevitable and tiresome 'Ken Burns' effect![12]

The abstract picture has virtues and possibilities that the figurative still and the narrative cinema lack, though. One of these is precisely its dynamic openness of form and concomitant reorganization of time. It can be rotated, or disoriented, productively. As Ferren himself wrote in 1958 about the possibilities post-cubist abstraction afforded his generation of painters:

> We found ourselves with a pictorial space which was less finite, less easily contained, full of energy; not the negative space between two planes, but a space in which the mind moves freely and which permits a flux of emotion instead of a timeless fixity. Comparing the classical concept of space which still haunts French painting to our space is like comparing a still photograph to a movie. A painting by Pollock 'contains' time in a way that is new.
>
> (26)

And, of course, the upside-down picture is a figure of Hitchcock's picture's own inversion, in a sense, too, is it not? The same content that would be framed with horror, suspense, and morbid fascination in other movies is here – in the film its director claimed to be fondest of in his oeuvre – turned on its head: made droll, amusing, benign. The reorientation of the picture speaks to those more abstract, dynamic values of composition, color, and line that are such a source of inchoate pleasure in Hitchcock's pictures: values, however, that generally must serve or be subordinated to the flow of narrative in his, as in all Hollywood, movies. In *The Trouble with Harry*, in which narrative flow is not brisk or subtle, while the setting is uncommonly beautiful, these formal values come to the foreground. Hitchcock, who – as quoted above – did once compare himself to an abstract painter (McGilligan 2003: 476), wanted Ferren's pictures 'for their brilliant color, like the color of Vermont in the fall.' Ferren no doubt wanted the cinema not only for its paycheck,[13] but also for its dynamism, scale, and luminosity. In the same year that Hitchcock employed Ferren, his pictures, and his wife, the painter had been experimenting with 'bright, nearly translucent inks' on Orlon on paintings he conceived to be displayed in windows, producing a luminous glow like stained glass [Color plate 7].

In hanging Ferren's pictures at Wiggy's roadside stand in the autumn sunshine, as well as indoors in her post office and general store, Hitchcock revels in the ways that their chromaticity operates under different conditions (a few of the same pictures are to be seen outdoors and indoors – perhaps a continuity error, but an illuminating one). A theater poster quite prominently displayed inside Wiggy's shop points to the chromatic focus; it is for 'The Caravan Color Season at the Dorset Playhouse' [Color plate 8]. Ferren was also in the mid-fifties, after years of working strictly nonobjectively, returning cautiously to figuration. Indeed, many of the works seen in *The Trouble with Harry* are abstract but not nonobjective. 'The figure conceived in the Western Humanist Tradition,' Ferren wrote, 'has found its communicable art form outside of painting. To me, it is experienced better plastically and humanly in giant close-ups moving in sequence across a movie or TV screen' (1953: 13, 32). He felt that figuration was risky – it could be both reactionary and cowardly for artists in 1953 – but also might fruitfully reemerge from the 'matrix' of abstract expressionism, a 'matrix' he believed could either destroy painting or enable a 'leap' to an objectification of mental, emotional, and spiritual energies.

The power that such language imputes to painting may not be evident in these colorful canvases that are all too easily subsumed in mise-en-scène. It does not help that quite a few rather small canvases jostle for attention in the scenes into which they're crowded or that they are somewhat inconsistent in style (because Ferren brought along the work of 20 years) [Fig. 57]. One or two paintings seen at the very top edge of the film frame on a shelf of Wiggy's emporium look to me unlike Ferren work and might be by Stanley Marc Wright, an accomplished realist painter resident in Stowe, who claimed to have made paintings for the film. 'Hitchcock wanted to shoot in Wright's studio,' according to art historian James Saslow, the painter's nephew, but 'the artist refused to allow the drastic remodeling required.' Wright

**Figure 57:** *The Trouble with Harry.*

claimed to have made all the art in the film, which is obviously untrue (perhaps he did not know that Ferren was paid for his canvases and was present for some days during the shoot; one wonders whether he ever saw the finished film), and, since 'Forsythe was supposed to be the stereotypically earnest but penniless modernist that Wright never wanted to be,' to have 'had a bit of fun at the expense of the avant-garde by cranking out a wildly varied smorgasbord of swirling, daubish abstractions, some of them deliberately dreadful' (Saslow n.d.: 26). Few of the canvases seen in the movie could be characterized as such. Hitchcock probably employed Wright's work sparingly, if at all.[14]

In any case, even the 'honest' abstractions by Ferren seem at best to contribute a benign, spiritually and sensually vivid air to the scene. Certainly one senses through the admiration of Mrs. Wiggs, Miss Gravely, and the wealthy collector who takes up the whole lot, the director's own appreciation. Ironically, these pleasant, almost decorative elements of Hitchcock's film are not very unlike some of the works that were cast as ridiculous, dangerous, crazy, and degenerate in *Venus vor Gericht*. When cast in fiction films, whether to perform as ideological punching bags or as aesthetic diversions, such objects – dematerialized and removed from not only the space but also the cultural context of the studio or gallery – become players rather than objects. This is especially true of easel paintings like Ferren's. The large, more cinematic scale of contemporaneous works by New York School artists like Pollock, Motherwell, or Kline come to embody a relationship between painting and cinema in a way that the representation, or incorporation, of the portable easel painting cannot, as Ferren himself had observed.

Thus the 'Marlow' paintings in *The Trouble with Harry*, despite their considerable screen time (in the two mercantile locations they are displayed, paintings are almost continuously to be seen for a total of about fifteen minutes), have been much less noticed, appreciated, and analyzed than the often inferior portraits and pictures upon which plot points turn in other Hitchcock films. Upon entering the age of its technological reproducibility, according to Walter Benjamin, the work of art loses aura. When art comes into the aura of film, so to speak: when the object of art enters the space of its own symbolic appropriation – the classical fiction film – it gains a strange and paradoxical sort of invisibility, as well.

But even as these concrete objects disappear into the mise-en-scène – even unremarked – they continue to signify. Their signification is not fixed, however. As modernist, abstract works of the mid-century, Ferren's are indices of freedom, sensual experience, psyche, and spirit. Color and abstract form are difficult to describe and to discuss, but they are felt. Ferren's pictures participate, albeit somewhat whimsically, in a dialogue about art and value that in fact had some urgency in the postwar period. This dialogue is neither as obvious nor as polemical as the National Socialist case around which *Venus vor Gericht* was structured during the war, but Hitchcock must have been aware of the history of anti-modernist rhetoric and the ways that aesthetic signification was shifting during the Cold War when he changed Sam Marlow into a modern painter. The modernist works regarded as 'degenerate' by the National Socialist ethos of Zerlett's film signify, too, and not always as intended. Although the objects themselves are mostly lost to history – a couple recently recovered, battered from it – their withered aura persists to defy the morality tale into which they were abducted. That morality tale pitted modernism against classicism, a classicism framed as virtuous, heroic, and occasionally a little titillating. But classicism is not a stable signifier, either. In *The Song of Songs* the classical figure is less reactionary than risqué; it is about the body, but not the heroic political body of the Nazi period; rather, it is about the sexual body that is off limits in Hollywood. American censors must have been as outraged by Mamoulian's sculptural surrogates as the NS establishment by the art it declared degenerate. By 1934, a nude statue was as taboo in Hollywood as a nude actress.

When art and movies get mixed up with one another, political signifiers get mixed up, too. What to one man is sheer madness is pure freedom to another. One woman's paragon of virtue is another's sexual fetish. The aura of the art object decays; the still image moves; the three-dimensional object becomes a mere projection, or shadow, but no more of one than the actor next to it. The mortal flesh and the solid inanimate thing begin to merge. The very notion of the 'real' withers, as well.

## Notes

1   For the most influential articulations of the 'Abstract Expressionism, Weapon of the Cold War' position, see Cockroft (1974), Kozloff (1985), Shapiro and Shapiro (1978), and Guilbaut (1983). Among more recent work to question the assumptions of this view, in addition to Tanga (n.d.), see: Jachec (1991), Craven (1999), and Cernuschi (1999).

2   John Ferren interview with Paul Cummings, 7 June, 1968, transcript, Archives of American Art, Smithsonian Institution, Washington, D.C.

3   'Ferren's return to the United States that year was voluntary, but his subsequent stay was not. He came back to New York initially intending to remain for a circumscribed period of time. It was supposed to be a temporary hegira before his eventual return to Europe. By the time Ferren was ready to return to Paris, however, he was unable to renew his visa because of the impending war and was, effectively, stranded in his home country' (Price 2011: 103). The OWI was a temporary governmental agency established during the early stages of the war that consolidated government information services on June 13, 1942 (Price 2011: 137ff).

4   'The Irascibles' refers to a group of eighteen American abstract painters who – with ten supporting sculptors – signed an open letter to the president of The Metropolitan Museum of Art, rejecting the museum's exhibition *American Painting Today – 1950* and boycotting the accompanying competition. 'The Irascibles' were famously pictured in a group photograph, taken on 24 November, 1950 and published in *Life* magazine 15 January, 1951.

5   A reproduction of Pablo Picasso's *Pitcher and Bowl of Fruit* (1931), as identified in private correspondence by Steven Jacobs.

6   Most sources list Sam's family name as 'Marlowe.' But the paintings are clearly signed 'Marlow,' without the final 'e,' and the name is not otherwise seen on the actual film titles, so I have chosen to spell it as the artist did.

7   Hitchcock and producer Herbert Coleman went to considerable lengths to commission a portrait for *Vertigo*. There is extensive correspondence in the files held by the Margaret

Herrick Library, dating from 1956 and 1957, related to an Italian commission. However, the Carlotta portrait finally used was a late substitution resulting from a casting change, as the previous had been painted to resemble Vera Miles, who was replaced due to her pregnancy by Kim Novak. Producer Coleman asserts in an interview that Ferren painted the picture and it is generally accepted that he did, although there is no archival evidence to confirm this.

8  In *Pollock* (Ed Harris, 2000), there is a scene set at the opening reception of that exhibition, in which Lee Krasner (Marcia Gay Harden) scolds Guggenheim (Amy Madigan) for not including American artists.

9  Interview with Rae Ferren, 22 June, 2009.

10  Royal Cortissoz (1869–1948) was an American art historian and art critic for the *New York Herald Tribune* from 1891 until his death. He was known for his traditionalism and antipathy toward modernism.

11  *The New Yorker* gives no source for its revised information on Ferren's signing practices. We cannot know whether he was in on the joke. To the best of my knowledge, however, he generally signed right-side-up in the lower right. It could be just a joke, or perhaps Ferren decided he preferred the particular canvas displayed at MoMA inverted. Peggy Guggenheim opened The Art of This Century gallery at 30 W. 57th Street, New York, on 20 October, 1942, in a space designed by Frederick Kiesler. The gallery was a major exhibition venue for contemporary art, particularly European modernism, until it closed in 1947, when Guggenheim returned to Europe. Guggenheim had purchased two works from Ferren in 1941 (Price 2011: 135).

12  On the still image in cinema, see Stewart (1999), Guido and Lugon (2012), and Auerbach (2007).

13  According to Paramount Production records (Margaret Herrick Library), Ferren was paid $2,500, plus all expenses for his trip with Rae to Vermont for the shoot.

14  I have looked closely at the works in *The Trouble with Harry* with Marshall Price, foremost scholar of the work of John Ferren, and, although he cannot definitively identify any of the works seen in the film, he recognizes all, or virtually all, as being consistent with Ferren's oeuvre (Personal communication, 14 July, 2010). Perhaps Hitchcock only approached Ferren after finding Wright's work inadequate. Unfortunately, there is scant evidence, one way or the other.

# Chapter 4

Art for the Apocalypse: *The Damned* (1961)

Every alert citizen of our society realizes, on the basis of his own experience as well as his observation of his fellow-men, that anxiety is a pervasive and profound phenomenon in the middle of the twentieth century. The alert citizen, we may assume, would be aware not only of the more obvious anxiety-creating situations in our day, such as the threats of war, of the uncontrolled atom bomb, and of radical political and economic upheaval; but also of the less obvious, deeper, and more personal sources of anxiety in himself as well as in his fellow-men – namely, the inner confusion, psychological disorientation, and uncertainty.

(Rollo May, 1950: 3)

*The Damned* begins with a pan from the sea to sublime views of the cliffs along the English Channel coast near Portland in Dorset. As the credits run and James Bernard's somewhat desolate, then progressively dissonant modern score plays, the camera slowly pans and tilts, journeying from the long view of the coast to a rocky outcropping in the foreground. When it encounters Elisabeth Frink's sculptures – dark, disfigured fragments upon the ground and rocks – they appear at first to be the charred remains of bodies [Fig. 58]. That these are scenes of an abandoned disaster or a post-apocalyptic landscape is certainly the impression conjured by the music, Arthur Grant's black-and-white cinematography, Richard Macdonald's austere (and uncredited) production design, and the savage, scarred surfaces of Frink's works. Only near the end of the sequence, when a couple of such works, an equine head and one of her fallen men, appear on man-made structures – armatures or pedestals for working – along with a sculpture credit, can we *perhaps* conclude otherwise. With a cut, both sound and image change entirely: from the rugged, barren cliffs to views of the busy, touristed attractions of Weymouth, the seaside town nearby, beginning with the esplanade and a percussive rock-and-roll song, 'Black Leather,' which we soon enough associate with a biker gang whose actions comprise one of the narrative threads of this 'patchwork' film. This cut takes us from a scene that expresses the existential soul of the film and a setting to which we shall return, to a scene that enters into the narrative proper, and in which the protagonists are gradually introduced. The abrupt and graphic change in image and sound underscores the powerful contrast between the two proximate locations, which was very much the director's intention (Ciment 1985: 199–200).

Joseph Losey was on the verge of a third act in 1961, on the very brink (as it were) of the collaboration with Harold Pinter and the art house films for which he may be best remembered, or at least most admired now. An engaged Communist and former member

**Figure 58:** *The Damned* (Losey, 1961/1963). Works by Elisabeth Frink as seen in opening title sequence.

of the Federal Theater Project who had worked with Brecht, Losey was about 40 when he directed *The Boy with Green Hair* (1948), his first feature film in Hollywood. Losey made five more there before moving to England, blacklisted for refusing to cooperate with the House Un-American Activities Committee (HUAC). He began directing in the United Kingdom under a pseudonym in 1954, and took pretty much what came his way, instilling each undertaking with his own distinct sensibility. Losey finished *The Damned* in England in 1961 but Hammer Films did not release it until 1963 (then with severe cuts), and it was not seen in the United States until 1965, further changed and retitled *These Are the Damned*. *The Damned* was Hammer's title, probably an attempt to underscore genre by reference to – as well as to capitalize on – the success of Wolf Rilla's 1960 *The Village of the Damned*,

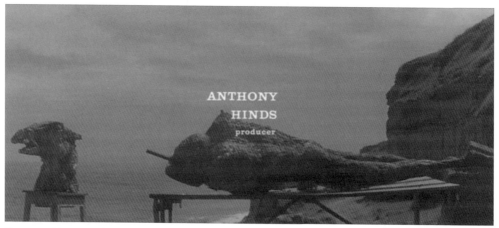

**Figure 59:** *The Damned.*

another film about dangerous, unnatural children of the age of anxiety.[1] Losey had planned to call the film *The Brink*, a title that evokes the emotional, physical, political, and existential edginess of the story.[2] Much as the imagery and associations of Chris Marker's titular jetty, Losey's title conjures a geographical edge, a historical threshold, an existential verge. This strange, arty genre film – a hybrid of science fiction, horror, and social commentary, adapted by Evan Jones from *The Children of Light*, a contemporary novel by H.L. Lawrence, *The Damned* in fact has much in common with *La Jetée* (1962, one year later), with its generic hybridity, apocalyptic omen, underground imagery, and evocative use of sculpture. *The Damned* tells the story of Simon Wells (Macdonald Carey), an American tourist who arrives in Weymouth, is lured into a trap by a young woman, Joan (Shirley Ann Field), mugged and beaten up by her brother King (Oliver Reed) and his gang. Later, Joan – perhaps remorseful – approaches Simon at his yacht, and, partly to defy her overprotective brother, she befriends and speeds away with Simon. King mobilizes his gang; their pursuit becomes threatening, turning Joan and Simon into fugitives. In their flight, the two break into and shelter in the studio 'birdhouse' of the sculptor Freya Nielson (Viveca Lindfors) – who scares them off as she returns – then flee again, scale a security fence, and fall down a cliff face. Slightly injured, and followed in short order by King, they stumble upon the top-secret compound under the rocks where Freya's friend Bernard (Alexander Knox) oversees the confinement and experimental education of nine irradiated children.

As Dave Kehr notes, *The Damned* is 'a transitional work that stands between Losey's last un-self-conscious genre piece [...] and later art-house career' (2010). The film was beautifully photographed (if unevenly acted) on location in Dorset, a region selected for its consonance with the narrative, and even for topographical associations echoed by sculptor Elisabeth Frink's avian imagery, according to Losey:

> I wanted a place that combined something absolutely bleak and wild and very ancient, which is Portland Bill, with something traditionally British, and that is Weymouth, of course, in the Bay. Portland Bill – bill does mean beak – is a kind of beak of bare rocks. In fact, it's a place where the British were developing germ warfare and also undersea warfare. So it was a very secret place, strange [...]. The Victorian-Edwardian seaside resort was absolutely ideal for contrast because it was obviously a kind of place for the Teddy boys, whose name is a diminutive for Edward because they affected Edwardian dress. They came out of poverty, unemployment, which was rife there as against these few old sea hotels which nobody went to excepting dying *rentiers*.
>
> (Ciment 1985: 199–200)

*The Damned* in some ways anticipates by a decade elements of Stanley Kubrick's 1971 *A Clockwork Orange*. It brings an American tourist into a violent confrontation with the gang of Teddy Boys and ultimately into a deadly, dystopic government experiment with radioactive children. When asked about the affinities by interviewer Michel Ciment, Losey acknowledged that *The Damned* did 'in a way anticipate' Kubrick's film but added, 'I could never have made

*Clockwork Orange* [...] I went to see it and [...] I simply had to leave because I knew I was going to be physically sick. I think it's a beautifully made picture and I would love to aspire to some of the technical and artistic things that Kubrick has achieved here, but I find it basically anti-social. Whereas I think my film is basically the reverse' (1985: 200). Losey's admitted sensitivity to and implicit distaste for Kubrick's film reflects his temperament, his leftist politics, and his sensibility, as characterized by Dan Callahan. 'The dominant themes of Losey's eclectic work are emotional instability, emotional and physical violence and perverse sexual power plays [...]. He has a mania for settings that express states of mind, and his camera movements are always abnormally sensitive and skittish' (Callahan 2003). This characterization suggests what would have drawn Losey to the work of Elisabeth Frink, who figures humanity in terms of animality and masculinity (there are almost no female figures in her large oeuvre[3]) and whose style, it could be said, also manifests an 'abnormal' sensitivity.

Losey's and screenwriter Evan Jones's considerable changes to Lawrence's story included changing a young British fugitive (a 25-year-old architect who is wanted for the murder of his unfaithful wife) into a middle-aged American tourist and the addition of a major character: the sculptor, played by Lindfors, whose cliff-top studio – referred to in the scenario as the 'birdhouse' – is a key location and whose works function as visual omens of the social and technological apocalypse to come. According to screenwriter Jones, sculptor Freya Neilson was conceived expressly to employ the work of Elisabeth Frink (Dame Elisabeth Jean Frink, CH, DBE, RA, 1930–1993) – with whom Losey had recently become acquainted – and whose scarred, distressed, figural works of the period included anthropomorphic birds, winged men, fallen men, horse heads and other morbid ciphers of existential dread, which they embody in the film at the same time as they figure art as a redemptive alternative to the cold-bloodedness of both lowbrow Teddy Boy and highbrow Government scientist.[4] The character of Freya herself stands for this view, as Losey made clear. Asked about the bird imagery in the film, which Michel Ciment found 'ambiguous because the bird is a symbol of freedom, but at the same time there is something threatening about the birds in the sculptures of Elisabeth Frink,' the contrarian Losey responded by connecting Frink's imagery to other elements of the narrative and mise-en-scène:

I don't think it's ambiguous at all – because the bird images of the helicopters, particularly when we get the three of them, is very sinister. And now even more so because of Vietnam and Angola [...] they were birds with no wings. They were always sort of blinkered science fiction warriors with masks for faces and tiny wings. You never feel about those birds that they can take flight [...]. Freya, the artist, represented the necessity and the right, if you can exercise it, to make your judgments on the merits of each case, which represents some kind of freedom.

(1985: 202)

Losey's response suggests that he wanted to shift the discourse of freedom from animal to artist and was perhaps attracted to Frink and her work precisely because of the way in which it eroded and troubled the more conventional symbolism and iconography of birds (is it coincidental, one wonders, that *The Damned*, although made somewhat earlier, and Hitchcock's *The Birds* were released the same year?). And Losey perhaps perceived the actual artist as most fittingly to embody the righteous artist. In an interview, Frink recalled that Losey originally wanted the strikingly handsome sculptor to play Freya herself and she was prepared to do so until the role evolved into a more central and complex one, requiring an actor (Kent 1985b).

**Figure 60:** Elisabeth Frink at her Fleming Close studio in Chelsea, ca. 1961, with the large *Bird Man* sculpture used in *The Damned*. Photo courtesy the Estate of Elisabeth Frink.

The numerous sculptures in bronze and plaster seen in *The Damned* represent her then current and recent works and range from small, tabletop figures to monumental over-life-sized works, including a couple in progress. Frink not only lent these but also was on location for their shooting and coached Lindfors on performing the sculptor's method of building up plaster, which was then ferociously worked and carved. According to Evan Jones, Frink was around for all the location shooting, seemed to thoroughly enjoy the process, and became quite good friends with Losey and members of the crew. There is no evidence that she was paid. She did receive a prominent screen credit, however, and there is anecdotal evidence that Frink welcomed the exposure, and that it enhanced her career (Jones 9 July, 2011 interview; Gardiner 1998: 197). In terms of its material presence in *The Damned*, it could be argued that Frink's sculpture performs the film's most major role. Its eloquent hybridity, liminality, equivocality, and edginess are those of the film, in terms of genre, politics, and emotion.

> In Suffolk during the war there was a whole bunch of very jolly Polish airmen who used to come to the house. My mother made them feel very much at home. They'd sit around and drink a lot of vodka and be very noisy. Then they'd go off in their flying machines – and sometimes they got killed. We were right next door to an operational aerodrome, and sometimes we'd see the planes coming home on fire.
>
> Elisabeth Frink (Lucie-Smith 1994: 15)

Frink's father was an officer. She was not quite nine years old when Britain declared war and the Allied flyers, flights, and accidents she saw on fields near her childhood home in Suffolk while her father was away fighting made a huge impression on her. Outwardly fearless and tomboyish and excessively admiring of the masculine and martial virtues she associated with

**Figure 61:** *The Damned.*

her father, she was evidently inwardly affected and developed insomnia (a condition from which Losey also suffered) and recurring, violent nightmares, including those of burning, falling men (Gardiner 1998: 8, 46, 80, 134). Frink studied art at Guildford School of Art, then Chelsea School of Art. She was influenced by, among other sculptors, Auguste Rodin, Alberto Giacometti, Germaine Richier, and, as with many of her peers, Henry Moore, the dominant British artist of the period. Moore's drawings of London bomb shelters were iconic images for wartime England, and his 1943 sculpture of the Madonna and Child for the Church of St. Matthew, Northampton closely echoed images of mothers with young children seen in many of the drawings. But if Frink's work is, like Moore's, organic – both figurative and abstract – it is in some respects very opposite. While Moore's oeuvre abounds with smooth, sinuous, undulating, biomorphic variations on the female form, often reclining, Frink developed a style and iconography of rough, sinewy, broken, and virtually decomposing figures, animal, hybrid, and – when human – almost always male, and generally, when not fallen, vigilant and aggressive. Frink's abstraction is external; the figures are abstract in their thingness, their objecthood. They are figures turned to things, tormented, expressionist facture and facticity taking the place of individuation and verisimilitude. Powerfully affective, their affect is surface, not countenance or gesture. Many of the sculptures are fragments – partial bodies – and several are of hybrid figures, including variations on Frink's most well-known motif – the bird–man.

The *Birdman* was another idea that possessed her, possibly inspired by the work of the French sculptor Germaine Richier, […] possibly too by César, […] and certainly by photographs of the death of the Frenchman, Leo Valentin, in 1956 during a flight of a few miles with wooden wings […]. Valentin's story brought out her horror of heights. She had stuck the *Paris Match* photos on the wall of the studio, where they remained, and

**Figure 62:** *The Damned.*

she began from there, developing the idea into a form of bird man unrelated to Valentin. That someone had dropped in space as he had terrified her, and it is possible that this fear was locked in with childhood experiences [...]. She had nightmares of great black wings beating past her until the end of her life, as if she were at the epicenter of a tornado; of bombers, limping back from raids, which might suddenly fall from the sky; even about falling through space herself, and tried to expel them in her sculpture.

(Gardiner 1998: 80)

Elisabeth Frink's career was marked by unusually early success. Having studied sculpture with Bernard Meadows, Frink had her first exhibition at the Beaux-Arts Gallery, London, while still a student in 1951; it was well received. The Tate Gallery bought a bird and Frink received some commissions; the next year – at just 22 – she was exhibited at the Tate, and in 1953 she won one of the British prizes (there were preliminary national rounds) in the international competition for the Monument to the Unknown Political Prisoner, a controversial Cold War undertaking that never, ultimately, resulted in a monument.[5]

Frink was loosely associated with and the only woman artist among an avant-garde circle of British sculptors, many of whom had been pilots during the war. 'The craggy rhetoric of their angular forms spoke of their terrible experiences – of fear and anxiety in the face of danger,' Sarah Kent (1985a) notes, implicitly invoking the structure of feeling that Herbert Read characterized as a 'geometry of fear' in the essay he wrote for the British Pavilion exhibit at the 1952 Venice Biennale:

These new images belong to the iconography of despair, or of defiance [...]. Here are images of flight, of raged claws 'scuttling across the floors of silent seas', of excoriated flesh, frustrated sex, the geometry of fear [...]. Their art is close to the nerves [...]. they have seized Eliot's image of the Hollow Men, and given it an isomorphic materiality. They have peopled the Waste Land with their iron waifs.[6]

(Read 1952: np)

Read's criticism was informed by psychoanalysis – Freudian, Kleinian, and at this point, Jungian – as well as Surrealism and Existentialism, and he would have seen these symptomatic and disturbing forms as socially productive, according to David Hulks. 'It was nothing less than the artist's duty, Read and his followers argued, to face society with its "darkest imaginings," [...] "to give shape to the compensatory values and content of which it is unconscious."' (96). Frink was a half-generation younger than most of the male peers and had not been included in the Biennale selection accompanying Read's essay. But, along with an entire generation, she was a bystander to some of the same 'terrible experiences,' the existential, psychological, social, economic, and physical upheaval and devastation of the war, which, along with the fascinations and horrors of her childhood, very much informed her work of the postwar period, which had distinct formal affinities with those artists and was dominated by cycles of birds. Of these Frink said, 'the birds at that time were really expressionist in feeling [...] that

**Color plate 1:** Frame from the special dream sequence John Ferren designed for *Vertigo* (Hitchcock, 1958).

**Color plate 2:** Mrs. Wiggs (Mildred Dunnock) and Sam Marlow (John Forsythe) in *The Trouble with Harry* (Hitchcock, 1955).

**Color plate 3:** *The Trouble with Harry.*

**Color plate 4:** *The Trouble with Harry.*

**Color plate 5:** *The Trouble with Harry.*

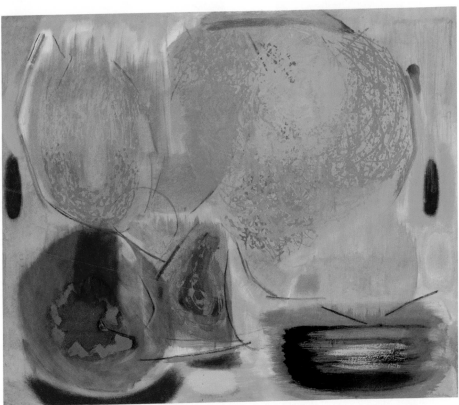

**Color plate 6:** John Ferren. *Summer Landscape*, 1951. Oil on canvas. Photo: courtesy of David Findlay Jr. Gallery, NYC.

**Color plate 7:** John Ferren, as seen in 'New Means for Moderns,' in *Life*, Vol. 37, No. 21 (22 November, 1954): 162.

**Color plate 8:** *The Trouble with Harry.*

**Color plate 9:** Saul Kaplan (Alan Bates) at work in *An Unmarried Woman* (Mazursky, 1978).

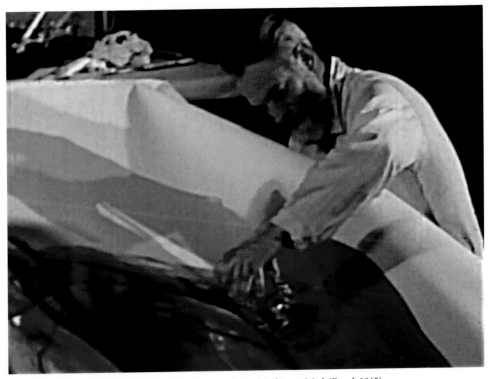

**Color plate 10:** Paul Jenkins as seen in *The Ivory Knife: Paul Jenkins at Work* (Engel, 1965).

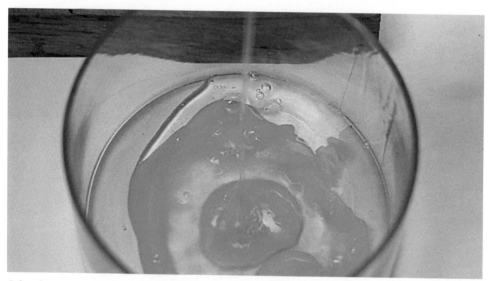

**Color plates 11 and 12:** *An Unmarried Woman.*

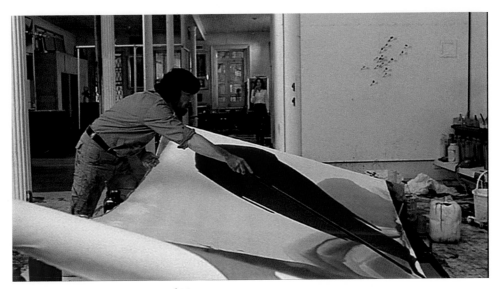

**Color plates 13 and 14:** *An Unmarried Woman.*

**Color plates 15 and 16:** *An Unmarried Woman.*

**Color plate 17:** 'Life Lessons' (Scorsese, 1989), from *New York Stories*, with Chuck Connelly's *Bridge to Nowhere.*

**Color plate 18:** 'Life Lessons,' Lionel Dobie (Nick Nolte) painting.

**Color plate 19:** June Gudmundsdottir (Greta Scacchi) and Griffin Mill (Tim Robbins) in *The Player* (Altman, 1992).

**Color plate 20:** *The Player.*

**Color plate 21:** *The Player*. Sydney Cooper's work as June Gudmundsdottir's.

**Color plate 22:** *The Player*.

**Color plate 23:** *Pride & Prejudice* (Wright, 2005).

**Color plate 24:** *Pride & Prejudice.*

**Color plate 25:** *Pride & Prejudice.*

**Color plate 26:** *Pride & Prejudice.* Elizabeth (Keira Knightley) and the Gardiners (Peter Wight and Penelope Wilton) in Sherwood Forest.

**Color plate 27:** *Pride & Prejudice.*

**Color plate 28:** *Pride & Prejudice.* First view of Chatsworth House.

**Color plate 29:** *Pride & Prejudice*. Elizabeth and the Gardiners in Chatsworth's Great Hall.

**Color plate 30:** *Pride & Prejudice*. The Great Hall's ceiling, painted by Louis Laguerre.

**Color plate 31:** *Pride & Prejudice*. Elizabeth and the *Veiled Vestal* (1847) by Rafaele Monti.

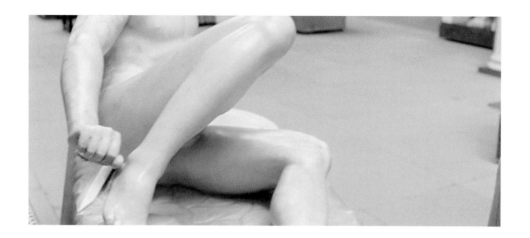

**Color plates 32–34:** *Pride & Prejudice.*

**Color plates 35–37:** *Pride & Prejudice.*

is, emphasis on beak, claws and wings – and they were really vehicles for strong feelings of panic, tension, aggression and predatoriness' (Kent 1985a: 10–11).

Panic, tension, aggression, and predatoriness are manifest in spades in *The Damned* and are often connected to Frink's imagery. Within five minutes of the start, Simon (Carey), the American visitor, has been brutally beaten and robbed by a gang, having been lured by Joan (a very pretty but wooden Field), sister of King (Reed), the leader of a biker gang. He affects the sartorial style of a Teddy Boy, while most of his gang wears black leather. Losey contrasts the unruly aggression and predatoriness of the displaced working class (indeed servant class) that this gang represents to that of the more 'elevated' protagonists of the other axis of the story, the sculptor Freya and secretive government scientist and 'public servant,' Bernard (Knox, who, like director Losey, was blacklisted and unable to work in the United States at this time).[7] The exposition presents Freya and Bernard as ex-lovers, still friendly (in an edgy way) and connected by the 'birdhouse,' the beautifully situated, remote cottage studio and terrace overlooking the sea at cliff's edge on his property that she rents in summer. In the film's second scene, Freya brings Bernard his rent in the form of one of her sculptures, one that she calls 'my graveyard bird,' a harbinger of themes to come[8] [Fig. 63]. It unfolds that Bernard's secrets – which will ultimately be the death of Simon, Joan, King, and Freya – involve his perverse utopian experiment with deadly, irradiated children.

One learns only at the film's climax that the children's 'mothers were exposed to an unknown kind and level of radiation by an accident' and that Bernard believes these survivors, who are themselves radioactive and immune to its fatal effects, are the only hope for the survival of mankind, which he is convinced will soon be annihilated by nuclear fallout. The sequence in which we are introduced to the children reveals the political topography of *The Damned*. It starts, echoing the credit sequence, with a long, aerial shot that pans from the sea – where Simon and Joan are rowing a dinghy toward the shore and

**Figure 63:** Freya (Viveca Lindfors), Bernard (Alexander Knox), and a Frink sculpture in *The Damned*.

the bill upon which stand Bernard's house and Freya's birdhouse – accompanied by score and the sound of gull cries. A cut to another long shot of seascape shows a long view of Bernard's house atop the cliff. Another cut shows a different view of the coast and sea, and then a reverse tracking shot reveals this to be the view through the window of a building in Bernard's secret compound, where a team of experts conducts the education and controls the upbringing of the irradiated children by remote. A Frink sculpture – one of her *Bird Men* or *Sentinel* figures ca. 1961, it appears – that begins the scene standing on the window sill, is not only part of the mise-en-scène, along with at least two other of her works and several other modernist artworks and furnishings of the period, but also part of the action and the dialogue [Fig. 64]. As the camera tracks backward, it gradually reveals a group of men (and later one woman) in a conference room. A uniformed officer, Major Holland (Walter Gotell), grabs the Frink figure and says, 'like a bird in a gilded cage, eh Dingle?' His reply from Mr. Dingle (Brian Oulton), a grumpy schoolteacher type – 'more like a gilded bird in a rather rusty cage' – leads to an extended disagreement that reveals tensions around class and the institutions of education and military, while underscoring the way that the bird and flight iconography of Frink's work relates to some of the salient themes of the film: freedom and imprisonment.

The imprisoned children whose education and well-being is the business of these technocrats, soldiers, and teachers, it is established, have never seen in the flesh any people besides themselves, except occasionally men who enter, when absolutely necessary, in full hazmat gear, and who look so alien that the kids, who have only a classical British education upon which to base their conclusions, refer to them as 'the black death,' unknowingly projecting their own toxicity onto the interlopers (although it is also possible we are meant to infer that the children have been raised to fear them). The children are interned behind and below the massive stone cliffs upon which much of the action takes place, in a cave that,

**Figure 64:** *The Damned.*

at its forbidding edges, is dark and rough-hewn – like the natural formations outside and the sculptures associated with them from the outset – but at its center is a chic, albeit airless and impenetrable, high-tech, modernist boarding school, in which the children have been raised to care for and educate themselves with remote assistance from the team above, led by Bernard, rather a Wizard-of-Oz-like figure, with whom they communicate by closed-circuit television[9] [Fig. 65].

When Simon and Joan, then later King, encounter the children, they find a preternaturally civilized culture of nine 11-year-olds who are (paradoxically, given that they are supposed to be radioactive) ice cold to the touch, well-educated, and well-spoken, seemingly very mature but at the same time terribly naïve, in the thrall of fantasy and family romance. They tell Simon and Joan that they had hoped that they were their parents, coming to rescue them; at the same time several of them cherish strange fantasies about their situation and origins. They have discovered one obscure, unfinished corner of the cave that is inaccessible to the video cameras that constantly survey them and there have established a sort of clubhouse, where they have dedicated fantasy 'memorials' to made-up parents using pictures cut out from magazines and art books. At age 11, the children are between childhood and adolescence: just beginning to rebel, conspire, and chafe at the Draconian constraints and obscurities of their world. A leitmotif of the script is the phrase, 'when the time comes ...', used repeatedly by Bernard to defer answering the children's existential questions, as well as some practical ones, and parroted by them in their attempts to master the mysteries of the Platonic cave-cum-modernist crypt-like universe to which they have been confined all their lives.

*The Damned's* dismal, dystopian narrative is fraught with political, social, existential, and psychological horrors. Class antagonism, technocratic hubris, and Oedipal abjection are funneled into a crucible of deadly conflicts, all of which can be read as both political and psychosexual allegory. At the time the film was made, at the height of the age of anxiety,

**Figure 65:** *The Damned.*

the underground complex in which the children are confined would have evoked the bomb shelters that were so familiar during the last war and the fallout shelters that were at the ready for the next. This real-world imagery was layered with utopian and dystopian images of the high-tech spaces of security and control belonging to the cold war popular imagination, which also had real-world correlatives. At other levels, the cave is, of course, a paradigmatic image for philosophy and psychology. These levels of meaning that pertain to mise-en-scène are found, too, in the narrative.

The world of the film is strangely parentless. Not only are the nine children orphans; so are King and Joan. And none of the adult characters are parents, although both Joan and Freya display maternal feelings toward the children. It is as though the nuclear family has been destroyed, replaced by nuclear technology. This parentlessness might seem ironic, in that the Atomic age was the heyday of the nuclear family, but it reflects aspects of recent British history and society that form the background to the world in which both novel and film were conceived. World War II wreaked havoc on families all over the world. In Britain, thousands of children lost one or both parents and thousands more were separated from their families in massive evacuations to the countryside. Elisabeth Frink, a child during the war, as noted, grew up in the countryside, so avoided evacuation. But due to her home's proximity to Stradishall, where there was a RAF base, and Great Wratting, with its airstrip, 'Lis could hear continual aerial activity from the house – bombers taking off for raids on Germany, and returning, sometimes badly shot up and in flames [...]. In the summer of 1941, a Wellington crash-landed in a field [...] only a couple of hundred yards away' (Gardiner 1998: 11). Finally, for her safety, Frink was sent away to her godmother at Chypraze, near Exmouth, Devon, where Saturday art classes at a convent school with a French nun, Sister Vincent-Paul, fostered her artistic talents (5, 11–14). Frink was already scarred by the war in the skies around her and by the absence of her father to whom she was very close and who survived the war but was a career officer and away fighting with the British Expeditionary Force. Her earliest work, at 13 – 'very frightening drawings that she saw as images of the apocalypse' – reflected the trauma and angst of her generation (Gardiner 1998: 14). Frink's mature work continued to give form to anxieties that were widespread in postwar Britain and beyond and that society itself was forced to meet on many fronts.

The social and psychological traumas and upheavals associated with the many thousands of bereaved, orphaned, and institutionalized children were the source of considerable theoretical, institutional, and governmental agitation and change in the postwar period. A psychoanalysis dominated by object relations, the pre-Oedipal reformulations that Melanie Klein innovated in the 1930s and brought with her to Britain, and that took several more turns in the work of theorists of the war- and immediate postwar-years (including D.W. Winnicott, John Bowlby, Emmanuel Miller, and Michael Ballint), was central to policies and institutions that became prominent in the crucible of a society at war and ravaged by it, including the Tavistock Institute, 'a center of analytic innovation [that] described itself as a mixture of Freud, managerial innovation, and sociology' (Zaretsky 2004: 253). Old-fashioned Freudianism turned toward children and their individual and group misfortunes, too; Freud's daughter,

Anna, exiled from Vienna and active as an analyst in England from 1938, and carrying on her father's legacy after his death there the following year, became director of the Hampstead Nurseries for homeless children. In 1944, with Dorothy Burlingham, she published *Infants Without Families*, the result of a four-year study of the Nurseries, and in 1945 established the journal, *The Psychoanalytic Study of the Child* (Zaretsky 2004: 269–271).

Explicitly parentless Joan and King, as well as the other members of the gang, the youths of 1960 in *The Damned*, would have been born just before or during the war and can be imagined to belong to a generation of orphans, evacuees and witnesses to unmanageable horrors. King's aggression, particularly, is given an obvious psychosexual pathography, one that can be seen in Freudian or Kleinian terms. He is wildly volatile and proprietary about Joan (who is of age), although he uses her as bait to lure mugging victims like Simon. He is convinced of the sexual predatoriness of all men. Joan reveals that he locked her in a cupboard when she dared go out with a boy once and accuses him of locking her up and trying to prevent her being a woman because he has never had a girl. The implication is that King projects onto other men his taboo incestuous desires and/or onto her an unacceptable desire for men. In one of *The Damned*'s most powerful scenes, Losey uses Elisabeth Frink's sculptures to suggest and provoke these unruly, distorting psychic urges – distinctly paranoid, probably homoerotic, and certainly Oedipal. King (whose name was Rex in the novel) has traced the runaway Simon and Joan to Freya's birdhouse (whence they fled when they saw her returning) and there confronts the sculptor. Here, not for the first time, Frink's sculptures seem to play the dual role of art objects (material and cultural) and what Melanie Klein would call 'partial' objects – archaic, phantasied internalizations that are the psychic source of introjections and projections. As King suspiciously interrogates Freya – who knows nothing of Joan and Simon – and accuses her of amorality, he is manifestly affected by the sculptures that surround him. He puts his hands to the neck of a life-sized *Warrior* (ca. 1954), with a strangely erotic strangulating action [Fig. 66]. The editing creates

**Figure 66:** Freya and King (Oliver Reed), with Frink's *Warrior* in *The Damned*.

**Figure 67:** *The Damned.*

a distinctly paranoid atmosphere, with a cut from a shot of King suddenly looking back over his shoulder to close-ups of two other sculptures in the room; it is as though he is responding to the blind 'look' of the gaunt male figure or beastly *Horse's Head* (ca. 1954; see Shaffer et al., catalogue no. 20; fig. 61). The tension then escalates as King inserts his fingers into the hollow eye sockets of the *Warrior* (1954, see Shaffer et al. 1984, catalogue no. 22), calls Freya's work 'nasty', spits at it, and then – grabbing an axe – runs outdoors and attacks a supine plaster figure, breaking it into pieces. When Freya screams and tries to restrain him, the two struggle on the ground, rolling together to the very edge of the cliff – to the brink – the action almost indistinguishable from a sexual assault.

While King acts out his psychic abjection, on people and objects, Bernard is his temperamental opposite: cool, rational, and withholding; his is more a case of sublimation (the redirection of unacceptable impulses) – he collects art rather than destroying it – but his repressed instincts may mirror King's. The scenario uses the elevations of its locations to map out the 'terrain' of psychic outcomes[10]: the repressed character has created an underground world, buried in stone; inside it is very orderly, modern, and rational, but still a prison. The well-behaved children use a recording of Byron's 'The Prisoner of Chillon' to obscure their rebellious planning. While Bernard's underground world is characterized by repression, Freya, on high, *expresses*, through art – high art – what Bernard *represses*. 'If I could explain these,' she says of her sculptures, 'I wouldn't have to make them.' The critics explain, though. Paul Mayersberg notes that, 'the bird suggests man's desire to be free – not the illusory freedom of sailing away, but a freedom from fear and oppression, a freedom of the spirit.' However, Mayersberg notes, 'the sculpture Freya gives to Bernard is a "graveyard bird." Bernard's project is associated with death and the same bird recurs as a menacing shadow behind him when he addresses the children on a closed-circuit TV screen' (1963: 33) [Fig. 68]. I would note, relative to this, that when King and his gang are stalking Joan

**Figure 68:** *The Damned.*

and Simon, King's position is in a graveyard, whence he communicates with his minions by whistling phrases from a song ('Black Leather'), like a bird ... a graveyard bird. It should also be noted that Freya's name is that of a Norse goddess, one whose iconography connects to Frink's. Freya is something of a bird-goddess; she wears a cloak of falcon feathers and she receives those who die in battle. As Gilles Ménégaldo observes, the use of Frink's sculptures not only contrasts creative instincts with destructive ones, but they are also resonant, in their 'tormented, incomplete, hybrid aspects', with the themes of nuclear apocalypse and physiological mutation' (My translation; 2000: 64).

These incomplete, hybrid aspects signify on a psychic register, too. They not only suggest partial objects but also dissolution of the human – a crisis of personhood – that Julia Kristeva would call 'abjection.' Elissa Marder's observation that 'one of the defining traits of being human is the incorporation of animal figures within the psyche, [...] uncanny traces of our radical alterity' (2012: 60) is part of her larger theoretical investigation into the primal scene and 'how, throughout human history and culture, humankind has attempted to reconcile the conceptual abyss between the apparently self-evident materiality of the maternal body and the radical unthinkability of the event of one's own birth' (2). Marder substitutes for 'Mother' the term 'maternal function' that permits a view of *The Damned*'s parentless spaces as symbolic:

> The maternal function operates at the outer limits of the human [...] opens up a strange space in which birth and death, *bios* and *techné*, the human and the nonhuman are brought into an intimate and disturbing proximity with one another [...]. the maternal function has always been that of an ambiguous 'container' (the womb) that fails to contain the unruly contradictions at work in the concept of birth. The 'womb' that holds the body before the beginning of life is structurally indistinguishable from the 'tomb' that holds

the body after the end of life. Indeed, in mythology, literature, and art the womb is often depicted in strikingly technological terms.

(2–3)

This notion of the maternal function connects the dots between the excessive, almost hysterical anxiety that characterizes *The Damned*, its strangely motherless world, its Cold War politics, the uncanny spaces – both primordial and futuristic – of its 'strikingly technological' subterranean lab school and the abject, incipient, partial, bestial forms of Elisabeth Frink's sculptures.

I am in my mother's room. It's I who live there now.

Samuel Beckett, *Molloy* (1951, trans. 1955)

In a review of an exhibition of Frink's work at Waddington Galleries exactly contemporaneous with the production of *The Damned*, Jasia Reichardt captured how the tension or equivocation in Frink's work between human figuration and inhuman thingness is an existential achievement:

[...] the falling men, the anxious bird figures, the ovoid heads that, like corroded stone, seem to disintegrate into shapeless and uncontrollable forms, reveal a sense of tension which arises directly from the predestined situation in which the subject finds itself. Whether the man has actually fallen, or is in the process of falling, he becomes in his strange and undignified way, a mere object [...]. Yet, he is elevated from the state by becoming a sort of symbol. The fragility, which is suggested by the very idea of a bird, is contrasted by the powerful, enigmatic and formidable bird-image Frink presents. The obvious tension is the result of this contrast, and of the artist's conscious choice to react to the quality in the bird which is that of the bird of prey. Thus Frink's art is the art of anguish, not the anguish of Rodin's hell, but rather that of Beckett's Molloy, where no human ideals and feelings are spared, but can only be reconstructed from the inevitable disintegration they must undergo. But Frink's concern with anguish never becomes objective, and her works convey the impression of an experience relived again and again.

(1961: 22–23)

Reichardt's articulation of what she referred to as Frink's 'Brutalism,' a sense of existential predestination, an anguish 'relived again and again,' illuminates the mise-en-scène of *The Damned*, with its vivid contrast between outside and inside: the austere sublimity of the exterior landscape and the high-tech sterility of the cave. Just as that cave in which the irradiated children dwell is philosophically Plato's and psychologically the womb-tomb – the secure, controlled container that expresses the inconceivable and inextricable origin and end of being (when King enters and touches one of the chilly children, he proclaims,

**Figure 69:** *The Damned.*

with horror, that they are dead) – the Frink sculptures are philosophically symbols of the human condition – of futility and mortality – and at the same time, psychologically, the partial objects, the parental imagoes, and the incorporated animals of archaic, infantile phantasy.

Losey ends the film by returning to and repeating for a third time the movement from sea to land with which he opened the film. This time the movement is connected to a machine – an avian machine – the helicopter. It tracks another that will follow, hovering over Simon's yacht until it is ascertained that he and Joan, already sick, have died of radiation poisoning and can neither infect nor inform the outside world of the lethal experiment they have stumbled upon. The children, who had escaped, have been rounded up by 'the black death', the men in hazmat suits, and returned to their prison; King, pursued by the helicopter and already sick, has crashed through the rails of a bridge, and to his death in the frigid waters. The camera-copter pulls away from the other machine and the receding craft and turns back toward the shore and the Portland Bill, atop which Bernard stands, aiming a pistol. He shoots Freya, who had been using what little time she knew was left to her now that she had been exposed to radiation and to Bernard's secrets to work on her massive bird–man sculpture.

She falls. An aerial shot follows the loud chopper's own shadow as it circles around the fallen figure; then there is a cut to a longer shot of the solitary *Bird Man* on the brink, 'a piece of sculpture', according to the screenplay, 'which expresses man's inspiration and his blindness', facing out to sea, the sound of the chopper fading.[11] A series of shots of the desolate rock faces below, buffeted by waves, is accompanied by the plaintiff score, the sounds of screeching gulls, and the echoing screams of the entombed children, whose cries for help – the last shot, a picture-postcard view of the Weymouth esplanade, assures us – will never be heard. Frink rejected the notion that her birdmen had anything to do

**Figure 70:** *The Damned.*

with the myth of Icarus (Kent interview 1985: 45). But for Losey, perhaps, it was a different matter.

## Notes

1 In *The Village of the Damned*, a fairly faithful adaptation of the novel *The Midwich Cuckoos* by John Wyndham, all the inhabitants of an English village lose consciousness and recover simultaneously some time later. It unfolds that all the women of childbearing age were somehow impregnated; they all give birth, prematurely, on the same day, to uncannily similar children, with some odd physical and exceptional mental attributes, including preternatural intelligence and telepathic powers. As the children grow older, it becomes increasingly clear that they are inhuman, the spawn of some alien invasion. Rilla's film starred George Sanders and Barbara Shelley and was released by MGM.

2 "'The Brink" was my title […] and insisted on by me. But I lost. I liked the two meanings […]. We toyed with the idea of "The Abyss", but that seemed very pretentious. And *The Damned* was entirely theirs, and I opposed it' (Losey, quoted in Ciment 1985: 204). The screenplay and shooting script held at the British Film Institute (BFI) Library preserve the history of the film's various titles, with *Children of Light*, the title of the source novel, crossed out and replaced with *The Brink* on some pages and with *The Damned* on others.

3 Frink's *Walking Madonna* (1981) for the Salisbury Cathedral is a significant exception.

4 Evan Jones recalls that Losey expressly believed that art was a moral 'counterbalance' to the destructive violence seen in both Bernard's officially sanctioned actions and the Teddy Boys' criminal ones (interview with author 9 July, 2011).

5 This international competition, organized by the Institute of Contemporary Arts (ICA), London, with a public announcement in 1952, was controversial from the outset, perceived by the USSR and other Eastern Bloc countries as a Cold War provocation, a charge that,

according to Robert Burstow, was not entirely unjustified. The idea for the exhibition was that of Anthony J.T. Kloman, an American former gallery director and US cultural attaché; and although it was not known at the time, there was CIA involvement. In a well-researched and informative article, Burstow contrasts the actual complexities and aesthetic concerns of this postwar sculpture competition – in which the abstract winning entry by Reg Butler (selected by a jury that included Herbert Read, Alfred Barr Jr., and Will Grohmann, among others) caused some consternation, with the much more well-known arguments about abstract painting, Abstract Expressionism particularly, and its role in Cold War politics, as discussed in my previous chapters. On the competition and Butler's winning design, never realized, see also Tate's catalogue entry for Butler's working model for the sculpture (1955–1956): http://www.tate.org.uk/art/artworks/butler-working-model-for-the-unknown-political-prisoner-t02332/text-catalogue-entry.

6 The sculptors exhibited in the 'New Aspects of British Sculpture' section of the Pavilion were: Robert Adams (1917–1984), Kenneth Armitage (1916–2002), Reg Butler (1913–1981), Lynn Chadwick (1914–2003), Geoffrey Clarke (b. 1924), Frink's teacher, Bernard Meadows (1915–2005), Henry Moore (1898–1986), Eduardo Paolozzi (1924–2005), and William Turnbull (1922–2012).

7 Evan Jones recalled that Macdonald Carey, too, was in exile due to the blacklist, the character of Simon changed so that he could be cast, but I do not have independent evidence of this (interview with author, 9 July, 2011).

8 Frink also at this time was at work on a series of very similar birds called *Harbinger Birds*.

9 The set includes classic mid-century furnishings designed by Eames, Eero Saarinen, George Nelson, and Finn Juhl, among others, such as were sold by Herman Miller, Knoll, and Heywood-Wakefield.

10 'Losey, almost alone except for Wyler among contemporary directors, makes brilliant use of different levels. A Losey film, in fact, looks rather like a contour map drawn up on scale paper. This is particularly noticeable in *The Damned*, where the minus 10 level means the children living in their prison under the cliff; zero is sea level, the beach at Weymouth, the atomic scientists' control-room, the little town besieged by the motor-cycle gang; and the plus 50 level is the cliff-top where Freya vainly erects tortured sculptures which seem already ravaged by radiation sickness and death' (Jacob 1966: 65).

11 From a much thumbed and hand-annotated screenplay and shooting script of *The Damned* held by BFI Library's Special Collections. The monumental sculpture appears to be the *Bird Man* (1959, see Shaffer et al. 1984, catalogue no. 62) that was cast in cement as a London County Council commission for the Sedgehill School in the Greater London district of Bellingham, until it was irreparably damaged and finally removed. The school building itself was recently torn down and replaced with a new building.

# Chapter 5

Object Choices: *An Unmarried Woman* (1978) and *The Player* (1992)

[…] the works' apparent excess of visibility remains linked to a manifestation of the invisible.

(Barry Schwabsky on the paintings of Paul Jenkins)

Between Joseph Losey's *The Damned*, made in black-and-white in Britain in the early 1960s – with its dystopian story of postwar political angst, its austere setting, and symbolic and expressionist use of Elisabeth Frink's grim sculptures – and *An Unmarried Woman*, the colorful seriocomic tale set among New York City's haute bourgeoisie and art world that Paul Mazursky wrote, produced, and directed in 1978, seems an enormous historical and cultural breach. In terms of both history and the structures of feeling associated with the two films and the art in them – from the geometry of fear to what one might call a phenomenology of pleasure – we have traversed a series of dramatic economic and political vicissitudes – landing on the other side of the Atlantic Ocean, the space race, the Vietnam War, and the Women's Movement – a spatiotemporal ellipsis that seems greater than the 17 years and overnight flight that divide the worlds of the two films. In between, the relationship between art and film became immensely complex and expansive, with technological innovations making moving-image technology more portable and affordable at a time when art-world traditions of craft and métier were breaking down, allowing artists easier access first to film, then video, technology. Painters, photographers, and other visual artists – most famously Andy Warhol, but also artists associated with Fluxus, and postmodern and minimalist practices, made films and videos, incorporated film and video into performances and installations, and experimented in television, radically expanding cinema and the fine arts. As cinema expanded beyond the screen, art – happenings, performance, installations, video, multimedia, and conceptual practices of all sorts – moved out of and transformed the museum and gallery.[1]

By 1978 there was conceptual art of all stripes and were numerous alternative galleries, cooperatives, and art spaces in SoHo, but the SoHo of Mazursky's film, despite its realist texture, shows little evidence of the conceptual, performative, multi- and intermedial, and collective practices that had exploded the art world of the previous decade. Art in *An Unmarried Woman* is such that a gallery can sell and collectors can buy. Certainly this is not unrealistic. The saleable art object did not disappear from the contemporary art scene in the 1960s and 1970s. Indeed, the contemporary art market was on the verge of a boom at this moment and several SoHo galleries would become premier retailers of blue-chip art merchandise. However, there is by definition a temporal and cultural lapse between the moment and spirit of an avant-garde and its mass cultural recognition. Thus, Mazursky's fictional artists represent the more established and establishment end of the SoHo artistic spectrum, while the more radical and experimental practices that had thrived in SoHo are scarcely to be seen (except in some of the flyers affixed to warehouse walls and light posts in the street scenes). It is fascinating, if a bit vertigo inducing, to think about the mixing of real art and artists in fictional situations as well as its conceptual opposite: fictional artists in real situations.

Saul Kaplan, the fictional British-born artist played by Alan Bates in *An Unmarried Woman*, is a painter. His large abstract compositions suggest Abstract Expressionism, Color Field painting, and other practices established a generation earlier, in the 1950s [Color plate 9]. In fact, actor Bates was born just a few years after and grew up just over a hundred miles away from Elisabeth Frink, the sculptor whose work was featured in *The Damned*. Had Saul Kaplan been a real rather than a fictional artist, he might have rubbed elbows with Frink at London art parties in the 1960s as he does in *An Unmarried Woman* with numerous actual New York artists, invited to populate a SoHo loft party as extras, along with some of their artworks. Further, while director Mazursky was born the same year as Frink (1930), Paul Jenkins (1923–2012), the real painter whose works play Kaplan's, was seven years older than she and had lived and worked between Paris and New York from 1953, the year Frink finished her studies and began teaching at Chelsea. So, although the worlds of Losey's and Mazursky's films seem radically separate, the artworks in them are not. Both oeuvres are related to high modernist developments of American and Western European art of the postwar period, the 1950s particularly. Thus – to review the dialectic of real and unreal modernism considered in the previous two chapters – one might imagine Saul Kaplan being acquainted with Frink, or her fictional counterpart, sculptor Freya Nielson (played by Viveca Lindfors in *The Damned*), and even John Ferren, or his character, Sam Marlow, the painter protagonist of Hitchcock's *The Trouble with Harry* (1955). Although the Hitchcock and Mazursky films are separated by almost a quarter of a century, their protagonists not only share a métier – abstract painting – but they also both paint in Vermont (Saul departs SoHo by station wagon for his annual five-month sojourn there at the end of *An Unmarried Woman*). In that summer of 1978, Sam Marlow, had he been a real rather than a fictional artist, would probably have been painting there still, in his fifties, maybe living happily with Jennifer and selling his paintings at the country store. Indeed, to shift back again from fiction to reality, Paul Jenkins had a great deal in common with John Ferren, who created the Sam Marlow pictures. The two abstract colorists were both American artists whose mature careers were grounded in Paris – Ferren's before the war and Jenkins's after – and were both associated with the New York School in the 1950s, with Ferren an older and Jenkins a younger member.

But if there is a striking parallel between the art in Hitchcock's and Mazursky's films, as well as its signification, much had changed in Hollywood and in the real world between 1955, when Sam quite counter-intuitively promised Jennifer, 'if you marry me, you'd keep your freedom,' and 1978, when Erica Benton (Jill Clayburgh), the protagonist of *An Unmarried Woman* becomes unmarried, embarking reluctantly on her journey to independence. This film – a sort of independent-Hollywood hybrid, written, directed, and produced by Mazursky for 20th Century Fox – about the end of an upper-middle-class Manhattan marriage and its aftermath, from the point of view of the rudely betrayed wife, was a critical and financial success, but also controversial.[2] Roger Ebert's paean was typical of the mainstream reaction:

> [...] we have to understand how completely Erica was a married woman if we're to join her on the journey back to being single again. It's a journey that Mazursky makes into one of the funniest, truest, sometimes most heartbreaking movies I've ever seen. And so much of what's best is because of Jill Clayburgh, whose performance is, quite simply, luminous.
>
> (1978)

I will return to luminosity, that of performers and especially that of paintings. Ebert's sense of the film's truth, its essential realism, was a typical popular-critical response and aligns with Mazursky's own intentions. 'I wanted to do a movie about the middle-class women who have very happy lives, a lot of opportunity, for whom things are good,' he said in an interview, 'but who in essence, are psychological slaves. They really live through their husbands, through the man' (Fox 1978: 30). But, although some feminist critics had positive, if equivocal things to say about *An Unmarried Woman* (Marsha Kinder and Charlotte Brunsdon, for instance), the most polemical among them, along with many critics on the left, savaged the film for trafficking 'in a type of feminist chic, which made visible some of the concerns of the Women's Movement, but trivialized or caricatured them, thus deflecting their political force' (Brunsdon 1982: 21) and for degenerating into romanticism and cliché. Todd Gitlin and Carol Wolman's review in *Film Quarterly*, with its derisive tone, was exemplary:

> The plot of *An Unmarried Woman* has the familiarity of a string of clichés. Stockbroker husband (Murphy) reveals he has been having an affair with a younger woman, and leaves charming, witty, pretty wife Erica (Jill Clayburgh), secretary at an art gallery, and daughter Patty (Lisa Lucas); Erica is furious; Patty feels bereft; Erica gets depressed; Erica fights off predatory men; Erica gets support from a group of woman friends; with help from a female therapist, Erica learns to become unmarried; seven weeks after husband has left, therapist urges Erica to get involved with men; after a one-night stand with one artist, Erica meets Mr. Right ('Saul Kaplan,' played by Alan Bates) and falls in love with him; Mr. Right is sexy, honest, ingratiating, friendly to Patty, desirable to Erica's friends, and, not last, a devoted and commercially successful artist; Mr. Right has trouble respecting Erica's hard-won freedom. Fade out on Erica fighting for privileges in her new relationship.
>
> (1978: 55–56)

However it was received, the film hit a cultural nerve and consolidated the sense of there being a trend of new sorts of films about new sorts of women in the new Hollywood.[3] And whatever its clichés, it is my contention that the feminist themes of *An Unmarried Woman* and its interest in women and gender are complicated by and even secreted within its use of real art. The real art used in the film was situated, too, within real – and realist use of – place.

In addition to being one of the first mainstream films to expressly narrativize themes arising from second wave feminism, *An Unmarried Woman* was one of the first to use the artist lofts and galleries of New York's SoHo as a setting. By the mid-1960s artists had begun to take up lofts in abandoned industrial buildings south of Houston Street in Manhattan as studios, some also illegally residing in them. In 1971, zoning laws were revised to permit artists to reside and work in their spaces. By the time Mazursky set his film there, SoHo had been well established as the new center of the New York, and arguably American, art world for almost a decade. Between 1968 and the early 1970s, dozens of galleries had opened in the neighborhood, including Paula Cooper (the first), Leo Castelli, André Emmerich, Sonnabend, as well as alternative spaces and artist cooperatives (Petrus 2007).

In the film, Erica works at Rowan Gallery, 'played' by a real gallery: OK Harris, which opened in 1969 on West Broadway, one of the first major SoHo galleries. Its founding director, Ivan Karp (1926–2012), typecast in a very small role in *An Unmarried Woman*, plays gallerist Herb Rowan. 'Originally, I had eleven lines of dialogue, then they were cut,' Karp is quoted in *Art News* as having said. 'But it would have been a disruptive force in the art world since I would have gone straight to Hollywood,' he concluded, his tongue certainly in his cheek (Anon 1978: 40). Karp had, in fact, earned a film diploma and had worked as an editor for a couple of years before his career as a gallerist and had already had his proverbial 15 minutes of media fame, having stood, smirking, next to the notoriously laconic Andy Warhol for a television interview in 1964.[4] At least two works by Warhol – *Campbell's Soup II (Chicken 'N Dumplings)* and *Mao*, both screen prints from series – are to be seen among others in the OK Harris stable in scenes at Rowan Gallery in the film. As noted in Gitlin and Wolman's synopsis, in the film's third act, Erica becomes involved with Saul Kaplan, a British-born New York artist who meets her when he is hanging his one-man show at the gallery. Paul Jenkins was the Abstract Expressionist painter who lent his art, loft space, and instruction of Bates in his signature – and very photogenic – technique, a sort of fluid action painting which is employed dynamically in the film, as both realist detail and metaphor.

According to a 20th Century Fox press release, 'SoHo: Art Capital of the World,' 'Bates was sent in London a short film on how Jenkins works, and when the actor arrived in New York he spent a week taking lessons from Jenkins in his loft studio on lower Broadway.'[5] That short film had to have been Jules Engel's *The Ivory Knife: Paul Jenkins at Work* (1965), the only such documentation of Jenkins. The entire 16-minute color film consists of shots of Jenkins working in his studio to a modernist score composed by Irwin Bazelon. In longer shots, one can see how Jenkins typically works on a tilted canvas, often physically maneuvering it to direct the pathways of poured paint. Closer shots show the pouring, pooling, melding, and diffusion of colors and water, and the strikingly photogenic, bearded Jenkins occasionally channeling, pushing, or pulling the paint with his signature tool, an ivory knife [Color plate 10]. There is no paintbrush in evidence; nor is there any voiceover explanation. The film expresses cinematically how central process itself is to Jenkins's aesthetic and the meaning of the paintings he referred to as 'phenomena.' While the studio press release claimed that Bates worked with Jenkins for a week preparing for the part, a contemporary article in *People Magazine* maintained that the apprenticeship was longer.

For a month before the film went into production, Jenkins instructed the English actor three afternoons a week. 'I made Alan mix the spectrum of colors to get a sense of fluidity and viscosity,' Jenkins recalls. 'I let him choose his colors – he was strongly drawn to vibrant orange – and made him do throws of acrylic paint and water on the canvas. As we went along, what grew stronger was Bates' concept of painting itself.'

(Collins 1978: 46)

The longer apprenticeship period is echoed by the contemporary account in the pages of *Art News*, which also quotes Jenkins.

[T]he actor spent nearly a month with the artist to see how an artist lives and works. Bates, says Jenkins, turned out to be a natural artist. 'I told him, "If you ever want to give up acting, you've got a second career here." It was alarming.' Alarming? 'Because he was so damned good.'

Jenkins noted it was a bit harrowing at times to have camera crew, light technicians and actors traipsing through the loft he has occupied on 13th Street since 1963 (before that it belonged to Willem de Kooning), and consequently he 'painted more at the time than during a month of Sundays.' It was 'well worth the experience,' however. Like many of the artists represented in the film, Jenkins even appeared for a split second in one of the scenes as an extra.

(Anon 1978: 40)

The film is scrupulous about naturalizing (and acknowledging) art and artists. Dozens are featured and credited in one of the first examples of a mainstream film set in a *real* art world, one in which the material realities of art explicitly include space, facture, sex, gender, commerce, and class. The critiques of the romanticization of the Kaplan character and the haute bourgeois milieu of the film notwithstanding, Mazursky's avowed approach to representing the art world rejected the typical artist myth – there's no abject, starving, or suffering artist in sight – and is not unlike his attitude toward the scenario's sexual politics. 'You know, American film has never dealt with the artist with any real honesty,' he says. 'Because they're flesh-and-blood people, real people, who have egos, who talk about money, who think about sex, who eat […]' (Fox 1978: 30).

*An Unmarried Woman* was shot entirely on location in New York and the naturalism of setting – interior and exterior – extends from the lofts and galleries of SoHo to the Bentons' Upper Eastside milieu and beyond. The albeit selective material realities of the mise-en-scéne – in this case not only 'real' objects but also real places and even real people – operate on multiple levels and lend the film complexities that many of the contemporary critiques ignored. Foremost among these reality effects are those related to art objects, especially Jenkins' works and his practice, as performed by and with Alan Bates. But a correlative to the real-art world of the film, to which I shall return, is to be found in the therapist whom Erica sees when struggling with the emotional fallout of being left. Interestingly, Gitlin and Wolman, and other critics, singled out this element of the scenario with particular contempt. Of the therapist, Tanya (Penelope Russianoff), they maintain, 'her therapy is shallow and incompetent. She serves as a mouthpiece for trendy seventies egotism, making the astounding proclamation that it's always wrong to feel guilty' (1978: 57). Ironically, perhaps, the role of the therapist was played by a real psychotherapist, a fairly prominent one. Penelope Russianoff (1917–2000) had a clinical practice and was on the faculty of the New School for Social Research from 1960 until the 1990s. In two scenes shot in her own consulting room, she sits, cross-legged, close to Clayburgh on cushions on the floor (in a third scene, accompanied by her probable lesbian partner, Tanya encounters Erica at a SoHo loft party).

Mazursky [...] had projected a scene in which Erica (Clayburgh) seeks help from a therapist who is a short, fortyish woman with a European accent. However, at the

**Figure 71:** Penelope Russianoff and Jill Clayburgh in *An Unmarried Woman* (Mazursky, 1978).

suggestion of director Claudia Weill [...] Mazursky cast the six-foot-two-inch, sixtyish American psychologist Penelope Russianoff as Erica's therapist. In fact, Russianoff is the real-life author of a book, *Why Do I Think I'm Nothing without a Man?*, which addressed many of the same problems Erica faces in the film. According to Russianoff (personal communication, 1984), Mazursky did several takes of the scene between Erica and her therapist in which Clayburgh read lines that Mazursky had scripted while Russianoff ad-libbed a number of different responses.

(Gabbard and Gabbard 1987: 138)[6]

The results, according to the Gabbards (one of whom is a practicing psychoanalyst), produced 'one of the most sympathetic images of psychotherapy in American film [...]' Moreover, not only did Mazursky permit Russianoff to improvise her lines, the dialogue about guilt that offended Gitlin and Wolman really reflected a strong feminist strain in her practice and her writing. In that scene Tanya assures Erica that feelings are okay – anger, depression, fear – but balks when Erica responds by saying she feels guilty. Calling it (ambiguously) a man-made emotion, Tanya urges Erica to try to turn off the guilt, a feeling which, in her essay, 'Learned Helplessness,' published shortly after her appearance in the film, Russianoff characterizes as symptomatic of the propensity of women to blame themselves for men's infidelities and failings (1979: 34–35).[7]

The Gabbards' assessment of the sympathetic portrayal of psychotherapy, despite mixed reviews and criticism from some among Russianoff's profession, was confirmed by an increase in her clientele, including celebrities, after the film's release. According to her *New York Times* obituary, 'it increased her practice and earned her a book contract' (Saxon 2000). The exposure was similarly salutary for Paul Jenkins's career, although *People Magazine* claimed 'the 54-year-old master hardly needed Hollywood to become a star. His paintings bring up to $20,000 and already in the permanent collections of institutions like the Museum of Modern Art' (Collins 1978: 46); Paul Mazursky claims that Jenkins's prices doubled as a result of the film (personal communication, 22 February, 2011).[8] That Russianoff's and Jenkins's careers *could* be impacted by their participation in *An Unmarried Woman* speaks to the realism and, moreover, the *reality* of their presence and work in the film, despite its fictional frame. To grasp the strength of this reality effect, imagine viewers of *Equus* (Sidney Lumet, 1977) or *Bad Timing: A Sensual Obsession* (Nicolas Roeg, 1980) – to name just two of the many other fiction films of the period that feature scenes of psychotherapy – seeking out Richard Burton (who played Dr. Martin Dysart in the former) or Art Garfunkel (Dr. Alex Linden in the latter) for treatment. The absurdity of this conceit depends not only on the disturbing representations of those two psychiatrists but also on the obvious star status of the actors *and* fictionalization of the psychiatric and psychoanalytic process in those, as in most films (see Gabbard and Gabbard 1987). Almost as absurd is the thought of viewers seeking out the works of fictionalized artists whose oeuvres were works for hire or studio pastiches in films such as *The Rebel* (aka *Call Me Genius*, 1961), even many of those made for fiction films by 'legitimate' artists, as I shall discuss later in this chapter regarding Sydney

Cooper's paintings for *The Player*. If Jenkins's reputation and market were enhanced by his work in *An Unmarried Woman*, that was possible in large part because of the realism with which his work, practice, and milieu was shown.

According to Mazursky, he originally asked Jules Olitski (1922–2007) – with whom he shared a mutual friend – to lend his art for the film. Olitski – a major abstract painter whose canvases of the 1970s often consisted of diffuse, luminous, sometimes almost monochromatic, colored fields – declined but introduced the director to Jenkins, whose loft was in the same building (actually not in SoHo, but on 13th Street in Greenwich Village). Mazursky's interest in Olitski suggests that scale, abstraction, color, and luminosity – characteristics common to Olitski's and Jenkins's oeuvres – may have been at some level integral to the conception of the fictional painter's practice. The Jenkins works used in the film – displayed in the fictional Rowan Gallery and hung and in progress in his loft – are large. Jenkins's technique, enacted by Alan Bates, and as evident in the Engel film, is bodily but unlike the more aggressive, spasmodic, and existential gesture of the most celebrated action painter, Jackson Pollock, whose practice also – famously – was captured on film, by Hans Namuth, in 1950. Jenkins's process has a sensual grace and his canvases a liquid luminosity and lyrical chromaticity that are cinegenic and lend themselves, in the context of the film, to embodying sexual pleasure, specifically female sexual pleasure. Here, among the privileged classes of New York in the 1970s, the politics signified or embodied by art are related less to the geopolitical threats of the atomic age and more to the social and personal convulsions of the women's movement and the sexual revolution.

### … something about abstraction that we may not want to know

In 2007, Barry Schwabsky, reviewing Paul Jenkins's one-man exhibition at the Redfern Gallery for *Artforum*, remarked that the artist had 'been exhibiting his paintings regularly since his first show in 1954, yet in recent decades his work has flown under the critical radar.' Schwabsky continued, 'even his moment of pop-cultural notoriety, when his studio and painting method were lent to the macho but sensitive character played by Alan Bates in Paul Mazursky's 1978 movie *An Unmarried Woman*, is nearly forgotten – as such moments usually are, with any luck' (480). The snobbish aside about pop-cultural notoriety is all too typical of art establishment attitudes toward the movies. But Schwabsky's explanation of establishment ambivalence about Jenkins is incisive:

By and large, abstract painting has anchored its claims to seriousness in a principled rejection of hedonism – a sensualistic impulse that is undoubtedly inherent, insofar as abstract painting means, fundamentally, playing with colors, forms, and materials without regard for anything else. This means that abstraction has developed precisely by working against itself, pitting austerity against a native tendency toward indulgence.

Leaving austerity out of the equation, Jenkins tells us something about abstraction that we may not want to know.

(480)

What is it that we may not want to know about abstraction? Something that has to do with hedonism, sensuality, play, and indulgence? Does abstract art threaten to return the repressed? I think Schwabsky's implication is that at some level we regard an abstract painting (that we perceive as) uninhibited by certain formalist measures of restraint as masturbatory: that it speaks of ludic, infantile pleasures like playing with ourselves, our food, our shit. If so, Jenkins's work is interestingly deployed in *An Unmarried Woman*, in which it is narratively connected to sex, food, and even to shit.

Shit is introduced early in *An Unmarried Woman*, in the first scene, in fact. The opening credits play – accompanied by Bill Conti's sax-dominated, jazzy score (in passages very reminiscent of Gato Barbieri's for Bernardo Bertolucci's 1972 *Last Tango in Paris*) – over a long aerial shot that begins on the east side of the Queensboro Bridge with a wide establishing view of lower Manhattan, travels and pans north, showing the city's most iconic skyscrapers (including the twin towers of the World Trade Center, the Empire State, and Chrysler Buildings), moves in on and along the FDR Drive, to a pedestrian bridge that crosses the highway at 71st Street, where we cut to a traveling shot of Erica and her husband Martin on their morning jog. Along the esplanade, Martin steps in dog shit. This is a realist touch (and a topical one, as 1978 – the year of the film's release – was also the year New York became the first US city to enact a so-called pooper-scooper law), but Mazursky uses it to reveal a great deal about the marriage and the politics of the relationship. While Martin overreacts, swearing and complaining that the shoe is ruined – shouting at passing traffic, 'come on out and take a crap on me – everybody else is' – as if the shit was left there as part of a conspiracy to ruin his day, Erica laughingly and cheerfully takes the shoe (which, she notes, only cost $35) in hand and attempts to scrape the shit off it, kneeling down near the grass to do so. Her good-natured servility is not without a certain amount of laughter at his expense and seems to exacerbate Martin's irritation. He ends up provoking a fight, telling Erica that the longer he's married to her the more she reminds him of his mother, then charging that she wanted him to step in it. Mazursky's espoused critique of the psychological slavery of even middle-class women in marriage is given a Freudian footing here, with the boy inside the man despising the woman who cleans up his shit.

The following scene, one of the film's most commented upon, begins, after implied morning make-up sex (a 'quickie') in the conjugal bedroom, and effortlessly pulls off a great deal of important exposition. The setting and furnishings establish the class to which the jogging couple belongs; the bedroom window offers elevated views of Manhattan high-rises. Over the bed in which Erica lolls, post-coital and happy, while Martin dresses for work, is a framed, contemporary print and nearby are two others (one probably by Victor Vasarely), which realistically reflects that the Bentons are of a class that can collect and also establishes a sensibility, as well as an association between abstract art and sex, that will intensify later. (These prints are relatively small; one has a relatively dull, brown-and-white palette, compared to the Jenkins paintings, while two others display bright, varied colors.) Elsewhere in the apartment are other colorful paintings and prints, including what appear to be (or are similar to) works by Kenneth Noland, Alfred Jensen, Jules Olitski, and others). Martin, kissing Erica goodbye, asks her what her plans for the day are. The question and her answer – that she's meeting friends for lunch and then going into the gallery – reveal that although she has a job, it is the part-time job of a woman of leisure, a lady who lunches. The scene also introduces the Benton's teenage daughter Patti and establishes a warm, frank family ambiance. When Martin and Patti have left for work and school, the camera lingers on Erica, herself lingering in bed with a happy smile on her face. Music from *Swan Lake* is heard playing on the radio or stereo. As Charlotte Brunsdon observes, the following part of the scene, [Fig. 72]

[...] has two functions. Firstly, to present Erica to us as 'subject' – active, desiring agent – and secondly, as spectacle, as object of our gaze [...]. As the music starts, Erica begins a semi-ironic fantasy commentary on her own successful debut dancing the lead in *Swan Lake*. The substance of this privileged view into the central character's privacy is her fantasy of being appreciatively watched! In a change to long-shot, Erica rises, and, in the diegetic imagination of being watched, quickly and neatly adjusts her bikini knickers to fully cover her buttocks as she begins to dance. Narratively, this is a scene which functions to give 'more depth' to the central female character – fantasising about being a

**Figure 72:** *An Unmarried Woman.*

ballerina, taking pleasure in her body. However, the sequence also functions quite clearly within the tradition of 'woman displayed as erotic spectacle.'

(1982: 25–26)

Brunsdon's analysis of the double function of this scene is persuasive, although she does not mention that Clayburgh's performance hardly evokes that of an actual dancer; it is more self-consciously clownish than balletic and, although she is scantily clad, the spirited, goofy dance around the apartment is shot in long, mobile shots; she is not particularly eroticized. In another early scene, Erica undresses for bed as the film regards her rather matter-of-factly and her husband doesn't spare her a sideways glance, a realist and revealing detail (one that is explicitly countered near the end of the film when Erica somewhat jokingly asks Saul, 'am I only a sexual object to you?' 'No,' he answers, 'you're a bright, willful, curious woman ... who is *also* a sexual object'). Perhaps the lolling-dancing scene has a third function. Viewed in the larger narrative context, many of the details of these first two scenes of married life take on dialectical meaning.

Mazursky sets up structural parallels between scenes before and after the un-marriage. Several of these parallels involve sex. Erica's first sexual foray after the separation is with Charlie (Cliff Gorman), a brash, macho artist who had been introduced before the break-up, in the first gallery scene, disparaging a show on view and coming on to Erica. Venturing out to a bar on her own, she runs into an acquaintance, Jean (Novella Nelson), a black woman artist, who introduces her new lover, Edward (Raymond J. Barry), and espouses some very

**Figure 73:** *An Unmarried Woman.*

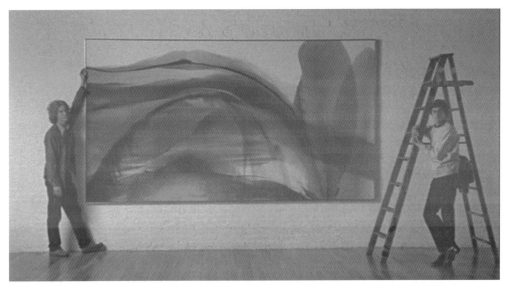

**Figure 74:** *An Unmarried Woman.*

liberated ideas about sexual relationships. Then Charlie appears and soon learns of Erica's separation. It is she who suggests they go to his place. At Charlie's loft, amidst his large, somewhat surrealist sculptures (wood carved to look fluid, melting and biomorphic),[9] an awkward, funny, singularly unerotic sex scene ensues. Charlie warns Erica that he doesn't get involved and she confesses that she's nervous and has only slept with one man in seventeen years. Her head gets stuck in her pullover as she undresses and Charlie has to help extract her. She becomes self-conscious, when stripped to her bra and panties, so runs across the loft to turn out the lights [Fig. 73]. Things haven't proceeded far before she is impaled by a splinter and Charlie has to perform a second extraction. Then Erica suffers a fit of ticklishness and is laughing a bit hysterically when finally overcome – evidently – by desire. With a cut, it is over, and it is Erica who is dressed and leaving, as Charlie, in just his underwear, suddenly seems involved. He asks if he may see her again, the next day. She demurs by quoting him: 'I'm a short-term guy.'

The next time Erica has sex, it is a 'quickie', during her lunch hour, with Saul, whom she has just met during the installation of his show (a scene that had begun with a close-up shot of a section of painting, then zoomed out, included Ivan Karp's appearance, and discussion about at what height the large canvas – Jenkins's *Phenomena Waves Without Wind*, 1977 – ought to hang) [Fig. 74]. Mazursky cuts from Saul, in the gallery, suggesting they take lunch together to Erica sitting next to him at the end of his bed, dressing. Again, as it was with Charlie, it is she who dresses and leaves and Saul, who stays behind, in his robe, expressing some chagrin at Erica's almost business-like attitude (the sex was good, she said; but felt empty). These scenes contrast in many ways to the earlier scene with Martin. There is little of the domestic languor and playful leisure seen at the beginning. But Mazursky emphasizes that Erica is active, not passive. She goes to their places, she dresses afterward, and leaves. The men, now, are the ones who remain behind undressed. The contrast is less about role reversal, however, than it is about allowing Erica, as she puts it, to 'experiment,' to express active sexual agency with emotional caution. Erica has, after all, been hurt. But sexual relations have been established as of primary importance for her.

Another parallel the scenario establishes involves shit. Leaving Jean and Edward's loft party together, Erica and Saul walk and talk through the SoHo night. At the party, they had encountered Charlie, who, drunk, behaved indiscreetly and badly, finally provoking Saul to fight. Saul exemplifies a kind of present-day chivalry, simultaneously expressing respect for Erica's autonomy and a strong, unambiguous, almost possessive desire for her. As he is telling her about himself and his background – ironically, that he is a simple man with simple tastes, except for in shoes, as he has bad feet – he steps in shit, as Erica points out, laughing. In contrast to Martin, earlier, Saul himself laughs (although Mazursky has managed to establish that his shoes are expensive, while Martin's were not), sits down on a stoop, with equanimity takes responsibility for his own shit, so to speak; and launches into a tongue-in-cheek disquisition about his extensive knowledge of different dogs and their dog-doo. Erica does not even try to clean up his mess. As the scene continues Saul tells Erica a lot about his background, including an anecdote (a parable?) about the origins of art. He says that during a bad row between his parents, who ran a London deli, his mother threw a jar of pickled herring at his father, missing. The resulting splatter on the wall, he says, inspired him to become an abstract expressionist.

Moving from shit to hurled food (a motif that returns at the end of the film), Mazursky continues the joke – or analogy – between action painting and food in a later sequence, one in which Saul and Erica's relationship has clearly become more domestic, intimate, and comfortable. It follows the film's most romantic scene, in which the two dance and embrace in the darkness of Saul's loft to a record of Billie Holiday singing 'I'm Yours,' faintly illuminated only by bluish light that enters through tall industrial windows (reminiscent of Michael Snow's 1967 *Wavelength*), from the street. The next morning Saul is working, pouring colors across a large tilted canvas. A close-up of bright orange paint spilling over the white ground cuts to another of bright yellow egg yolks, broken into a bowl [Color plates 11–14]. The scene cuts between shots of Saul pouring red, then deep blue veils of color that wash down over white canvas, and across a rainbow array of color at the bottom edge, pooling at the base, and Erica, who, preparing eggs, also emerges from the kitchen, walking toward the studio area where he works, bursting with pleasure and possibility. 'I feel great! I feel happy,' she says. 'I don't know what's going on. This is craziness. I don't understand anything anymore. I feel … I like to do things, you know? I want to travel.' 'We'll travel,' says Saul, still painting. 'I want to see Greece,' she goes on. 'I want to see Persia. I would like to go to Tibet,' adding playfully, 'I'd like to open up a little restaurant – nothing fancy – just a little something where I sing, under a spotlight.' Erica is experiencing the prospect of what Penelope Russianoff, the real therapist who played Tanya, called, 'a whole new world […]

as women unlearn helplessness and begin to feel exhilaration by taking charge of their own lives, instead of accepting a dependent position' (1979: 36–37). The dialogue goes on, in a similar vein, as Erica heads back to the kitchen for the eggs and returning with them, sits down with Saul on a bench along the wall, flanked by paint and supplies. They eat the eggs (which he finds 'delicious') directly out of the pan, as the discussion becomes more serious: Erica's exhilaration about freedom, adventures, challenges, educational and professional possibilities is met by his passionate desire for her, to live with her, and his offer – according to conventions of which she has grown suspicious – to support her in order to have her. The scene ends after Saul expresses his passion by picking Erica up and spinning her around and reluctantly lets her go home, appeased by her invitation to come to her place for dinner and to meet Patti. She writes her address in paint on the floor. 'I like your style,' says the artist. She leaves and he goes back to work, pouring paint as yellow as the egg yolk across his canvas.

Art critic Carter Ratcliff offered a clever, rather facile, double-edged interpretation of this juxtaposition of action painting and eggs: '[…] cross-cutting between Clayburgh's scrambling eggs and Bates's spreading paint suggests that art and artists have the power to spice up any menage. Of course, the woman may still have to do the cooking' (1978: 14). And Ratcliff is not wrong (there is a certain sexism here), merely superficial. The scenario explicitly acknowledges not only that Erica's eggs are delicious (or so Saul says) but also that they are spicy (when Saul comes to dinner, Patti mentions that her mother's scrambled eggs with hot sauce is one of her specialties). So, any spicing up of the ménage is mutual. Both eggs and hot sauce, of course, are rich in metaphorical potential. Erica may bring the eggs and hot sauce to the relationship and Saul the ivory knife and 'explosive eruptions of paint and passion' (Bennett Schiff, quoted in Norland 1971: 20)[10] but the results are delicious and colorful enough to induce inexplicable, whirling joy. It is difficult – no, impossible – to convey with words the aesthetic properties of the Jenkins paintings that are used in these scenes, the process by which they're seen being made (by Bates), and the affective and metaphoric connections drawn between them and the action of the narrative. There, on screen, they give form to things that cannot be articulated: sensation, emotion, pleasure; vital, internal phenomena. Indeed, from about 1958, Jenkins's titles for his paintings began with the word 'Phenomena.' 'The word phenomenon came to me after finishing a painting which happened with no preconceived idea. The sensation of the experience happened with me, not outside of me as though it were done by a medium. The discovery came within the act […]' (Jenkins, 1958: 13).

There is an element of the mystical, as well as the phenomenological, in the way that Jenkins and some of his critics articulate his work. Indeed, Jenkins himself developed a life-long fascination with mysticism, the occult, Buddhism, and other eastern religions, a facet of his work noted by Barry Schwabsky:

[…] The whiff of New Age spirituality about some of the titles here […] will put some viewers off, but Jenkins has a right to it, as the effects he seeks in his paintings are none other than the ones that mystical poets have sought for centuries: 'Shattered and refracted light, indefinite depths, weightlessness … and synthesizing these sensations and affects, an all-consuming clarity,' as Kenneth Rexroth once put it. In a way, abstract painting is the art most perfectly suited to evoke these, because it can convey sensations without representing (and thereby establishing a distance from) the bodies that experience them.

(2007: 481)

It may seem that there is a paradox in a practice at once mystical and hedonistic, to use Schwabsky's terms, but a kind of ecstasy is a common element, or outcome of both tendencies. Jenkins expresses an intensive merging of the spiritual, the psychological, and the sensory in his writings:

There are two kinds of light in painting which I move toward that become and relate to form. One is radiant, luminous light – that element which has its light from *within* [...]. The other is reflected light that appears as a mysterious substance on the surface [...]. When these two kinds of light interpenetrate I discover unique forms that have a psychic substance, forms that build, hold on to one another, become alive and certain [...]

Color is the hidden fact of your psyche and you make it real or not.

In abstract painting, I am amplifying reality, intensifying it in another way. Abstractions are extractions from nature. Concentrates of nature.

There is something inscrutable about the familiar, something unknown, and this unknown is what I try to discover by approaching it indirectly.

(1983: 194)

The notion of merging luminous and reflected light bespeaks the mystical but also conjures the salient qualities of Jenkins's use of light and color. His vivid, liquid, varyingly translucent veils of color construct mystery. As Helen Harrison notes, 'the mysterious, ineffable character of the veil, which both conceals and reveals the forms beneath it, has been exploited by artists of all cultures and eras' (1993: 5). Veils are, of course, associated with mysteries or secrets, both religious and sexual. Harrison observes the distinction of Jenkins's abstract veils from representational ones.

With the Phenomena series, [...] his veils of paint became even more ambiguous [...]. His technique of pouring layers of liquid enamel paint onto a primed and gessoed canvas (not staining into the fabric, as James Brooks and Helen Frankenthaler were then doing, and as Morris Louis and Kenneth Noland would do later) caused the colors to flow over the surface in a process of controlled improvisation. By painting wet on wet, so the colors interacted, he could suggest imaginary space, inviting the eye to probe the surface for hidden depths.

(6)

Harrison's language, which adds concrete, even haptic description of medium and process to Jenkins's evocative consideration of color and light, conjures the material correlative to his psychic and spiritual apperception. Moisture (wet on wet) is the vehicle that conveys something more immaterial, yet still sensational.[11] Although neither Jenkins nor many of his critics reference it explicitly, it is hard not to correlate this luminous, 'wet,' internal sensation with sexuality, specifically female sexuality. Certainly, in the context of *An Unmarried Woman*, where the appearance of Jenkins's work is not only associated with a sexual relationship but is seen before and after the sexual encounters the scenario 'skips' over, the paintings seem to perform as proxies for the acts that are not shown and, moreover, the experience of them that is invisible [Color plate 15]. The scenario cuts directly from the scene of Saul's paintings in the gallery to the aftermath of his and Erica's first sexual encounter and sex is also the ellipsis between romance and painting in the later sequence, where a sustained scene of painting follows the one of dancing in the dark loft. Indeed, in this context, suddenly the liquidity of Jenkins's pigments recalls the strange, almost surreal quality of Charlie's sculptures, by Toshio Odate – solid wood carved to look liquid, as though dripping or melting – in the scene of Erica' first sexual experiment. Intentionally or not, the art chosen for these scenes is suggestive, offering surrogate images of an invisible site of pleasure.

## The Colors of Imaginary Space and Hidden Depths

> Current opinion always holds sexuality to be aggressive. Hence the notion of a happy, gentle, sensual, jubilant sexuality is never to be found in any text. Where are we to read it, then? In painting, or better still: in colour. If I were a painter, I should paint only colours: this field seems to me freed of both the Law (no Imitation, no Analogy) and Nature (for after all, do not all the colours in Nature come from the painters?).
>
> 'La couleur ~ Color' (Barthes 1977: 143)

If the fluid, wet veils of Jenkins's paintings give form to that experience which is invisible – female sexuality – it is their striking arrays of luminous color that expresses that ineffable aspect of female pleasure it is tempting to call *jouissance*, as this Lacanian term has been adopted by Hélène Cixous, Catherine Clément, and Luce Irigaray, among others, to describe female pleasure as distinct from a phallic pleasure principle: as Other, beyond, mystical (Jones 1981). The term has also been used by Julia Kristeva, Roland Barthes, and other theorists, often in connection with color. Color, like *jouissance*, is surplus, beyond, in excess of form. Color is impossible to describe. It is probably this perception of color as sensational, uncontrollable, and excessive that Barry Schwabsky implicates when he observes that Paul Jenkins' work 'leaves austerity out of the equation' (2007: 480) A puritanical, suspicious attitude toward color, David Batchelor argues, is a widespread and ancient prejudice of Western culture:

> Generations of philosophers, artists, art historians and cultural theorists of one stripe or another have kept this prejudice alive, warm, fed and groomed. As with all prejudices, its manifest form, its loathing, masks a fear: a fear of contamination and corruption by

something that is unknown or appears unknowable. This loathing of colour, this fear of corruption through colour, needs a name: chromophobia.

Chromophobia manifests itself in the many and varied attempts to purge colour from culture, to devalue colour, to diminish its significance, to deny its complexity. More specifically: this purging of colour is usually accomplished in one of two ways. In the first, colour is made out to be the property of some 'foreign' body – usually the feminine, the oriental, the primitive, the infantile, the vulgar, the queer or the pathological. In the second, colour is relegated to the realm of the superficial, the supplementary, the inessential or the cosmetic.

(2000: 22–23)

Thus we can see how the very ambivalence about Paul Jenkins's work that Schwabsky remarked may also inform the reception of *An Unmarried Woman*. Rosalind Galt, drawing on the work of Batchelor among others, has detailed similarly iconoclastic attitudes toward color and the 'pretty' in film criticism, particularly postwar Marxist criticism and its legacy in academic film studies (2011). *An Unmarried Woman* is hardly the sort of film whose reception Galt wants to problematize (her case studies center on the works of Derek Jarman, Baz Luhrmann, Mikhail Kalatazov, and Ulrike Ottinger) and is itself more realist than 'pretty.' But perhaps sequestered within the critical disdain for its equivocally commercial status and bourgeois values is a discomfort with the way that the pretty paintings tell us something we don't want to know. Batchelor's inventory of that which is despised by the chromophobe ranges from what Galt would call pretty, past the feminine, the exotic, the excessive, the vulgar, and the pathological, to what Kristeva might call abject. Perhaps the something we don't want to know, then, is that the explosive array of color in the paintings is made of thin veils thrown over more archaic pleasures: comestible, scatological, and sexual.

In *An Unmarried Woman* a vital but invisible aspect of women's experience is given form through art. Moreover, while that form manages to express what Barthes called 'a happy, gentle, sensual, jubilant sexuality,' the process by which it comes into being is suggestive of the poignant aspects of the protagonist's story arc. Of Jenkins's practice, Jack Flam notes:

The notions of virtuosity and risk that underlie his painting not only comprise a crucial element of its imagery, but also are inseparable from his conception of the medium itself. Painting, for Jenkins, is an unending series of forays into the unknown, the acceptance of 'the paradoxical, the contradictory, the interference of chance' [...]. This conception of risk, which has determined Jenkins' course away from painting within repetitive formats and sustained his notion that the act of painting is in itself an act of discovery, forms [...] a fertile matrix for internal growth.

(1975: 92)

If the Jenkins paintings, then, act as objective correlatives for Erica's internal pleasure and experience, their process corresponds to her own risk-taking, forays into the unknown, acts of discovery, and internal growth. They are indices, or matrices, too, of a sort of feminist illumination or consciousness. Perhaps this is confirmed by the film's conclusion, in which Erica chooses to stay in New York rather than to accompany Saul to Vermont for the summer (five months, actually), as he has urged. Although the film is unambiguous in its portrayal of her love for Saul and his for her, it doesn't elect the cliché happy ending but rather allows Erica to jeopardize the relationship to commit to her own autonomy. In the final scene, an enormous canvas – (it is, in fact, *Phenomena Rain Palace*, 1976, a 77 x 87-inch acrylic) – is lowered from the window of Saul's loft to the SoHo street below [Color plate 16]. Saul and Erica receive it and as soon as he has confirmed that she has a handle on it, he gets into his packed station wagon and drives away, leaving Erica to manage and move the cumbersome but beautiful gift herself. The last shots of the film follow her as she navigates the painting through the busy city streets, with it sometimes protruding above the crowds and traffic like the sail of a boat. Drawing stares and struggling, she soldiers on with the outsized manifestation of her own desire and agency.

In order to focus on what is compelling about the way that sex, sex roles, and gender are framed in *An Unmarried Woman*, it is worth pausing to consider another film set in SoHo, one I have written about before: Martin Scorsese's 'Life Lessons,' his contribution to the portmanteau film, *New York Stories*, 1989 (2006: Ch. 7). Made and set about a decade later than *An Unmarried Woman*, its artist-protagonist, Lionel Dobie (Nick Nolte), like Saul Kaplan, is a successful, bearded painter, represented by a blue-chip gallery, and owner of not just his loft, but 'the whole building.' 'Life Lessons' is short – under an hour – but features sustained scenes of painting. In fact, the narrative is the story of the end of a relationship in terms of the making of a single painting. As with *An Unmarried Woman*, 'Life Lessons' used the work of a 'real,' legitimate contemporary artist, Chuck Connelly. Connelly was not quite as established as Jenkins – he was only in his early to mid-thirties at the time – but had been exhibiting for several years, and had annual solo exhibitions from 1984 at Annina Nosei Gallery, a prominent venue (where the now more renowned Jean-Michel Basquiat showed from 1981 to 1986). In that the only other Dobie (Connelly) works seen in 'Life Lessons' are seen just briefly at the very end, in the concluding scene set at Lionel's opening (and one other is occasionally glimpsed in the loft), the one painting that is made in the course of the film, *Bridge to Nowhere*, a monumental (7 ½ x 18 foot) canvas (similar in scale and dimensions to a movie screen) is somewhat more equivocally a 'real object,' in that it was obviously a work for hire, i.e. made *for and during* the film. However, as it was 'the centerpiece' of Connelly's exhibition at the Lennon, Weinberg Gallery, shortly after the film's release (Smith 1989) and is now in a public collection (The Tucson Museum of Art), it was and is clearly no mere movie prop [Color plates 17 and 18].

In Scorsese's film, the nature of the painting process shown and the style of the Connelly-Dobie painting itself offer a striking contrast to the process and style of the Jenkins-Kaplan paintings in Mazursky's. The process is represented as intense, spasmodic, aggressive, athletic, and tortured and is filmed such that the correspondences with Scorsese's own cinematic technique and style are evident. While Kaplan gently poured his luminous veils of acrylic, occasionally catching and channeling them with discreet movements of his ivory knife, Dobie stabs, dabs, slashes, trails, and thrusts at and over the ever darker, busier, and thicker impasto of his expressionist canvas with brushes and sticks. Although both artists work on a large scale and both practices derive from Abstract Expressionism, the resulting works could hardly be more different; Jenkins-Kaplan's works are more abstract and less expressionist, while Connelly-Dobie's are the opposite: much less abstract and more expressionist. *Bridge to Nowhere* is representational; it features a recognizably architectonic form, one full of angst and repetition, which Scorsese uses as a metaphor for Dobie's relationships. 'Life Lessons' parallels the making of the painting to the fraught, agonistic end of the artist's relationship with his current muse, Paulette (Rosanna Arquette), a much younger (ex-)lover-cum-studio assistant who, the story makes clear – in part by very allegorical use of the *Bridge to Nowhere* and its repetitive forms – is not the first and will not be the last woman to fill the ambivalent role of muse. She says she sometimes feels like a human sacrifice and she is, more or less, as I wrote:

> The story of Lionel Dobie and Paulette, finally, is a remake of an ancient story, or is it a myth? – the story of the genius and his muse. Scorsese sees Dobie's accomplishment as the gift of genius and the grace of sublimation [...]. With consummate irony and self-consciousness and not a little immodesty, Scorsese exposes in *Life Lessons* the sordid side of this [...] its psychic cost to both 'genius' and, especially 'muse,' as the artistic process consumes the 'relationship.'
>
> (2006: 156)

The woman in 'Life Lessons' is, finally, little more than a cipher – an idea of a woman – and although she plays a vital role in the protagonist's psyche, it is a role that can be (has been and will be) played by someone else. The film is in fact about the male artist's psyche and the painting that comes into view in the course of the narrative is its objective correlative.

As I have suggested already, the *Bridge to Nowhere* is not only an image of the protagonist's psychic disturbances and patterns, it is also an image of Martin Scorsese's. 'He is, after all, portraying himself,' I noted, 'in Lionel Dobie: the mature, celebrated, oft-married artist, renowned for his big, colorful, violent, action-packed, gestural, almost baroque *tours de force*' (2006: 156). *An Unmarried Woman*'s protagonist is a woman, Erica Benton, and it uses Paul Jenkins's paintings remarkably differently, as images perhaps *from*, but not *of* the artist's psyche, images that embody the ineffable aspect of feminine sexuality and aspirations. But perhaps Saul Kaplan is something of a self-portrait, too, and Paul Mazursky sees himself in the masculine but sensitive painter whose works allow 'a certain dynamism to be suffused in an aura of sensitivity' (Maria Amayo on Jenkins, 1979, quoted in Anon. 2009: 1). To Martin Scorsese's five wives (only four at the time of 'Life Lessons'), Mazursky has had only one, Betsy, to whom he has been happily married as of this writing for 60 years (already 25 in 1978). *An Unmarried Woman* is dedicated to her.

## The Woman ~~Artist~~ Does Not Exist

One of the truisms around gender and sexuality that *An Unmarried Woman* refuses is that for women in heterosexual relationships, romantic love, intimacy, and security take precedence over the simpler, base sexual drive that motivates their partners. The film establishes from the outset that Erica and Martin's sexual relationship is good and when the marriage ends, it is because *he* has fallen in love with someone else. Later, when he proposes reconciliation, Erica refuses, despite the obvious economic and familial advantages. She is represented as a complex subject and sexual agent who ultimately seeks autonomy and to divorce economic and emotional dependency from sexuality. I have argued that the paintings of Paul Jenkins both give form to invisible aspects of Erica's sexual subjectivity and are material correlatives to the process by which she asserts agency. In contrast, attitudes about gender and art in heterosexual relationships, according to Martin Scorsese's 'Life Lessons,' are powerfully delimited by myths of masculinity and genius. It, too, is something of a realist (albeit hyper-stylized) film but its reality – like its protagonist – is myopic. The woman in the picture, Paulette, has only one name because she really has only one function. The film portrays her insecurity, doubts, and frustration poignantly, but as givens and only from the outside. Although Paulette is an aspiring painter, there is little insight into her psyche; we see her drawings and paintings but we do not see her making them. While Lionel works, Paulette is generally in her bedroom, often on the telephone. We only see her in her studio when submitting herself masochistically to Lionel's critique [Fig. 75] and then, later, throwing a fit. Ultimately, she is a cipher, essentially the catalyst for the massive outpouring of temperamental, corporeal, and artistic expression that is the material correlative to *the* artist's (Dobie's) psyche. What happens to Paulette at the end of the story, when she finally leaves Dobie, could not matter less to the narrative. His masterpiece is done and, as the coda makes clear, the job of muse is readily filled ... so long as the desired woman's subjectivity, her agency, her reality can be held in abeyance. Even more than the generic fictional creature, she is unreal.

'Life Lessons' illustrates her surplus irreality by the way it employs the work of Susan Hambleton as Paulette's. Hambleton was several years out of the MFA (Hunter College, 1984) at the time Robin Standefer (credited in 'Life Lessons' as the Fine Arts Curator) chose her work for the film based on documentation on file at A.I.R. Gallery (founded 1972, the first artists-run gallery for women in the United States). The work ultimately used in the film, however, all derived from Hambleton's student years at The School of Visual Arts, where she completed her BFA in 1982, and Hunter, so (although Hambleton was a mature woman – a non-traditional student) not representative of a fully-developed oeuvre. The works are all, too, considerably smaller than the Connelly-Dobie works. Two or three canvases are perhaps as much as 5 or 5.5 feet long or wide, so of a considerable scale, albeit only a third the dimensions of *Bridge to Nowhere*; the remaining works range from small to mid-sized drawings and canvases. Further, most of the Paulette works are figural compositions – several with a solitary figure, one with two – that are characterized by an aura of indistinctness or incompleteness. Some of

**Figure 75:** Rosanna Arquette and Nick Nolte in 'Life Lessons' (Scorsese, 1989), from *New York Stories*.

these figures are schematic, genderless ciphers themselves; others are sketchy and undefined [Fig. 76]. Indeed, Hambleton – who signed a disclaimer permitting any use of the work and was paid a fee of $3,000 for the loan of it – says that the paintings seen are not hers but are based on drawings she lent (personal communication, 6 May, 2013).[12] Two or three of these are canvases with pale, bluish-gray fields and incipient, unfinished, thin figures, with their arms raised (the drawings from which they derive can be seen in the studio, as well). The two-figure painting in progress that Dobie says has a 'nice little irony' going on, is, ironically, based on a two-part drawing that Hambleton felt was 'mangled' by the film's translation of it to canvas.[13] You might say these canvases were made to appear like the work of an insecure artist, which is – to the extent that her artistic temperament is evident at all – a fair characterization of Paulette. So, while Chuck Connelly was hired to create a magnum opus alongside Scorsese, Susan Hambleton was essentially paid a fee to have her student drawings turned into weak paintings. The most substantial and chromatically rich works (enlarged copies of a sort of mystical still life and a copy of an expressionist, deep blue, almost extra-terrestrial figure from Hambleton's undergraduate portfolio) are seen very briefly in corners, while the vague, insecure, unfinished, ghostly simulations dominate the short scenes set in Paulette's studio,

**Figure 76:** A painting based on a student drawing by Susan Hambleton in 'Life Lessons' as Paulette's painting.

creating not only a profound contrast to the monumental, strong, crusty, dark facture of the Connelly-Dobie work but also reifying Paulette's own liminal substantiality.

And so it is with the woman artist in *The Player*, Robert Altman's 1992 satirical view of Hollywood. June Gudmundsdottir (Greta Scacchi), too, is arguably even more unreal than the usual movie character and her paintings manage to be concrete yet phantasmal manifestations of this equivocal status.

> *The Player* tells the story of Griffin Mill (Tim Robbins) a Hollywood producer who unintentionally kills a writer he thinks is threatening him, successfully evades being charged with murder, happily marries his victim's girlfriend, and successfully maneuvers his way to the top of the studio power structure by supplying a formulaic happy ending to a film not unlike those directed by Altman himself.
>
> (Self 2002: 215–216)

Fiction and reality are minutely imbricated in *The Player*. Some sixty-odd celebrities play themselves, while several stars play fictional characters. The resulting tension between the real and the fictional carries over to the film's mise-en-scène. Many real Hollywood locations are used. Classic movie posters around Mill's office function as witty intertexts to genre aspects of the narrative, including *M* (Joseph Losey 1951), *Murder in the Big House* (B. Reeves Eason 1942), *Highly Dangerous* (Roy Ward Baker 1950), and *Hollywood Story* (William Castle 1951), among others. Movie posters are, of course, reproductions that really have no 'original'; they are advertisements for movies. Meanwhile, June Gudmundsdottir (Scacchi), the cool, beautiful blonde whose writer boyfriend Mill murdered, makes – although not, she says, to sell – pale, filmy, cryptic, multimedia canvases that are very like her and at the same time – in a formal sense –evocative of cinema itself; in them, fragmented photographic images and words are seen as if through glass or a screen. June's paintings were made by Sydney Cooper, a then young and relatively unknown Los Angeles artist.[14]

The character of June – who always wears white (even to a funeral), seems to know no one, and exudes a rather immanent but innocent sensuality – recalls the rather spectral and obscure objects of desire from previous films about the movies, including Fellini's *8 ½* (1963), Fosse's homage to it, *All That Jazz* (1979), and Kazan's *The Last Tycoon* (1976). As noted, Altman has said of June that she does not exist. Of course, this can be said of any fictional character; but there is an added level of illusoriness here. While Saul Kaplan was fictional, it was not hard to imagine him in the real world, as I did at the beginning of this chapter. June Gudmundsdottir, on the other hand, seems unreal even in her fictional world, relative to the real actors playing themselves in *The Player*, as well as to the fictional characters: almost like a figment of Griffin Mill's imagination. This impression is initiated as June is introduced, at night, through a veil of reflective glass and translucent plastic in a scene where Griffin, stalking the home of her boyfriend – the writer whom he suspects of sending him anonymous, threatening hate mail – calls the house and speaks with her from a cellular phone, watching her all the while [Color plates 19 and 20].

Confirming that this scene was invented for the movie to underscore the constitutive voyeurism of cinema, Altman claimed that in her unreality, June embodies the movies. 'So I felt that to make this woman so interesting to him,' Altman said of June and protagonist producer Mill, 'I'd let him create her. I took the position that June Gudmunsdotter [sic] too doesn't exist' (Keogh 2000: 159). This relocation of June from a fictional reality to irreality, as Altman noted in another interview, represented a significant alteration to Michael Tolkin's novel, adapted for the film by Tolkin himself, and one that writer and director were not entirely in agreement upon. In Tolkin's novel, David Kahane's girlfriend was called June Mercator and she was a distinctly less romantic character and type of artist; she worked as an art director for Wells Fargo (i.e. 'paste-ups of interest-rate brochures'). Altman felt the character 'was too ordinary. I felt that we should make her a movie character. I tried to explain it to Greta: You're not a real person, you're acting in a movie, you don't have to find out the truth in this woman because there isn't any truth, she doesn't really exist' (159). Altman's interlocutor Keogh responded with a question: 'Is she like a blank movie screen on which you can project your desires?' 'Absolutely,' the director replied.

In other interviews, Altman repeated this claim and went even further, acknowledging June's allegorical aspect: 'To me, she doesn't even exist. She's a hallucination. She's the character a guy like Griffin would dream up for the hero of his movie to get involved with. Someone who had nothing to do with the movies – except that she's the ultimate movie character. She's the movies' (Smith and Jameson 2000: 170).[15] 'It's an allegory on an allegory, set inside an allegory,' he observed, elaborating on his critique of Hollywood: '[...] the arena is something that I know fairly well. But it's no different from the museum business or the newspaper business. Hollywood is the surrogate for what I am addressing, which is the cultural dilemma between art and commerce [...]' (Fuller 2000: 205). This dialectical commentary on art and commerce is precisely why Altman specifies that June doesn't even sell her art, as I have noted elsewhere:

> The languid narcissism that Scacchi brings to this, as to many of her roles, ultimately makes art seem less like a metier than a kind of organic emanation, but Altman needs her at the same time to symbolize art (as opposed to commerce) – an obscure object of desire for Griffin Mill, David Kahane, and Hollywood in toto.
>
> (2006: 137)

Sydney Cooper's paintings, then, had to play the paradoxical role of products of a nonexistent hand, the hand of doubly unreal artist, and yet at the same time signify art as a moral corrective to the base commerce of Hollywood. They exemplify the way material objects often become mere projections in the movies. In a very real sense, these works for hire are collaborations between director Altman and Cooper. They brainstormed the concepts for the works together and Cooper, who worked feverishly day and night to produce them in time for the shoot, says she felt, as she worked, as though Altman were there sitting on her shoulder, directing. In this sense, the production of June's work was almost like a performance and Cooper an actor. In contrast to the films discussed previously where, for the most part, extant works are cast as the fictional artists', sometimes alongside works made for the productions, here it was the artist herself who was cast and had to find a way to perform the practice of an artist who was not only fictional but who 'did not exist,' who personified the movies. It was Cooper's idea to use Polaroids in the work and the taking of pictures was added into the action [Fig. 77] [Color plates 21–22]. Similarly, punning wordplay that was improvised on set ('icy' > 'I see' > 'blue sea' > 'red sea'; see Smith and Jameson 2000: 166) corresponds to and follows from Cooper's choice to incorporate the written word in many of the pictures. This incorporation of photography and language – as with the voyeurism of the scene that introduces June and her work – draws constitutive elements of cinema into the images. This cinematic element afforded the artist an opportunity to explore something that cinema has that painting does not, she recalls: time. Citing the work of Gerhard Richter as a comparison, Cooper has remarked that the effect of veiling, layering, and, more consciously, gilding of her later work, induces a kind of kinetic (in-motion) effect and more time-based experience (Personal communication, 17 January, 2013).

**Figure 77:** Greta Scacchi and Tim Robbins in *The Player* (Altman, 1992).

Visually the works reinforce the obscurity, mystery and insubstantiality of the character, as well as her cool, mythic aura. They are 'veiled,' 'not clarifying,' according to Cooper. Using mostly a pale and cool palette – shades of white, violet, blue, and gray – and incorporating photographic images – some shot through plastic curtains – and words, the works are filmy and cryptic. There is little, according to Cooper, of her actual practice at the time; that was 'too substantial,' she notes, for so insubstantial a character and artist. The resulting images hover between a cool poeticism and conceptual obscurity. The photography of the three major scenes set at June's enhances these liminal properties of the fictional artist and her work. Two of the three are nighttime scenes and in those, especially, the lighting has a blue 'day for night' cast that merges the atmosphere of the space with that of the pictures, creating an almost dreamlike mood. According to Cooper, the scenes were shot in an incomplete section of a real house, staged by the production design team with a bit of input from the artist, and are lent a certain realism by minutiae of Cooper's studio: materials, tools, etc. Despite this element of realism, however, the final effect of the scene of art in *The Player* is one of irreality.

Sydney Cooper says that she was not yet a fully developed artist at the time of her work on *The Player* and, like the character whose works she created, she did not then have gallery representation. She never sold any of the June Gudmundsdottir works and was never approached to do so, although she had received a screen credit as the creator of June's artworks. She says she gave a few pieces away as gifts to people involved in the production and has retained the rest. This lack of a real world resonance of the art is striking and it is echoed by almost complete critical silence about June's work (and Cooper's role) in the literature on *The Player*, despite consistent interest in the character of June. This gap contrasts pointedly with the outcome of the Jenkins-Mazursky collaboration on *An Unmarried Woman*, where – although they, too, could be said to have performed imaginary parts – the material reality of the paintings, the renown of the artist, and the market were all recognized and enhanced. A studio press release drew attention and interest to Jenkins, SoHo, the real objects, and institutions that participated in Mazursky's film and the popular press followed suit. Accordingly, as with a number of other films that engaged contemporary art, including even Losey's *The Damned* (with its real and fictional woman artists), these real objects that had performed as actors in the movies had their independent existence and value confirmed and magnified. Sydney Cooper, on the other hand, despite having created an intriguing, original body of work – and although she made connections through the film that may have enlarged the audience for her work – saw absolutely no increase in publicity or market. Indeed, she says that she does not herself regard the June Gudmundsdottir works as part of her oeuvre, rather, more as movie ephemera.

The explanation for this discrepancy must be overdetermined, resulting from the conditions under which the work was created and employed, as well as the intersection of real world and fictional obscurity, which are not unrelated to gender. For, given the actual social and economic realities of the art world, a male artist – regardless of the fiction in which he lives – inevitably seems a more realist proposition than a woman artist. There is, as I have noted,

> a slippage between two alluring, enigmatic, sometimes threatening terms – art and femininity, a slippage that is both a persistent structural attribute of the classical film ethos and a symptom of the sociopolitical cultural flux of [the period] [...]
>
> Against the ever shifting dynamics in the relationship between art, movies and society, gender plays a protean and always rather mythic part. If she is not mere muse or object of art, but emerges as its supposed agent, the woman is an unnerving and problematic proposition.
>
> (2006: 137–139)

June Gudmundsdottir, the woman who does not exist, is also an artist who does not exist. When Griffin asks her where she shows; who her dealer is, she replies that she doesn't have a dealer. 'I couldn't sell these; they're never finished,' adding, 'they're just what I do [...] for myself [...] what I feel.' The dialogue is meant to point to the moral disparity between commerce (the venal player) and art (the ludic outsider). It also almost belies the illusory aura that surrounds June, possibly suggesting she is a self-realized subject who harbors a strong sense of self and expression (and does not need an income to survive). But, as I have noted, June's seeming organic, intuitive approach to art underscores myths of gender (immanence, narcissism) that are often used to relegate women artists to a secondary, a less heroic, less visible, less valued status.

The art world, like Hollywood and the world of cinema generally, was and is fraught with sexism and discrimination of all sorts. Thus, even when a major male artist's work, such as Jenkins's, can perform acts of feminist insight – arguably giving form to something as obscure and invisible as the Lacanian concept of *jouissance* – its reality effect survives and its metacinematic value is enlarged, while the obscurity of an unknown woman artist is magnified by her engagement to perform materially the mystique of an unknown woman artist who is an obscure object of desire, a fantasy, a screen, a projection. Because, always already – to quote Altman and again invoke Lacan – the Woman does not exist.

## Notes

1   See, e.g. Gene Youngblood (1970); Chrissie Iles (2001); John Alan Farmer (2000); Michael Rush (1999); Margot Lovejoy (2004).

2   *An Unmarried Woman* earned three Academy Award nominations: for Best Picture, Best Screenplay Written Directly for the Screen, and for Jill Clayburgh, as Best Actress, and numerous others, with Mazursky winning Best Screenplay from the Los Angeles Film Critics Association, the National Society of Film Critics, and the New York Film Critics Circle. Clayburgh shared the best actress award at Cannes with Isabelle Huppert.

3   'AN UNMARRIED WOMAN is one of a number of 1970s Hollywood films that could be read to address and construct, however obliquely, changing conceptions of the appropriate modes of femininity in contemporary Western culture. Films such as *Alice Doesn't Live Here Anymore* (Scorsese, 1974), *Three Women* (Altman, 1977), *Looking for Mr Goodbar* (Brooks, 1977), *The Turning Point* (Ross, 1978), *Julia* (Zinneman, 1978), *Girlfriends* (Weill, 1978), *Old Boyfriends* (Tewkesbury, 1979) can be loosely grouped together through their use of central female protagonists. In the main they can be seen as aimed at a specifically female audience, in a period where there has been increasing differentiation of target audiences.' (Brunsdon 1982: 20).

4   On Karp's career, see Cummings (1969). For the television interview, see http://youtube/deRMRh8Zjgg, excerpted from the film *Andy Warhol* (Kim Evans and Lana Jokel, 1987).

5   Margaret Herrick Library.

6   It is noteworthy regarding the film's realism and feminism that it was Claudia Weill who recommended Russianoff. Weill's own realist and feminist film, *Girlfriends* (1978) was released the same year as *An Unmarried Woman*. In fact, Weill, according to Marsha Kinder, 'said that Mazursky was helpful and supportive to her when she was making *Girlfriends* and stressed that the boxoffice [sic] success of his film "will help us all"'(1978: 46). Kinder's glowing review of *Girlfriends* appeared in the same issue of *Film Quarterly* as Gitlin and Wolman's pan of *An Unmarried Woman*.

7   It should be noted that Russianoff's essay concerns women of all classes and focuses at least as much on the damaging effects of 'learned helplessness,' among women in poverty as on the privileged classes.

8   Conversation with author.

9   Charlie's studio is certainly that of Japanese-born sculptor and woodworker, Toshio Odate (b. 1930), as the works seen in it are his, from a cycle of 'melting wood' pieces he did in the second half of the 1970s. Odate, who now lives and works in Woodbury, CT, is best known

now for his teaching and publications of traditional Japanese woodworking technique, tools, and cabinetry but was an active member of the avant-garde and conceptual art scene in New York from the late 1960s through the 1970s. See Kelley 2007: 160–162 and Wechsler 1997: 101–102, 168.

10 From Bennett Schiff's review of Paul Jenkins's November 1958 exhibition at the Martha Jackson Gallery, New York.

11 See also Elsen 1973: 24–25, on 'The Significance of Moisture.'

12 Hambleton related that the day she visited the Scorsese set, Connelly was notably 'aloof.' The power politics of the scenario seem to have been projected onto the real life situation. Ironically, Hambleton also noted, both she and Connelly were invited to show in a group exhibition some years later: 'Songs of the Earth: Twenty-Two American Painters of the Landscape,' at AHI Gallery, New York, 1994. Hambleton is now on the fine arts faculty at Eugene Lang College, of The New School, and The School of Visual Arts.

13 The 'nice little irony' here is that Hambleton received a credit as the creator of Paulette's work but very little of her actual work was shown.

14 The story of how she got the job is wonderful. According to Cooper, in preproduction, Altman had planned to commission the artwork from the artist son of a friend. Cooper, an artist, also made jewelry, and Lydia Tanji, a friend of hers working as a wardrobe supervisor on the The Player, came to visit, accompanied by Altman's confidante, producer, and some-time costume designer Scott Bushnell, to consider some of Cooper's jewelry for the film. When they told her that the narrative included a woman artist and that Altman – about whom she knew next to nothing – planned to hire a man, Cooper's feminist hackles were raised. 'Are you kidding?' she exclaimed, adding, 'what an asshole!' (an impression of which she was quickly disabused when she came to work with and know him, she says). Scott Bushnell thought Altman would be amused by Cooper's remarks, so related them. He was amused, and impressed, and called her in for a meeting, gave her the script, some guidelines, and 24 hours to come up with a proposal for the artwork. Cooper worked up some sketches and concepts, pitched them, and got the job. She created all the work seen in the film about six weeks, for about $6,000 plus materials. Cooper was on set for the art scenes and instructed Greta Scacchi briefly on technique. Scacchi, whose father was a painter, was a quick study, Cooper says (personal communication, 17 January, 2013).

15 This female allegorization of cinema itself is very similar to that in the adaptation of *The Last Tycoon* (1976), written by Harold Pinter and directed by Elia Kazan, as I analyzed it in *Art in the Cinematic Imagination* (2006: 42–48).

# Chapter 6

Subjects, Objects, and Erotic Upheaval at Pemberley:
*Pride & Prejudice* (2005)

In one of the key scenes in Jane Austen's 1813 novel, *Pride and Prejudice*, Elizabeth Bennet, touring Pemberley with her aunt and uncle, enchanted by the large and handsome property, particularly the views out the windows, and having been much surprised by the exceptionally generous and admiring 'portrait' painted by his housekeeper, encounters an actual painted portrait of the great estate's master, Mr. Darcy.

> At last it arrested her – and she beheld a striking resemblance of Mr. Darcy, with such a smile over the face, as she remembered to have sometimes seen, when he looked at her [...]. There was certainly in this moment, in Elizabeth's mind, a more gentle sensation towards the original than she had ever felt in the height of their acquaintance [...]. Every idea that had been brought forward by the housekeeper was favourable to his character; and as she stood before the canvas, on which he was represented, and fixed his eyes upon herself, she thought of his regard with a deeper sentiment of gratitude than it had ever raised before: she remembered its warmth, and softened its impropriety of expression.
>
> (2003: 234)

The text is really about the various representations jostling in the beholder's mind – the housekeeper's, the portraitist's, and her own prior, perhaps 'prejudiced' one – and the simultaneous self-consciousness with which Elizabeth comes to see Darcy seeing her (or imagines herself from his position) and begins to paint a new picture. The phrase, 'she fixed his eyes upon herself,' expresses this flux; Isobel Armstrong characterizes it as an 'amazing moment of syntactic ambiguity' (1980: xviii). This syntactic ambiguity also expresses something about the very experience of beholding a portrait whose subject's eyes are shown meeting those of the viewer's. Subjectivity itself is in motion and agency in question, in a sense, when the portrait exists as a testament to its subject's stature, status, wealth, authority, and character. The portrait can seem to subject the beholder to its gaze, turning the viewing subject into an object. Indeed Elizabeth, whom we can imagine to have been gliding past countless more indifferent works, is 'arrested' – herself made still – by the portrait.

In the novel – completed in 1797 but not published until 1813, after revisions in 1811–1812 – Elizabeth actually encounters at Pemberley two painted portraits of Darcy: first a miniature among a collection of portraits above a mantelpiece and then the more monumental portrait in the picture gallery, the one that 'arrests' Elizabeth in the account above. We might imagine the miniature to be along the lines of George Engleheart's 1798 portrait of Tom Lefroy, who is said to have had something of a courtship with Austen herself (Tomalin 1999: 119), and the grander portrait comparable to that of Charles Christie by Henry Raeburn (1800), both of the period in which *Pride and Prejudice* was written.[1] Indeed, for the Pemberley scene, the very popular A&E/BBC 1995 television adaptation of the novel displayed a painted pastiche of Colin Firth as Darcy, very much along the lines of the Raeburn picture, showing him finely dressed and presented in three-quarter pose, before a Romantic landscape background.

In the 2005 film adaptation *Pride & Prejudice*, starring Keira Knightley as Elizabeth and Matthew Macfadyen as Darcy, Pemberley is played by Chatsworth House, the grand estate that is the seat of the Dukes of Devonshire, and much of Elizabeth's tour was also filmed in its rooms [Figs. 78 and 79]. As mentioned in my introduction, there is a decided logic to this casting, as Chatsworth has been proposed as a prototype of Pemberley (Greene 1988).[2] The film substitutes Chatsworth's famous sculpture gallery (which was neither furnished nor built, however, at the time of Austen's visit or the writing of *Pride and Prejudice*) for the novel's picture gallery, and a sculptural bust of Darcy – a fine pastiche made of resin and marble dust by Nick Dutton – for the two painted pictures, in so doing, transforming not only the visual and spatial tropes of the scene, but its very meaning. In his DVD commentary, director Joe Wright calls the sculpture gallery scene, 'a short film about art.' But it might also be called a short film about sculpture, specifically, or even a short film about cinema. The use of a mobile camera here – which recalls the scene in which Catherine (Ingrid Bergman)

**Figure 78:** Chatsworth House, Derbyshire.

**Figure 79:** Sculpture Gallery, © Devonshire Collection, Chatsworth. Reproduced by permission of Chatsworth Settlement Trustees.

visits the National Museum of Naples in Rossellini's *Viaggio in Italia* (1954) – expresses what Kenneth Gross calls 'the relational fascination of sculpture' (2006: 130).

But while Rossellini's scene – set in a place that is as much mausoleum as museum – uses the statuary exhumed from the ashes of Vesuvius to bespeak the inextricability of sex and death, Wright's poignancy is rather less morbid. The director's commentary continues by recalling how it was decided upon seeing the sculpture gallery at Chatsworth during preproduction that it would be interesting to recast the portrait of Darcy in three dimensions and remarks – *incorrectly* – that the marbles at Chatsworth are all by Canova, observing as the camera pans up the gleaming torso of the *Sleeping Endymion*, 'that one's worth about fourteen million pounds' [Fig. 80]. Here production values take on an almost prurient aspect, and Wright continues as the camera caresses and tracks the marble anatomy of a recumbent naked Bacchante, 'I also like that this is about sex: this place, as well; that it's about her discovering the sensuality; that it's about bodies.'

In fact, of the statuary that stars in the scene, only one work – the *Sleeping Endymion* – is by Antonio Canova; and of the sixty some odd marbles in the Chatsworth collection, only five are by him, but Canova, his work, and particularly his *Endymion* were the inspiration for the gallery as realized after Canova's death in 1822, when William Spencer Cavendish, the sixth Duke of Devonshire (1790–1858), went to Rome 'to secure the release of *Endymion* from

**Figure 80:** *Pride & Prejudice* (Wright, 2005). Close-up of Canova's *Sleeping Endymion.*

Canova's studio' (Yarrington 2009: 45). Cavendish had commissioned the piece from Canova on his first trip to Rome in 1819 and it would become his greatest sculptural treasure. In those same years and after, the sixth Duke acquired numerous other sculptures, on the continent and in England. The 'gallery was intended for modern sculpture,' according to Cavendish himself, and most of the collection dates from the second quarter of the century and comprises neoclassical works in marble by leading sculptors, including Bertel Thorvaldsen, Rudolf Schadow, and numerous of Canova's fellow Italians, as well as a couple of Britons (Yarrington 2009: 44). The particular works that are seen, therefore, not only postdate the publication of Austen's novel by a decade or more and its inception by at least a quarter of a century and as much as a half century, they are not entirely representative of the Chatsworth collection. Clearly, they have been selected for their erotic potential and for the dynamics of looking that they evoke.

Wright's *Pride & Prejudice* is very much concerned with looking. The larger sequence to which the Pemberley scenes belong in fact begins with a shot, almost ten seconds long, of what experimental filmmaker Stan Brakhage would call 'closed-eye vision,' a bright, fluctuating, impressionistic image that suggests the sun as seen through closed eyes.[3] This shot dissolves into another, also about ten seconds long: an extreme close-up of Elizabeth's closed eyes, with shadow and sunlight playing across them, accompanied by the gentle sounds of a horse-drawn carriage rolling and swaying and a patient, pensive, somewhat bittersweet piano motif. To this piano motif, suddenly, is added an effusive, romantic swelling of strings, as there is a dramatic cut from the extreme close-up that suggests internal vision to the wide panorama of the external: a picturesque view of landscape, with an extreme long shot of the figure of Elizabeth standing on an outcrop overlooking the countryside of Derbyshire (filmed at Stanage Edge in the Peak District) [Color plates 23–25]. After a thirty-second or longer, slow, circular traveling shot that reframes the figure and landscape, a cut

**Figure 81:** Keira Knightley in *Pride & Prejudice.*

to a close-up of Elizabeth – hair blown by the wind and accompanied by an orchestration of the rather internal piano motif with the picturesque lyricism of the strings – suggests the heroine's complex emotional and experiential situation [Fig. 81].

The next scene sets up the visit to Pemberley – and reinforces the element of the picturesque – as Elizabeth and the Gardiners rest and picnic at the foot of an enormous ancient tree in Sherwood Forest [Color plate 26]. When it is proposed to her, Elizabeth, after some reluctance, consents to visit Darcy's estate and the scene cuts to a brief shot of a herd of deer running [Color plate 27], then to a series of shots describing the party arriving at Pemberley-Chatsworth: first one of the carriage moving in depth away from the camera on a long tree-lined drive, then a traveling pan that finally frames the estate like a picture postcard view, as the carriage arrives in front of the house [Color plate 28], then reaction shots, as first Elizabeth, then the Gardiners, rising from their seats into frame, express evident amazement at the sight and its grandeur [Fig. 82].

'I wanted to treat it as a piece of British realism,' Joe Wright is quoted as saying of his treatment of the English locations and settings in the film, 'rather than going with the picturesque tradition, which tends to depict an idealized version of English heritage as some kind of heaven on Earth.'[4] Although this ambition may have been achieved in some of the many grittier scenes in the film – those set in a 'dingy Longbourne,' as Linda Troost notes (2006: 22), and in Meryton, this particular sequence is striking for the beauteousness of its sights and the perfection of their framing (although dialogue in the picnic scene does suggest that the scenic stop was motivated by carriage problems, a nod to realism). This is, no doubt, because of the importance of contrasting Pemberley's (and Darcy's) fineness and attractions to Elizabeth's native situation and, especially, setting the stage for the scene of awakening desire that follows. Additionally, as Troost and others have noted, this was, in fact, a scene of tourism and its sights are modeled on those that visitors to the Peak District and Chatsworth (such as Austen herself) would have experienced in the late eighteenth and

**Figure 82:** Penelope Wilton and Peter Wight in *Pride & Prejudice*.

early nineteenth centuries and reflect descriptions and illustrations from guidebooks of the day. The genre of 'heritage' film that Wright implicitly impugns, as scholars including Troost and Belén Vidal have noted, is one that is in fact 'a hybrid genre with porous borders, a genre that is becoming less consensual and more political through its own staunch preference for emotional histories, and also more adventurous in its continuous incorporation of a popular historical iconography [...]' (Vidal 2012b: 4).[5]

With Elizabeth's rueful laugh and the gaping mouths of her aunt and uncle, the stage is set for a different sort of sight and attraction than the picturesque views heretofore have afforded, and the scene cuts to an overhead shot of the housekeeper, Mr. and Mrs. Gardiner and then their niece Elizabeth crossing the threshold of the frame across the floor of Chatsworth's painted hall [Color plate 30]. The photography almost perfectly captures the experience of visitors as described by the Duchess of Devonshire herself in her book about Chatsworth:

> Here is size and grandeur at last. Here people stop talking and look up and around, finding themselves in a vast space with little furniture but so much decoration that they hardly know where to start to take it all in. The brilliant colours of the painted upper walls and ceiling, the gilded wrought-iron balustrade, the swirls of foliage on walls and under balconies, and the starkly black and white marble floor make a rich and exciting start to the tour of the house.
>
> (Cavendish 2002: 52)[6]

Particularly dramatic is the film's cut from the overhead view of Elizabeth, looking upward as an affecting piano motif commences, to a rotating shot upward – clearly indicating her view – of the painted ceiling by Louis Laguerre, which portrays Julius Caesar's ascension to the heavens [Color plate 30]. Such edits in film, to views upward, often to the sky, tend to convey a feeling of spiritual opening up or out: a feeling of sublimity or awe. After a rotating pan and tilt – still representing Elizabeth's point-of-view – across the ceiling and then downward to the great stairs upon which her company has proceeded, the housekeeper calls to Elizabeth to 'keep up,' there is a cut to a close-up of Elizabeth reacting, then dashing toward the camera, out of frame, and then there is a cut to the scene in the sculpture gallery proper. This sequence, the main focus of my analysis, begins and ends with Elizabeth 'arrested' by statuary, as the musical motif develops. This arresting symmetry frames the themes of self-reflection and insight that are the narrative essence of the scene, for most of which Elizabeth is by herself among marbles.

Elizabeth's self-consciousness is expressed initially by her fascination before the *Veiled Vestal* (1847) by Rafaele Monti[7] [Color plate 31]. The sculpture, although chronologically too late by about half a century and not on view at Chatsworth until the late twentieth century, is important in establishing the mood and the meaning of the scene. Monti's *Veiled Vestal* functions doubly, or perhaps triply, as Elizabeth's reflection: her virginal sexual desire is figured as the flame the Vestal holds, and the Vestal's veil suggests that being lifted, figurally, from Elizabeth's eyes, a veil that has prevented her from seeing Darcy for what he is. The uncannily virtuosic, transparent veil made of marble not only foregrounds the paradoxical ontology of statues but also suggests the revelation of sexual desire, one of the film's distinct contributions to Austen's narrative. Films must always make this contribution to the written word, in a sense: that of the sensory. The iconography of the Vestal Virgin is overdetermined too; she is the guardian of the sacred fire of Vesta, goddess of hearth and home, so is also an image of Elizabeth as the potential mistress of Pemberley.

Before ending on Elizabeth, arrested again before the bust of Darcy, 'fixing his eyes upon herself,' the scene moves through the space of the sculpture gallery, alternating shots of Elizabeth alone, looking, and engrossed, with mobile shots of her and the objects of her gaze, and others that represent her point of view and virtually caress the three languorous figures that are singled out: Filippo Albacini's *Wounded Achilles* (1824); Canova's *Sleeping Endymion and his Dog* (1822); and Lorenzo Bartolini's *Recumbent Bacchante* (ca. 1834). Each of these marbles echoes especially well-known Hellenistic prototypes that provoke sensual contemplation.

Albacini's *Achilles* [Fig. 84] is clearly inspired by *The Dying Gaul,* a Roman copy of a Hellenistic bronze original of the late third century BC that commemorated the Attalid victory over the Galatians [Fig. 83]. One of the most celebrated of all antiquities, the marble figure was taken by Napoléon's forces to Paris and exhibited in the Louvre from 1797 to 1816 and then returned to Rome and the Capitoline Museums. It is famous for its extraordinary realism and pathos. Albacini's *Achilles,* like the Pergamene *Gaul,* is a paragon of lean, warrior masculinity – and Knightley is photographed gazing unambiguously at his masculinity! – but an almost masochistic abandonment replaces the Hellenistic figure's stoical endurance of his mortal wounds.

It is that atmosphere of abandonment that connects *Achilles* to the other male figure featured in the scene, Canova's *Sleeping Endymion* [Fig. 86]. The prototype for Canova's provocative statue is another of the most renowned antiquities, the Hellenistic *Sleeping*

**Figure 83:** *The Dying Gaul,* Roman marble copy of a Hellenistic bronze of the late third century BC. Rome: Capitoline Museums.

*Satyr* known as the *Barberini Faun* [Fig. 85]. Either a marble original of the Pergamene school (contemporary with the *Dying Gaul* or a bit later) or a Roman copy of remarkable quality, the *Faun* was discovered in Roman excavations of the Castel Sant'Angelo in Rome in the early seventeenth century, and displayed in the Palazzo Barberini until its restoration and sale in the early nineteenth century to Ludwig of Bavaria, among whose collection it can be seen at the Munich Glyptothek. A potent embodiment of Bacchic forces, the *Barberini Faun*, through the contrast between its brooding facial expression and slumbering carnal naturalness, exudes, according to Peter von Blanckenhagen, 'the melancholy of a creature who, suspended between animal innocence and human insight, has lost the one and not attained the other' (1975: 197, my translation). Canova borrows the *Faun*'s provocative image of languor but transfers it from the subject of the satyr to that of Endymion – a human mortal fixed upon as an object of desire by Selene, the goddess of the moon – displacing the more animal qualities of the prototype onto the sleeping shepherd's companion dog. *Endymion* is indeed a more intuitive recipient of this treatment. Satyrs, as Roland Barthes observes in *A Lover's Discourse,* are sexual aggressors:

**Figure 84:** Filippo Albacini, *Wounded Achilles*, Marble, 1824. © Devonshire Collection, Chatsworth. Reproduced by permission of Chatsworth Settlement Trustees.

The Satyr says: I want my desire to be satisfied *immediately*. If I see a sleeping face, parted lips, an open hand, I want to be able to *hurl myself upon them*. This Satyr – figure of the Immediate – is the very contrary of the Languorous. In languor, I merely wait: 'I know no end to desiring you.'

(155)

Barthes's reflections are not occasioned by the paradoxes of the *Barberini Faun* – a languorous satyr such as his would hurl himself upon – but they do put them in relief and point to some distinctive properties of the Hellenistic originals, as well as their neoclassical legacy, featured in *Pride & Prejudice*. Peter von Blanckenhagen's essay, 'Der Ergänzende Betrachter: Bemerkungen zu einem Aspekt Hellenistischer Kunst'/'The Completing Beholder: Thoughts on an Aspect of Hellenistic Art' observes that around the late third century BC a new tendency became manifest in sculpture, one in which figures – often sleeping, inwardly focused, or otherwise turned away from the environment – made new imaginative demands upon their beholders. One of the most exemplary instances of this tendency is another celebrated antiquity, *The Sleeping Hermaphrodite* [Fig. 87], known through at least two Roman copies

**Figure 85:** *Sleeping Satyr (Barberini Faun)*, Marble, ca. 220 BC.
Munich: Staatliche Antikensammlungen und Glyptothek.

(at the Louvre and Terme museums) of a Hellenistic bronze original. The *Hermaphrodite* is an obvious influence on the third figure that Elizabeth contemplates at Pemberley, between her reflection upon herself (in the form of the *Veiled Vestal*) and her confrontation with the marble Darcy: Lorenzo Bartolini's *Bacchante* [Fig. 88]. But just as Canova's *Endymion* is a somewhat tamer revision of the *Barberini Faun*, Bartolini's sculpture subdues many of the disquieting properties of its prototype, starting with its hermaphrodism, which J.J. Pollitt observed could not 'simply be a rococo joke. Perhaps it is a serious votive associated with fertility cult. [...] Or does it express a complex psychological and philosophical view of the psyche, the Platonic idea that on a spiritual level the natures which we call female and male become one?' (1986: 149).

170

**Figure 86:** Antonio Canova, *Sleeping Endymion*, Marble, 1822.
© Devonshire Collection, Chatsworth. Reproduced by permission of
Chatsworth Settlement Trustees.

I have dwelt on these problems of Hellenistic sculpture because it seems that they are reiterated in the sculptures selected for the scene and their presentation. Wright notes in his commentary that this is one of the only scenes in which he did not have Elizabeth clad in the usual dark, earthy colors that expressed her own nature, implying that the sartorial style and palette reflect the objects around her: make her statuesque. This is clear as this scene comes to its climax and the subjective camera that performs Elizabeth's unembarrassed and curious gaze has moved over and across the genitals of one male figure, the slumbering torso and upturned neck of another, and tracked up to the backside of the Bacchante giving way to an objective view, in which Knightley and the nubile tambourine player echo one another and Elizabeth is 'arrested' by the gaze of the bust of Darcy [Color plates 32–37]. The camera figures this 'arrest' by moving from a shot of Elizabeth from the point of view of the bust, to a tracking view of it, then cutting to an over the shoulder shot of Elizabeth, riveted

**Figure 87:** *Sleeping Hermaphrodite,* Roman marble copy of the 2nd century CE after a Hellenistic original of the 2nd century BC. Paris: Louvre, Borghese Collection; purchase, 1807.

before it. The dynamics of the moment underscore the observation that Kenneth Gross makes in *The Dream of Moving Statue*, that the myth of the statue that comes to life has a shadowy opposite, or reversal: the myth of the person turned to stone: 'fictions of animation are tracked by stories of living creatures who turn into stone, whether out of need, wish, or fear, … images of animation and petrification circulate around each other, … they collide and parody each other' (Gross 2006: 9).

Although there is no overt fantasy of animation or petrification here, it is exactly a troubling, all too reversible movement between subject and object that lends the scene its poignancy. We see the gaze mobilized in two ways in this scene: in Elizabeth's sensual appraisal of – and pleasure in – the paradigmatically 'absorptive' (to use Michael Fried's term) neo-Hellenistic marbles and in her suddenly self-conscious, deeply affective confrontation with the portrait bust. Fried (1980) noted the emergence in eighteenth-century French painting of formal and thematic contrivances that 'absorb' painterly figures, warding off the beholder's self-consciousness about looking; his articulation of a turn in the relationship between 'theatrical' and 'absorptive' paintings and beholders in the age of Diderot is not entirely unlike Peter Blanckenhagen's sense of a shift in the relationship between sculpture and beholder in the late third century BC. Although Fried treats French painting as a special case and demands that it be understood as an autonomous ontological development in the history of painting, not a politically or culturally symptomatic one, it is interesting to note that the neoclassical sculptural paradigm on display at Chatsworth, as well as the fictional events and objects of Austen's world, bear historical proximity to the paintings of David in which Fried's narrative of absorption culminates. There is absolutely no disputing that the turn of the eighteenth to nineteenth centuries constitutes one of Western history's most profound paradigmatic shifts: the foundation of modernity. Is it possible that *Pride*

**Figure 88:** Lorenzo Bartolini, *Recumbent Bacchante*, Marble, ca. 1834. © Devonshire Collection, Chatsworth. Reproduced by permission of Chatsworth Settlement Trustees.

*& Prejudice* might help us locate another such shift: a change in the relationship between cinema and beholder at the turn to the current century?

Scholarly investigations of Wright's adaptation have suggested as much. One, by Joyce Goggin, persuasively analyzes the cinematography of *Pride & Prejudice* with an eye to the impact of interactive media, especially 'the video game aesthetic, frequently mobilized to communicate an intensified state of mind or sensory perception and to invite viewer involvement.' 'Elizabeth circles the statues while actively looking […].' This scene, Goggin observes, uses subjective movement characteristic of video games to 'provide the spectators with the illusion of freedom of movement […].' She notes, moreover, with reference to Laura Mulvey's claims about visual pleasure and classical cinema, that compared to the 1940 MGM and 1995 BBC *Pride and Prejudice* adaptations – in which the portrait scene was respectively absent and conflicted – the 2005 version 'foregrounds Keira Knightley as the looker, the owner of the gaze.' Goggin concludes that this film addresses a young feminist (or post-feminist) viewer who does not remember or adhere to the classical Hollywood paradigm in which women are to be looked at and the gaze was, if not strictly a male prerogative, certainly a vexed one for female viewers (2007).

The central visual experience figured in this scene of sculpture was augured by images of 'closed-eye vision' and the closed eyes of the protagonist, which could be regarded as a cinematic correlative to those Hellenistic figures that, because absorbed in their own pain and slumber, invited our participatory completion. Elsewhere in the film, too, Wright notes in his commentary, the spectator's imaginative engagement is induced through means not altogether typical of classical cinematic identification and suture. 'She's looking at us,' he remarks of a scene in which Elizabeth, supposedly looking at herself in a mirror, stares directly into the lens. 'We are her,' Wright adds (a possible nod to Flaubert?). In the Pemberley scene, this film adaptation of *Pride & Prejudice* has transformed a narrative moment from one in which Elizabeth Bennet's prejudice is overcome by a revelation about Darcy's essential goodness and moral probity into one in which sexual repression is overwhelmed by a sensual exchange between art and beholder. In doing so, it may allegorize the young woman's claim and accedence to sensual pleasure, sexual agency and freedom: in art, cinema, and perhaps in life. Any seeming conservatism of those neoclassical art objects, which solicit the beholder's dynamic and embodied gaze, is belied by a film and a cultural moment in which the active female gaze is a newfound possibility and central preoccupation. They are neoclassical art for a post-classical cinema.

## Where the Camera Comes into Play

This is where the camera comes into play, with all its resources for swooping and rising, disrupting and isolating, stretching or compressing a sequence, enlarging or reducing an object. It is through the camera that we first discover the optical unconscious.

(Benjamin 2008: 37)

This key sequence renders the spatial and temporal experience of the neoclassical sculpture into an exemplary, and very contemporary, cinematic turn. As with *The Song of Songs*, the film with which this study began, *Pride & Prejudice* is concerned with embodiment, with the erotic, temporal and spatial demands of sculpture, although it must be observed how different are the reactions to sculptural nudes of Dietrich's Lily and Knightley's Elizabeth; the former, as befits the female protagonist of a classic Hollywood exercise in structuring the gaze, feels embarrassed, threatened and implicated upon entering Waldow's atelier, while the latter – perhaps a more sophisticated but a no less innocent character – displays frank appreciation and curiosity. Although the figurative sculpture used in both films, as well as in *Venus vor Gericht*, can be characterized as neoclassical, the signification of the style in films – as I have noted already – is neither transparent nor stable. From the first half of the nineteenth century and inspired by the sculpture of Antiquity, the sculptures seen in the Pemberley scene are, arguably, the least modern of the objects that star in the unreal situations (fiction films) I have discussed in this book. Most of them predate the discovery of photography. Certainly, if modern, they are far from modernist, belonging to the end of a period of European art – the Renaissance and Baroque periods, roughly speaking – known for what Walter Benjamin called a 'secular worship of beauty' (2008: 24), when aesthetic values grew more important and increasingly separable from religious ritual. Yet their idealized anatomical verisimilitude and gleaming white stillness invite a regard and hint at revelations that would appear anachronistic and disorienting had *Pride & Prejudice* attempted to show them otherwise. This scene about art – about sculpture, cinema, and sexual looking – borrows and preserves some of the cool erotic aura of the marble bodies, an aura that to a considerable extent, as per Benjamin, does emanate from 'their unique existence in a particular place.' Although it has been obvious, since even before Kuleshov, that cinematic geography is inherently artificial, *Pride & Prejudice*, by attending to the spatial and material properties of these works – and situating them within the larger touristic frame and the phenomenology of vision – manages to preserve, or harness something auratic.

The inexplicably transparent marble veil of Monti's *Vestal Virgin* exemplifies this harnessed aura. It is deployed metaphorically and yet its astounding virtuosity is such as no reproduction, copy, or prop could achieve. 'The mysterious, ineffable character of the veil, which both conceals and reveals the forms beneath it, has been exploited by artists of all cultures and eras,' as Helen Harrison was quoted in the previous chapter, by way of introducing the ambiguous veils of abstraction in the paintings of Paul Jenkins. It is hard to be as different from the uncanny verisimilitude of the white neoclassical marbles of the first half of the nineteenth century as are those brilliantly chromatic non-objective paintings of the second half of the twentieth. But the veils and virtuosity that are found in both Chatsworth's Hall of Marbles in *Pride & Prejudice* and Paul Jenkins's paintings as created in *An Unmarried Woman* have somehow defied the propensity of cinema to diminish the object of art and to decay its aura, while also performing metaphorically, probing the surface for hidden depths, giving form to the invisible phenomena of pleasure and desire.

It is certainly both scale and, especially, process – that they are seen being made – that enable the Jenkins paintings to achieve this. Indeed, of the paintings seen in the films considered here, the only ones that really begin to stand up to the cinema's regard and perform in ways that perhaps exceed their scripted parts are either large (Jenkins's, Connelly's) – or at least shown filling the frame (Cooper's) – *and* are seen, closely, being made. In facture is texture – presence – and becoming. The static, two-dimensionality of the modernist easel paintings seen in *Venus vor Gericht, Muerte de un ciclista* (in those two cases also denuded of color), and *The Trouble with Harry* causes these material and substantial objects to become insubstantial: mere images. The decay of the aura complete, the images are subordinated not only to cinema but also to narrative. The striking vicissitudes of the meaning of modernist abstraction in those three films – madness, degeneracy, decadence, hollowness, inscrutability, freedom! – follow from this decay. Sculpture too can be and is often subordinated to picture and story, but – again – its scale and three-dimensionality make spatial and temporal demands on the camera that permit, indeed often demand that it be engaged more dialectically.

Although it may be, as I wrote in my introduction, that 'films do not and filmmakers, film audiences and scholars (of film studies or art history) cannot – without the help of archives, press releases, and other documentary accounts, like Harry Horner's – really distinguish a fine oil painting by a major painter from a reproduction, an imitation, or from significantly lesser works seen on the screen,' there are properties of artworks – those having to do with time and space and with process – that can, when engaged by the film, defy this incapacity, this essential medial indifference. 'In the fine arts – the collectible ones – the connoisseur's work depends on the material presence of the object and in movies the object is, like the actors, always absent,' I continued. But, as I have noted, in some instances artworks perform much more like actors, even 'stars' (as Mamoulian insisted), than as props. Perhaps, despite their ontological absence, then, it is not very different to respond to and appreciate the roles of Canova's *Endymion* in *Pride & Prejudice* or Frink's *Warrior* in *The Damned*, than it is to respond to and appreciate the roles of Keira Knightley or Oliver Reed. Authenticity, then, is not exactly the point; it is their ability to play the role.

Moreover, does it really matter to us?' I continued, moving on to more intractable questions.

What difference does it make whether a painting in a movie is 'real': an authentic object with provenance, as opposed to a photomechanical reproduction, an imitation, or an anonymous daub? Film itself is photomechanical; fiction is imitation; anonymity is the proper condition of the mutely indexical excess that constitutes the impression of reality on screen. And as Benjamin noted, the value of that unique, original object – the object that through its physical duration in space and time 'bears the mark of history' and partakes of cultural tradition – has been liquidated in the age of technological reproduction. Mass media – film especially – has shattered tradition and 'substitutes a mass existence for a unique existence.'

Well, clearly it matters to me. Presumably it matters to the artists! Perhaps it matters to the (other) actors. As Olivia de Havilland could not – take after take – properly perform her abject ascension of the stairs in *The Heiress* (1949), after her character Catherine's abandonment, until director William Wyler filled her suitcase with heavy props, realizing only when she threw it at him in frustration that the empty bag was too buoyant, so too perhaps can an actor more properly respond to art when it is 'real.' The suitcase looked real but, being empty, did not feel it. So can it be with art.[8] 'Mutely indexical excess' does not constitute the impression of reality on screen when part of that reality is a museum, a gallery, or an artist's studio, scenes of art, art making and looking. In those cases, the impression of reality is diminished forcefully by the use of props, daubs, poor imitations, pastiches, or copies.

Although 'the value of that unique, original object – the object that through its physical duration in space and time "bears the mark of history" and partakes of cultural tradition' – has been *diluted* and too often monetized in the age of technological reproducibility, it has not been entirely liquidated. So long as painters paint and sculptors sculpt, it cannot be. And although the cinema is wont to make the other arts its own by domination and incorporation – and often succeeds – as a medium that preserves the indexical trace of the material world, it occasionally preserves with the index of the art object – with its material specificity and historical genesis – its capacity to affect the unreal situation in which it finds itself, even sometimes to exceed it.

## Notes

1   There exist two miniatures by Engleheart of Tom Lefroy from the last years of the 18th century; one has remained in the possession of the Lefroy family and the other was purchased by antique dealers Judy and Brian Harden at a Christie's London auction on 6 November, 2001 (sale 6495, lot 192; http://www.christies.com/lotFinder/lot_details. aspx?intObjectID=3103663, accessed 22 February, 2014) and sold by them amidst considerable attention in June 2008. See: 'Pictured: Face of the "good-looking, pleasant young man" who inspired Jane Austen's Mr Darcy,' *Mail Online* (10 June, 2008): http://www. dailymail.co.uk/news/article-1025400 (accessed 22 February, 2014). Raeburn's portrait of Charles Christie, Esq. is in the permanent collection of the Philadelphia Museum of Art.

2   Janine Barchas has just recently disputed the theory that Chatsworth is Pemberley's prototype in a blog post on the Johns Hopkins University Press website, proposing instead, with careful reasoning, Wentworth House in Yorkshire (2013).

3   'Closed-eye vision' expressed Brakhage's sensitivity to optical sensations that traversed the closed eyelid from without, as well as those that emerged from within the mind and the optic nerve. As William Wees notes, the concept 'includes hypnagogic imagery, phosphenes, and the grainy visual "noise" perceptible when we are in a dark room or have our eyes tightly closed' (Wees, 1992: 3).

4   In the booklet that accompanies the 'deluxe' DVD edition of the film.

5   There is an impressive body of literature already on Wright's *Pride & Prejudice* – in relation to the heritage film, issues of adaptation, history, narrativity, etc. including, in addition to Linda Troost's 'Filming Tourism, Portraying Pemberley' (2006) and Vidal's books (2012a; 2012b), essays by Sarah Ailwood (2007), Joyce Goggin (2007), Lydia Martin (2007), Anne-Marie Paquet-Deyris (2007), and others.

6   Deborah Vivien Cavendish, the Dowager Duchess of Devonshire (born 31 March, 1920), was born Deborah Freeman-Mitford, and is the youngest and last surviving of the Mitford sisters.

7   The 6th Duke of Devonshire visited Monti's studio in Milan, Italy, on 12 October, 1846 on his way to Naples. He ordered the marble sculpture on 18 October, placing a £60 deposit on the following day. The sculpture was ready to be dispatched to England in April 1847, and the Duke appears to have displayed it in Chiswick House, west of London. http://www.chatsworth.org/art-and-archives/art-library-and-archive-collections/ highlights/sculpture/a-veiled-vestal-virgin

8   The fact that Alan Bates apprenticed with Paul Jenkins and that Jenkins's loft and studio was a set for *An Unmarried Woman*, along with accounts I heard from Mazursky, from Chatsworth preparators and curatorial staff about the details of accommodating and assisting with the *Pride & Prejudice* production, from Evan Jones about Elisabeth Frink and *The Damned*, and from Sydney Cooper about *The Player*, substantiate my sense that the material, economic and affective presence of art would likely have been palpable on these sets.

# Bibliography

Ailwood, S. (2007), '"What are men to rocks and mountains?" Romanticism in Joe Wright's *Pride & Prejudice*', Special issue of *Persuasions On-Line*, 27: 2, http://www.jasna.org/persuasions/on-line/vol27no2/ailwood.htm. Accessed 12 March 2010.

Allen, R. (2006), 'Hitchcock's color designs', in A. Dalle Vacche and B. Price (eds.), *Color: The Film Reader*, New York: Routledge, pp. 131–144.

Andrew, D., ed. (1997), *The Image in Dispute: Art and Cinema in the Age of Photography*, Austin: University of Texas Press.

Anon. (1931), 'Katchamakoff in notable sculpture show', *Art Digest*, 5, 15 May, p. 6.

Anon. (1933), 'PARAMOUNT SUES MARLENE DIETRICH', *The New York Times*, 3 January, Amusements Section, p. 18.

Anon. (1941), 'Venus vor Gericht', *Illustrierter Film-Kurier*, 3214.

Anon. (1978), 'Mazursky in Soho (The 'Vasari' Diary)', *Art News*, 77: 6, pp. 38–40.

Anon. (1980), 'Deutsche Zensoren: "Das Hohe Lied" verboten', *Film und Fernsehen*, 8: 12, p. 45.

Anon. (2007), *Paul Jenkins in the 1950s: Space, Color, and Light*, New York: D. Wigmore Fine Art.

Anon. (2009), *Paul Jenkins in the 1960s and 1970s: Space, Color, and Light*, New York: D. Wigmore Fine Art.

Armstrong, I. (1990), 'Introduction', in J. Kinsley (ed.) and J. Austen, *Pride and Prejudice*, Oxford, UK: Oxford University Press, pp. vi–xxvi.

Auerbach, J. (2007), *Body Shots: Early Cinema's Incarnations*, Berkeley: University of California Press.

Austen, J. (2003), *Pride and Prejudice*, New York: Barnes and Noble.

Bach, S. (2011), *Marlene Dietrich: Life and Legend*, Minneapolis: University of Minnesota Press.

Bailey, C. (1979), *Ferren: A Retrospective*, New York: Graduate School and University Center of the City University of New York.

Balio, T. (1993), *Grand Design: Hollywood as a Modern Business Enterprise, 1930–1939*, in C. Harpole (ed.), *History of the American Cinema, Vol. 5*, Berkeley: University of California Press.

Barber, B. (2009), *Trans/actions: Art, Film and Death*, New York and Dresden: Atropos.

Barchas, J. (2013), 'Will the real model for Pemberley please step forward?', *JHU Press blog*, 26 September, http://jhupressblog.com/2013/09/26/will-the-real-model-for-pemberley-please-step-forward/. Accessed 22 November 2013.

Bardem, J. A. (2008), 'Report on the current state of our cinema (1955)' (trans. M.C. King), *Death of a Cyclist*, Criterion Collection DVD booklet, pp. 22–23.

Barron, S., et al. (1991), 'Degenerate Art': The Fate of the Avant-Garde in Nazi Germany, Los Angeles County Museum of Art.

—— and S. Eckmann (1997), Exiles + Emigrés: The Flight of European Artists from Hitler, Los Angeles County Museum of Art.

Barthes, R. (1977), Roland Barthes by Roland Barthes (trans. R. Howard), New York: Hill and Wang.

—— (1978), A Lover's Discourse (trans. R. Howard), New York: Farrar, Strauss and Giroux.

—— (1981), Camera Lucida: Reflections on Photography (trans. R. Howard), New York: Farrar, Strauss, and Giroux.

Batchelor, D. (2000), Chromophobia, London: Reaktion.

——, ed. (2008), Colour (Documents of Contemporary Art), London: Whitechapel Gallery and Cambridge, MA: MIT Press.

Bazin, A. (1967), 'The Ontology of the Photographic Image', in What is Cinema? Vol. 1 (ed. and trans. Hugh Gray), Berkeley: University of California Press, pp. 9–16.

Benjamin, W. (2008), 'The work of art in the age of its technological reproducibility', Second Version, in M. W. Jennings, B. Doherty and T. Y. Levin (eds.), The Work of Art in the Age of Its Technological Reproducibility, and Other Writings on Media (trans. E. Jephcott, R. Livingstone, H. Eiland et al.), Cambridge, MA: Harvard University Press, pp. 19–55.

Bernstein, M., ed. (1999), Controlling Hollywood: Censorship and Regulation in the Studio Era, New Brunswick: Rutgers University Press.

Blanckenhagen, P. H. von (1975), 'Der Ergänzende Betrachter: Bemerkungen zu einem Aspekt hellenistischer Kunst', in E. Homann-Wedeking (ed.), Wandlungen: Studie zur Antiken und Neueren Kunst, Munich: Institut für Klassische Archäologie der Universität München, pp. 193–201.

Brody, R. (2010), 'Radio activity', DVD review of The Damned, The New Yorker, 5 April, p. 86.

Brunsdon, C. (1982), 'A subject for the seventies: Charlotte Brundson traces the construction of an "Independent" heroine', Screen, 23: 3–4, pp. 20–29.

Burstow, R. (1997), 'The Limits of Modernist Art as a "Weapon of the Cold War": reassessing the unknown patron of the Monument to the Unknown Political Prisoner', Oxford Art Journal, 20: 1, pp. 68–80.

Callahan, D. (2003), 'Joseph Losey – great directors', Senses of Cinema, 25, 21 March, http://sensesofcinema.com/2003/great-directors/losey/. Accessed 4 February 2013.

Carter, E. (2007), 'Marlene Dietrich: the prodigal daughter', in G. Gemünden and M. R. Desjardins (eds.), Dietrich Icon, Durham and London: Duke University Press, pp. 186–207.

Caute, D. (1994), Joseph Losey: A Revenge on Life, New York: Oxford University Press.

Cavendish, Duchess of Devonshire, D. (2002), Chatsworth: The House, London: Francis Lincoln.

Cernuschi, C. (1999), 'The politics of Abstract Expressionism', Archives of American Art Journal, 39: 1/2, pp. 30–42.

Chametzky, P. (2010), Objects as History in Twentieth-Century German Art: Beckmann to Beuys, Berkeley: University of California Press.

Chris, C. (2012), 'Censoring purity', Camera Obscura, 27: 1, pp. 97–125.

Ciment, M. (1985), Conversations with Losey, London and New York: Methuen.

Cockroft, E. (1974), 'Abstract Expressionism, Weapon of the Cold War', *Artforum*, 12: 10, pp. 39–41.

Collins, N. (1978), 'His paintings co-starred, but well before "Unmarried Woman" Paul Jenkins made his splash', *People Magazine*, 9: 24, 19 June.

Cowan, M. and K. Sicks (2012), '28 March 1935: Premiere of Triumph des Willens presents Facism as unifier of communal will', in J. M. Kapczynski and M. D. Richardson (eds.), *A New History of German Cinema*, New York: Camden House, pp. 255–261.

Craven, D. (1999), *Abstract Expressionism as Cultural Critique: Dissent During the McCarthy Period*, Cambridge, UK: Cambridge University Press.

Culbert, D. (2002), 'The impact of anti-semitic film propaganda on German audiences: *Jew Süss* and *The Wandering Jew* (1940)', in R. A. Etlin (ed.), *Art, Culture, and Media Under the Third Reich*, Chicago: University of Chicago Press, pp. 139–157.

Cummings, P. (1969), 'Oral history interview with Ivan C. Karp, 1969 Mar. 12', *Archives of American Art*, http://www.aaa.si.edu/collections/interviews/oral-history-interview-ivan-c-karp-11717. Accessed 14 August 2010.

——— (1975), 'Oral history interview with Salvatore Scarpitta, 1975 January 31–February 3', *Archives of American Art*, http://www.aaa.si.edu/collections/interviews/oral-history-interview-salvatore-scarpitta-12727. Accessed 21 October, 2012.

Dalle Vacche, A. (1996), *Cinema and Painting: How Art is Used in Film*, Austin: University of Texas Press.

——— (2008), 'Cinema and art history: film has two eyes', in J. Donald and M. Renov (eds.), *The Sage Handbook of Film Studies*, London: Sage, pp. 180–198.

Danks, A. (2007), 'Great directors: Rouben Mamoulian', *Senses of Cinema*, 42, February, http://sensesofcinema.com/2007/great-directors/mamoulian/. Accessed 1 November 2012.

Deutsche Kinemathek Museum fur Film und Fernsehen (2011), 'Newsletter No. 99', Marlene Dietrich Collection, Berlin, http://marlenedietrich.org/pdf/News99.pdf. Accessed 10 December 2012.

Doherty, T. (1999), *Pre-Code Hollywood: Sex, Immorality, and Insurrection in American Cinema, 1930–1934*, New York: Columbia University Press.

Durgnat, R. (1963), 'Review of *The Damned*', *Films and Filming*, 9: 8, May, pp. 24–25.

Ebert, R. (1978), 'A Man and a Woman', *Film Comment*, 14: 2, March–April, pp. 26–29.

Eddy, M., A. Smale, P. Cohen and R. Kennedy (2013), 'German officials provide details on looted art', *New York Times*, 5 November, http://www.nytimes.com/2013/11/06/arts/design/german-officials-provide-details-on-looted-art-trove.html?smid=pl-share. Accessed 7 November 2013.

Edgerton, G. R., ed. (1988), *Film and the Arts in Symbiosis: A Resource Guide*, Westport: Greenwood Press.

Elsaesser, T. (1992), 'Mirror, Muse, Medusa: *Experiment Perilous*', *Iris*, 14–15, pp. 147–159.

Elsen, A. (1973), *Paul Jenkins*, New York: Harry N. Abrams.

Etlin, R. A., ed. (2002), *Art, Culture, and Media Under the Third Reich*, Chicago: University of Chicago Press.

Evans, J. (2007), 'Pudovkin and the censors: Juan Antonio Bardem's Muerte de un ciclista', *Hispanic Research Journal*, 8: 3, pp. 253–265.

Farmer, J. A., ed. (2000), *The New Frontier: Art and Television, 1960–1965*, Austin: Austin Museum of Art.

Felleman, S. (1997), *Botticelli in Hollywood: The Films of Albert Lewin*, New York: Twayne.

—— (2006), *Art in the Cinematic Imagination*, Austin: University of Texas Press.

—— (2011), 'Decay of the aura: modern art in classical cinema', *Jump Cut* 53, http://www.ejumpcut.org/archive/jc53.2011/FellemanDecayAura/. Accessed 2 April 2013.

Ferren, J. (1953), 'Symposium: the human figure', *Art Digest*, 28: 4, pp. 12–13, 32–33.

—— (1954a), 'An artist pursues the reality beneath the appearance', in R. M. MacIver (ed.), *The Hour of Insight: a Sequel to Moments of Personal Discovery*, New York and London: Harper & Bros/Institute for Religious and Social Studies, pp. 51–59.

—— (1954b), 'New art and old morals – another view', in R. M. MacIver (ed.), *New Horizons in Creative Thinking: A Survey and Forecast*, New York and London: Harper & Bros/The Institute for Religious and Social Studies, pp. 133–138.

—— (1958), 'Epitaph for an avant-garde', *Arts*, 33: 2, pp. 24–26, 68.

Fitzsimmons, J. (1953), 'A John Ferren profile', *Art Digest*, 27: 10, 15 February, pp. 11, 25, 26.

Flam, J. (1975), 'Paul Jenkins and the aesthetics of risk', *Arts Magazine*, 50: 2, pp. 92–94.

Fox, T. C. (1978), 'Interview with Paul Mazursky', *Film Comment*, 14: 2, pp. 29–32.

Frascina, F., ed. (1985), *Pollock and After: The Critical Debate*, New York: Harper & Row.

Fried, M. (1980), *Absorption and Theatricality: Painting and Beholder in the Age of Diderot*, Berkeley: University of California.

Friesen, L. (2011), 'Hermann Sudermann, Mennonite playwright and novelist from the boundary', *CMW Journal*, 3: 4, http://www.mennonitewriting.org/journal/3/4/hermann-sudermann-mennonite-playwright-and-novelis/. Accessed 26 October 2012.

Fulks, B. A. (1984), 'Walter Ruttmann, the avant-garde film, and Nazi modernism', *Film and History*, 14: 2, pp. 26–35.

Fuller, G. (2000), 'Altman on Altman', in D. Sterrit (ed.), *Robert Altman: Interviews*, Jackson: University Press of Mississippi, pp. 188–210.

Gabbard, K. and G. O. Gabbard (1987), *Psychiatry and the Cinema*, Chicago: The University of Chicago Press.

Galt, R. (2011), *Pretty: Film and the Decorative Image*, New York: Columbia University Press.

Gambill, N. (1983), 'Harry Horner's design program for "The Heiress"', *Art Journal*, 43: 3, pp. 223–230.

Gardiner, S. (1998), *Elisabeth Frink: The Official Biography*, London: HarperCollins.

Gardner, C. (2004), *Joseph Losey*, Manchester: Manchester University Press.

—— (2006), 'From mimicry to mockery: Cold War hybridity in Evan Jones's *The Damned, Modesty Blaise* and *Funeral in Berlin*', *Media History*, 12: 2, pp. 177–191.

Gehler, F. (1984), 'Das Lied der Lieder', *Film und Fernsehen*, 12: 8, p. 13.

Gemünden, G. and M. R. Desjardins, ed. (2007), *Dietrich Icon*, Durham and London: Duke University Press.

Giesen, R. (2003), *Nazi Propaganda Films: A History and Filmography*, Jefferson and London: McFarland.

Gitlin, T. and C. Wolman (1978), 'Review of *An Unmarried Woman*', *Film Quarterly*, 32: 1, pp. 55–58.

Goergen, J. (1989), *Walter Ruttmann: Eine Dokumentation*, Berlin: Freunde der Deutschen Kinemathek.

Goggin, J. (2007), 'Pride and Prejudice reloaded: navigating the space of Pemberley', Joe Wright's *Pride & Prejudice* (2005), Special issue of *Persuasions On-Line*, 27: 2, http://www.jasna.org/persuasions/on-line/vol27no2/index.html. Accessed 12 March 2010.

Gottlieb, S., ed. (2003), *Alfred Hitchcock: Interviews*, Jackson: University Press of Mississippi.

Greene, D. (1988), 'The original of Pemberley', *Eighteenth-Century Fiction*, 1: 1, pp. 1–23.

Gross, K. (2006), *The Dream of the Moving Statue*, University Park: Pennsylvania State University Press.

Guido, L. and O. Lugon, eds. (2012), *Between Still and Moving Images*, New Barnet, Herts: John Libbey.

Guilbaut, S. (1983), *How New York Stole the Idea of Modern Art* (trans. A. Goldhammer), Chicago: University of Chicago Press.

Gunning, T. (2007), 'In and out of the frame: paintings in Hitchcock', in W. Schmenner and C. Granof (eds.), *Casting a Shadow: Creating the Alfred Hitchcock Film*, Chicago: Northwestern University Press, pp. 29–47.

Hake, S. (2001), *Popular Cinema of the Third Reich*, Austin: University of Texas Press.

Hamilton, G. H. (1993), *Painting and Sculpture in Europe, 1880–1940*, New Haven: Yale University Press.

Haralovich, M. B. (2007), 'Marlene Dietrich in Blonde Venus: advertising Dietrich in seven markets', in G. Gemünden and M. R. Desjardins (eds.), *Dietrich Icon*, Durham: Duke University Press, pp. 162–185.

Harrison, H., I. Sandler, A. Gibson et al. (1993), *The Abstract Spirit: John Ferren (1905–1970)*, Stony Brook: The Stony Brook Foundation.

Hearn, M. (2010), '*The Damned*', Columbia Pictures/Sony Pictures Home Entertatinment, Region 2 DVD edition.

Hopkins, L. (2000), 'Mr. Darcy's body: privileging the female gaze', in L. Troost and S. Greenfield (eds.), *Jane Austen in Hollywood*, Lexington: University Press of Kentucky.

Horner, H. (2002), 'Designing *The Heiress*', in E. Smoodin and A. Martin (eds.), *Hollywood Quarterly: Film Culture in Postwar America, 1945–1957*, Berkeley: University of California Press, pp. 180–185.

Hulks, D. (2006), 'The dark chaos of subjectivisms: splitting and the geometry of fear', in B. Taylor (ed.), *Sculpture and Psychoanalysis*, London: Ashgate, pp. 95–114.

Hüneke, A. (2008), '"Entartete Kunst" in Einem NS-Film', *Recherche Film und Fernsehen: Zeitschrift der Deutschen Kinemathek*, 4, pp. 42–45.

Iles, C. (2001), *Into the Light: The Projected Image in American Art, 1964–1977*, New York: Whitney Museum of American Art.

*Iris*, No. 14–15 (Fall 1992), Special number: 'Le Portrait Peint au Cinéma/The Painted Portrait in Film'.

Jachec, N. (1991), '"The Space Between Art and Political Action": Abstract Expressionism and ethical choice in postwar America, 1945–1950', *Oxford Art Journal*, 14: 2, pp. 18–29.

Jacob, G. (1966), 'Joseph Losey, or the camera calls', *Sight and Sound*, 35: 2, pp. 62–67.

Jacobs, L. (1991), *The Wages of Sin: Censorship and the Fallen Woman Film, 1928–1942*, Madison: University of Wisconsin Press.

Jacobs, S. (2007), *The Wrong House: The Architecture of Alfred Hitchcock*, Rotterdam: 010 Publishers.

———— (2011), *Framing Pictures: Film and the Visual Arts*, Edinburgh: Edinburgh University Press.

Jenkins, P. (1958), 'A cahier leaf', *It Is: A Magazine for Abstract Art*, 2, p. 13.

———— (1983), *Anatomy of a Cloud,* with S. D. Jenkins, New York: Harry N. Abrams.

Jones, A. (1981), 'Writing the Body: Toward an Understanding of "L'Ecriture Feminine,"' *Feminist Studies*, 7: 2, pp. 247–263.

Kahn, E. M. (2009), 'Behind the screen: a look at *Summer Hours* with François-Renaud Labarthe', *Antiques*, 10 June, http://www.themagazineantiques.com/news-opinion/current-and-coming/2009-06-10/behind-the-screen-a-look-at-summer-hours-with-franois-renaud-labarthe/. Accessed 22 June 2010.

Katchamakoff, A. (1965), *Atanas Katchamakoff: Lescovetz, La Quinta*, Los Angeles: Zeitlin & Ver Brugge.

Kehr, D. (2010), 'The icons of suspense collection: Hammer films', *New York Times*, 2 April, http://www.nytimes.com/2010/04/04/movies/homevideo/04kehr.html?ref=arts&_r=0. Accessed 3 April 2010.

———— (2011), 'Chopin, Schubert and Dietrich (the latter nude)', DVD Review of *The Song of Songs, The New York Times*, 3 June 2011, http://www.nytimes.com/2011/06/05/movies/homevideo/marlene-dietrich-in-song-of-songs-on-dvd.html. Accessed 21 October 2012.

Kelley, K. (2007), 'Toshio Ōdate', *Encyclopedia of Asian American Artists*, Westport, CT: Greenwood Press, pp. 160–162.

Kent, S. (1985a), *Elisabeth Frink: Sculpture and Drawings, 1952–1984*, London: Royal Academy of Arts.

———— (1985b), Interview with Elizabeth Frink, ICA Talks, *British Library Sounds*, 13 March, http://sounds.bl.uk/Arts-literature-and-performance/ICA-talks/024M-C0095X0164XX-0100V0. Accessed 17 August 2012.

Keogh, P. (2000), 'Death and Hollywood', in D. Sterrit (ed.), *Robert Altman: Interviews*, Jackson: University Press of Mississippi, pp. 156–162.

Kimmelman, M. (2010), 'Art's survivors of Hitler's war', *New York Times*, 30 November, http://www.nytimes.com/2010/12/01/arts/design/01abroad.html. Accessed 1 December 2010.

Kinder, M. (1978), 'Review of *Girlfriends*', *Film Quarterly*, 32: 1, pp. 46–50.

———— (1993), *Blood Cinema: The Reconstruction of National Identity in Spain*, Berkeley: University of California Press.

———— (2008), 'Creating a modern Spanish cinema', *Death of a Cyclist*, Criterion Collection DVD, accompanying booklet, p. 19.

Koehler, R. (2009), 'A second look: death of a cyclist', *Cineaste*, 34: 3, pp. 72–74.

Koepnick, L. (2002), *The Dark Mirror: German Cinema Between Hitler and Hollywood*, Berkeley: University of California Press.

———— (2007), 'Dietrich's face', in G. Gemünden and M. R. Desjardins (eds.), *Dietrich Icon*, Durham: Duke University Press, pp. 43–59.

Kozloff, M. (1985), 'American painting during the Cold War', in F. Frascina (ed.), *Pollock and After: The Critical Debate*, New York: Harper & Row, pp. 107–123.

Kracauer, S. (1947), *From Caligari to Hitler: A Psychological History of the German Film*, Princeton: Princeton University Press.

Kunsthistorisches Institut. (2010), 'Die Beschlagnahme der "Entarteten Kunst" 1937 und ihre Folgen', Freie Universität Berlin, 22 December, http://www.geschkult.fu-berlin.de/e/db_entart_kunst/geschichte/beschlagnahme/index.html. Accessed 19 April 2010.

Lacan, J. (1982), *Feminine Sexuality: Jacques Lacan and the École Freudienne* (ed. J. Mitchell and J. Rose, trans. J. Rose), New York: Norton.

Laemmle, C. (1976), '"The Ballyhoo Man", excerpted from "From the Inside"', *Saturday Evening Post*, 200 (1927), in T. Balio (ed.), 'The Business of Motion Pictures', *The American Film Industry*, Madison: University of Wisconsin Press, pp. 153–168.

Lawrence, H. (1962), *The Children of Light*, London: Consul Books.

Leahy, J. (1967), *The Cinema of Joseph Losey*, London: A. Zwemmer and New York: A.S. Barnes.

Lema-Hincapié, A. (2008), 'Existential crossroads in *Muerte de un ciclista*', in J. R. Resina (ed.), *Burning Darkness: A Half Century of Spanish Cinema*, Albany: SUNY Press, pp. 27–41.

Lévy, S., ed. (2003), *A Transatlantic Avant-Garde: American Artists in Paris, 1918–1939*, Berkeley: University of California Press.

Lovejoy, M. (2004), *Digital Currents: Art in the Electronic Age*, New York: Routledge.

Lucie-Smith, E. and E. Frink (1994), *Frink: A Portrait*, London: Bloomsbury.

Macklowe Gallery (2013), 'Boris Lovet-Lorski, 1894–1973', Decorative Artists, Artist Biographies, http://www.macklowegallery.com/education.asp/art+nouveau/Artist+Biographies/antiques/Decorative+Artists/education/Boris+Lovet-Lorski/id/140. Accessed 27 November 2013.

Marder, E. (2012), *The Mother in the Age of Mechanical Reproduction: Psychoanalysis, Photograph, Deconstruction*, New York: Fordham University Press.

Martin, L. (2007), 'Joe Wright's Pride & Prejudice: from Classicism to Romanticism', Special issue of *Persuasions On-Line*, 27: 2, http://www.jasna.org/persuasions/on-line/vol27no2/martin.htm. Accessed 13 February 2009.

Martin-Márquez, S. L. (1992), 'Codes and games in Juan Antonio Bardem's Muerte de un Ciclista', *Romance Languages Annual*, 4, pp. 511–515.

Marzo, J. L. (2006), *Arte Moderno y Franquismo: Los origenes conservadores de la vanguardia y de la politica artistica en españa*, http://www.soymenos.net/arte_franquismo.pdf. Accessed 3 September 2012.

—— (2009), *Arte Moderno y Franquismo*, Online Video, 2 November, http://www.youtube.com/watch?v=Z6Q2Sxs6r4A&feature=youtu.be. Accessed 17 December 2012.

May, R. (1950), *The Meaning of Anxiety*, Revised Edition, New York: W. W. Norton, 1977.

Mayersburg, P. (1963), 'Contamination', review of *The Damned*, Movie, 9, pp. 31–34.

McGilligan, P. (2003), *Alfred Hitchcock: A Life in Darkness and Light*, New York: Harper Collins.

Ménégaldo, G. (2000), '*The Damned*: l'écran et la statue', in D. Bantcheva (ed.), *L'univers de Joseph Losey*, Paris: Corlet, pp. 62–72.

Milne, T. (1970), *Rouben Mamoulian*, Bloomington: Indiana University Press.

Minturn, K. (1999), 'Peinture Noire: Abstract Expressionism and Film Noir', in A. Silver and J. Ursini (eds.), *Film Noir Reader 2*, New York: Limelight.

Morgan, R. C. (1998), *John Ferren: The New York Paintings, 1950s–1960s*, New York: Katharina Rich Perlow Gallery.

Mullins, E. (1972), *The Art of Elisabeth Frink*, London: Lund Humphries.

Mulvey, L. (1975), 'Visual Pleasure and Narrative Cinema,' *Screen*, 16: 3, pp. 6–18.

Museum für Kunst und Gewerbe (2012), 'Der Berliner Skupturenfund im Museum für Kunst und Gewerbe Hamburg', Online Video, Hamburg, 27 April, http://youtu.be/yc7q-dUWYaE. Accessed 7 November 2012.

Ng, D. (2009), 'Olivier Assayas' new film about art uses authentic masterpieces', Culture Monster blog, *Los Angeles Times*, 25 May, http://latimesblogs.latimes.com/culturemonster/2009/05/summer-hours-olivier-assayas-musee-dorsay-louis-majorelle-art-bracquemont.html. Accessed 22 June 2010.

Noble, C. and A. Yarrington (2009), 'Like a poet's dreams', *Apollo Magazine*, http://www.chatsworth.org/files/apollo.pdf. Accessed 29 April 2013.

Nordland, G. (1971), *Paul Jenkins Retrospective*, New York: Universe Books, in cooperation with the Museum of Fine Arts, Houston and the San Francisco Museum of Art.

Païni, D. and G. Cogeval (2001), *Hitchcock and Art: Fatal Coincidences*, Montreal: Montreal Museum of Fine Arts, 2001.

Paquet-Deyris, A. (2007), 'Staging Intimacy and Interiority in Joe Wright's *Pride & Prejudice* (2005)', Special issue of *Persuasions On-Line*, 27: 2, http://www.jasna.org/persuasions/on-line/vol27no2/paquet-deyris.htm. Accessed 12 March 2010.

Petropoulos, J. (1996), *Art as Politics in the Third Reich*, Chapel Hill: University of North Carolina Press.

————— (2002), 'From seduction to denial: Arno Breker's engagement with national socialism', in R. A. Etlin (ed.), *Art, Culture, and Media Under the Third Reich*, Chicago: University of Chicago Press, pp. 205–229.

Petrus, S. (2007), 'From gritty to chic: the transformation of New York City's SoHo, 1962–1976', 22 March, http://sohoalliance.org/documents/sohorevised.pdf. Accessed 11 November 2013.

Peucker, B. (1995), *Incorporating Images: Film and the Rival Arts*, Princeton: Princeton University Press.

————— (1999), 'The cut of representation: painting and sculpture in Hitchcock', in R. Allen and S. Ishii-Gonzales (eds.), *Alfred Hitchcock: Centenary Essays*, London: British Film Institute, pp. 141–156.

————— (2007), *The Material Image: Art and the Real in Film*, Stanford: Stanford University Press.

Pollit, J. J. (1986), *Art in the Hellenistic Age*, Cambridge, UK: Cambridge University Press.

Price, M. (2011), 'John Ferren and the development of Abstraction', PhD dissertation, New York: City University of New York Graduate School.

Ratcliff, C. (1978), 'Arty movies, locus Soho', *Art in America*, 66: 5, pp. 14–15.

Raubicheck, W. and W. Srebnick, eds. (1991), *Hitchcock's Rereleased Films: From Rope to Vertigo*, Detroit: Wayne State.

Read, H. (1952), 'New aspects of British sculpture', *Exhibition of Works by Sutherland, Wadsworth, Adams, Armitage, Butler, Chadwick, Clarke, Meadows, Moore, Paolozzi, Turnbull, organized by The British Council for the XXVI Biennale, Venice*, London: British Council.

—— (1964), *A Concise History of Modern Sculpture*, London: Thames & Hudson.

Reichardt, J. (1961), 'Modern art in London: Elizabeth [sic] Frink at Waddington Galleries', *Apollo*, 75, pp. 22–23.

Rham, E. de (1991), *Joseph Losey*, London: André Deutsch.

Riva, M. (1993), *Marlene Dietrich*, New York: Alfred A. Knopf.

Robertson, B. (1990), *Elisabeth Frink: Sculpture and Drawings, 1950–1990*, Washington, DC: The National Museum of Women in the Arts.

Rogers, S. A. (2011), 'The artist as cultural diplomat: John Ferren in Beirut, 1963–1964', *American Art*, 25: 1, pp. 112–123.

Rose, B. (1968), *Readings in Modern Art Since 1900: A Documentary Survey*, New York: Praeger.

Rosenbaum, J. (2007), 'Death of a cyclist', *Chicago Reader*, 18 January, http://www.chicagoreader .com/chicago/death-of-a-cyclist/Content?oid=924081. Accessed 9 February 2014.

Rush, M. (1999), *New Media in Late 20th-Century Art*, London: Thames & Hudson.

Russianoff, P. (1979), 'Learned helplessness', in P. Russianoff (ed.), *Women in Crisis*, New York: Human Sciences Press.

—— (1982), *Why Do I Think I am Nothing Without a Man?*, Toronto and New York: Bantam Books.

Sallitt, D. (2004), '*The Damned*', in G. Rickman (ed.), *The Science Fiction Film Reader*, New York: Limelight, pp. 146–152.

Sanders-Brahms, H. (2000), *Marlene und Jo: Recherche einer Leidenschaft*, Berlin: Aargon.

Sandler, I. (2003), *A Sweeper-up After Artists*, New York: Thames & Hudson.

Sanjek, D. (2002), 'Cold, cold heart: Joseph Losey's *The Damned* and the compensations of genre', *Senses of Cinema*, 21, http://sensesofcinema.com/2002/21/losey_damned/#5. Accessed 4 February 2013.

Saslow, J. M. (n.d.), *My Wonderful Adventure: The Art and Life of Stanley Marc Wright: American Contemporary Artist, 1911–1996*, Stowe, VT: Estate of Stanley Marc Wright.

Saxon, W. (2000), 'Penelope Russianoff, psychologist, dies at 82', *New York Times*, 5 September, http://www.nytimes.com/2000/09/05/nyregion/penelope-russianoff-psychologist-dies-at-82 .html. Accessed 19 November 2013.

Schmid, H. (2011), 'Edle Kunst, nur leider etwas schmutzig: Fälschung und Etartung im NS-Kino' ('Das Dritte Reich im Selbstversuch- Teil 9'), *Telepolis*, 8 May 2011, http://www.heise .de/tp/artikel/34/34199/3.html. Accessed 3 November 2012.

Schrödl, B. (2004), *Das Bild des Künstlers und seiner Frauen: Beziehungen zwischen Kunstgeschichte und Populärkultur in Spielfilmen des Nationalsozialismus und der Nachkriegszeit*, Marburg: Jonas Verlag.

—— (2011), 'Der Künstlerwahnsinn. Wie sich die Metapher der "Verführung" zum Nationalsozialismus und der Geschlechterkampft in einem Spielfilm der 1950er Jhre überlagern', in S. Fastert, A. Joachimides and V. Krieger (eds.), *Die Wiederkehr des Künstlers: Themen und Positionen der aktuellen Künstler/innenforschung*, Cologne: Böhlau Verlag, pp. 257–269.

Schulte-Sasse, L. (1996), *Entertaining the Third Reich: Illusions of Wholeness in Nazi Cinema*, Durham: Duke University Press.

—— (2004), 'Plastiken auf Celluloid: Frauen und Kunst im NS-Spielfilm', in H. Segeberg (ed.), *Mediale Mobilmachung I: Das Dritte Reich und der Film*, Munich: Wilhelm Fink Verlag, pp. 181–202.

Schwabsky, B. (2007), 'Paul Jenkins: the Redfern Gallery', *Artforum International*, 46: 1, pp. 480–481.

Self, R. T. (2002), *Robert Altman's Subliminal Reality*, Minneapolis: University of Minnesota Press.

Shaffer, P., B. Robertson, S. Kent, et al. (1984), *Elisabeth Frink, Sculpture: Catalogue Raisonné*, Salisbury, Wiltshire: Harpvale.

Shapiro, D. and C. Shapiro (1978), 'Abstract Expressionism: the politics of apolitical painting', *Prospects*, 3, pp. 175–214.

Shaw, T. (2006), *British Cinema and the Cold War*, London and New York: I.B. Tauris.

Sikov, E. (1994), *Laughing Hysterically: American Screen Comedy of the 1950s*, New York: Columbia University Press.

Smith, G. and R. T. Jameson (2000), 'The movie you saw is the movie we're going to make', in D. Sterrit (ed.), *Robert Altman: Interviews*, Jackson: University Press of Mississippi, pp. 163–181.

Smith, R. (1989), 'Critic's Notebook: The Art World Painted in Films', *The New York Times*, 5 April, http://www.nytimes.com/1989/04/05/movies/critic-s-notebook-the-art-world-painted-in-films.html. Accessed 20 April 2014.

—— (1993), 'Review of "John Ferren, the formative years: the 1930s in Paris and Spain"', *New York Times*, 27 August, http://www.nytimes.com/1993/08/27/arts/art-in-review-256993.html. Accessed 12 September 2008.

Spergel, M. (1993), *Reinventing Reality – The Art and Life of Rouben Mamoulian*, Metuchen and London: Scarecrow Press.

Stein, G. (1938), *Everybody's Autobiography*, London: William Heinemann.

Stewart, G. (1999), *Between Film and Screen: Modernism's Photo Synthesis*, Chicago: University of Chicago Press.

Stiftung Preussischer Kulturbesitz (2010), 'Ausstellung: Der Berliner Skulpturenfund. "Entartete Kunst" im Bombenschutt', Press Release, 8 November, http://hv.spk-berlin.de/deutsch/presse/pdf/101108_2_PM_Ausstellung.pdf. Accessed 23 December 2010.

Stoichita, V. I. (2008), *The Pygmalion Effect: From Ovid to Hitchcock* (trans. A. Anderson), Chicago: University of Chicago Press.

Stone, R. (2002), *Spanish Cinema*, Harlow: Longman.

Story, J. (1950), *The Trouble with Harry*, New York: Macmillan.

Studlar, G. (1988), *In the Realm of Pleasure: von Sternberg, Dietrich, and the Masochistic Aesthetic*, New York: Columbia University Press.

—— (2007), 'Marlene Dietrich and the erotics of code-bound Hollywood', in G. Gemünden and M. R. Desjardins, *Dietrich Icon*, Durham: Duke University Press, pp. 211–238.

Sudermann, H. (1909), *The Song of Songs (Das Hohe Lied)* (trans. T. Seltzer), New York: B.W. Huebsch.

—— (1914), *The Song of Songs* (trans. B. Marshall), London: The Bodley Head.

Tanga, M. (unpublished article), 'The politics of Abstraction: painting in the 1950s', http://www.academia.edu/1074462/The_Politics_of_Abstraction. Accessed 8 November 2011.

Temporary Services (2005), *Framing the Artists: Artists & Art in Film & Television*, 1, Chicago: Temporary Services.

Tolischus, O. (1931), 'Dietrich – how she happened', *Photoplay Magazine*, 35: 5, 19 April, pp. 28–29, 129.

Tolkin, M. (1992), *The Player*, New York: Vintage Contemporaries.

—— (1995), *The Player, The Rapture, The New Age: Three Screenplays*, New York: Grove Press.

Tomalin, C. (1999), *Jane Austen: A Life*, New York: Vintage.

Tomasevskij, B. (1971), 'Literature and biography', in L. Matejka and K. Pomorska (eds.), *Readings in Russian Poetics: Formalist and Structuralist Views*, Cambridge: MIT, pp. 47–55.

Troost, L. (2006), 'Filming tourism: portraying Pemberley', *Eighteenth Century Fiction*, 18: 4, pp. 477–498.

—— and S. Greenfield, eds. (2001), *Jane Austen in Hollywood*, 2nd edition, Lexington: University of Kentucky Press.

Truffaut, F. (1967), *Hitchcock*, New York: Simon & Schuster.

Tschauner, E. (1941), 'Benjamin Hecht macht in "Kunst"', *Filmwelt* (Berlin), 16, 18 April, pp. 410–411.

Tusell García, G. (2006), 'The internationalisation of Spanish abstract art (1950–1962)', *Third Text*, 20: 2, pp. 241–249.

Vidal, B. (2012a), *Figuring the Past: Period Film and the Mannerist Aesthetic*, Amsterdam: Amsterdam University Press.

—— (2012b), *Heritage Film: Nation, Genre and Representation*, London: Wallflower.

Waldman, D. (1982), 'The childish, the insane and the ugly: the representation of modern art in popular film and fiction of the forties', *Wide Angle*, 5: 2, pp. 52–65.

Walker, J. (1993), *Art and Artists on Screen*, Manchester: Manchester University Press.

Walker, M. (2005), *Hitchcock's Motifs*, Amsterdam: Amsterdam University Press.

Wechsler, J., ed. (1997), *Asian Traditions, Modern Expressions: Asian American Artists and Abstraction, 1945–1970*, New York: Harry N. Abrams, in association with the Jane Vorhees Zimmerlin Art Museum, Rutgers University.

Weedman, C. (2011), *Exilic Vision and the Cinematic Interrogation of Britain: The Joseph Losey and Harold Pinter Collaboration*, PhD Dissertation, Southern Illinois University Carbondale.

Wees, W. (1992), *Light Moving in Time: Studies in the Visual Aesthetics of Avant-Garde Film*, Berkeley: University of California Press.

Wemhoff, M. (2011), *Der Berliner Skulpturenfund: 'Entartete Kunst' im Bombenschutt*, Berlin: Museum für Vor- und Frühgeschichte (Staatliche Museen zu Berlin- Stiftung Preussischer Kulturbesitz)/Verlag Schnell & Steiner.

——, ed. (2012), *Der Berliner Skulpturenfund: 'Entartete Kunst' im Bombenschutt: Entdeckung, Deutung, Perspektive*, Begleitband zur Ausstellung mit den Beiträgen des Berliner Symposiums, 15–16 März, 2012, Berlin: Museum für Vor- und Frühgeschichte (Staatliche Museen zu Berlin- Stiftung Preussischer Kulturbesitz)/Verlag Schnell & Steiner.

Weschler, L. (1997), 'Paradise: the Southern California Idyll of Hitler's cultural exiles', in S. Barron and S. Eckmann (eds.), *Exiles + Emigrés: The Flight of European Artists from Hitler*, Los Angeles County Museum of Art, pp. 341–357.

Wood, R. (1989), *Hitchcock's Films Revisited*, New York: Columbia University Press.

Yarrington, A. (2009), '"Under Italian skies," the 6th Duke of Devonshire, Canova and the formation of the Sculpture Gallery at Chatsworth House', *Journal of Anglo-Italian Studies*, 10, pp. 41–62.

Young, P. (2006), *The Cinema Dreams Its Rivals: Media Fantasy Films from Radio to the Internet*, Minneapolis: University of Minnesota Press.

Youngblood, G. (1970), *Expanded Cinema*, New York: E.P. Dutton.

Zaretsky, E. (2004), *Secrets of the Soul: A Social and Cultural History of Psychoanalysis*, New York: Alfred E. Knopf.

Zuschlag, C. (1995), '*Entartete Kunst*': *Ausstellungsstrategien im Nazi-Deutschland*, Worms: Wernersche Verlagsgesellschaft.

———(2012), '75 Jahre Ausstellung »Entartete Kunst«', in M. Wemhoff, M. Hoffman and D. Scholz (eds.), *Der Berliner Skulpturenfund. »Entartete Kunst« im Bombenschutt, Entdeckung – Deutung – Perspektive*, Regensburg: Quick and Steiner, pp. 37–51.

# Index

Numbers in italics refer to pages on which illustrations appear. **CP** refers to an illustration in the folio of color plates.